THE BEST OF THE
DOLL READER®

VOLUME II

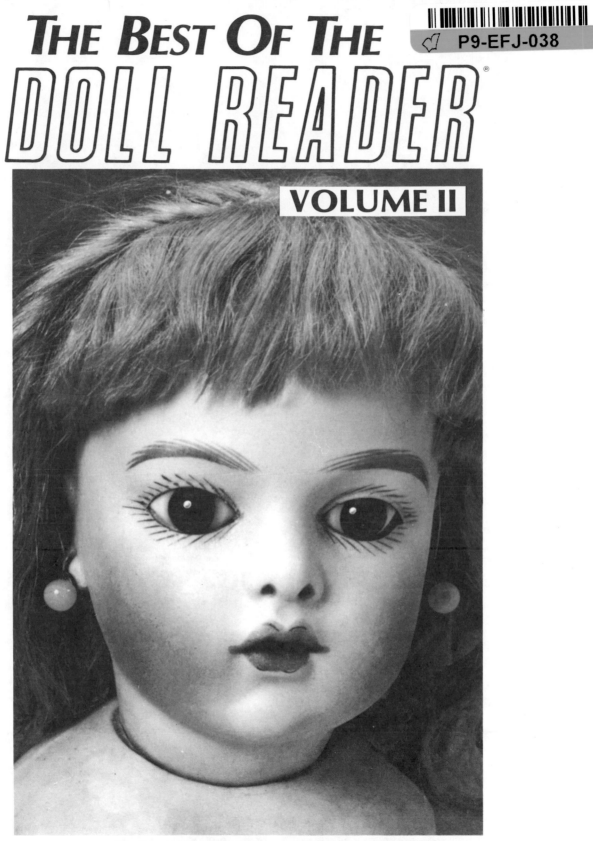

Article Reprints — 1974 to 1982
Compiled by Virginia Ann Heyerdahl

Published by  Hobby House Press, Inc.
Cumberland, Maryland 21502

FRONT COVER: Bru Jeune Doll. Marked: "Bru Jne 3" on head and both shoulders. Bisque head; blonde mohair wig over cork pate; fixed brown glass eyes; open/closed mouth; pierced ears; kid body with bisque forearms and wooden lower legs; paper label on abdomen; wearing white underclothes. c.1800. Height 14in (35.6cm). *Photo courtesy Sotheby's, London, England.*

BACK COVER: Contemporary Kathe Kruse dolls from Germany. Heads are plastic with attached wigs and brown painted eyes; the bodies are cloth and are fully-jointed. The large children are 18½in (47cm) *Daniel* and *Amelie;* the little boy is 13¾in *Otto.*

Additional copies of this book may be purchased at $10.95
from
Hobby House Press, Inc.
900 Frederick Street
Cumberland, Maryland 21502
or from your favorite bookstore or dealer.
Please add $1.25 per copy for postage.

Printed in the United States of America

ISBN: 0-87588-247-1

TABLE OF CONTENTS

Page 45 **Page 69** **Page 77** **Page 110**

ANTIQUE

6 **How To Buy An Antique Doll**
by Robert & Karin MacDowell

10 **Why Bisque Heads?**
by Dorothy & Evelyn Jane Coleman

13 **The Womanly Ideal of the 19th Century and Her Dolls**
by Estelle Johnston

18 **Chinas, Parians and Molded Hair Dolls**
by Robert & Karin MacDowell

23 **Dolls' Christmas of Yesterday**
by Elspeth

25 **Later Than You Think**
by Evelyn J. Coleman

29 **Dolls In Their Original Clothes Parts 1 & 2**
by Robert & Karin MacDowell

35 **Dolls' House Dolls**
by Magda Byfield

39 **The Margaret Woodbury Strong Museum Opens On October 12, 1982**
by Margaret Whitton

English

45 **English "Babies" of the 18th Century**
by Mary Hillier

49 **What Is Your Fortune, My Pretty Maid?**
by Betty Cadbury

52 **The "Model" Doll**
by Mary Hillier

56 **The English Pedlar Doll**
by Mary Hillier

French

61 **The "French" Selection - A Photographic Essay**
by Elspeth

65 **Dolls and Dolls' Accessories Sold in Paris 1870-1871**
by Dorothy & Evelyn Jane Coleman

69 **French Fashion Dolls "As Pretty As Hummingbirds"**
by Sybill McFadden

73 **Les Parisiennes - Tres Jolie - Tres Chic**
by Sybill McFadden

77 **The Marque Doll**
by Mildred Seeley

79 **On The Production of Dolls' Biscuit Heads In France**
by Claire Hennig

German

84 **Dolls in Europe - Germany**
by Dorothy S. Coleman

91 **Let's Look At Heubach**
by Shirley Buchholz

97 **Height Markings in Centimeters and Inches**
by Dorothy S. & Evelyn Jane Coleman

100 **The Collector's Mini-Digest on Kestner Dolls**
by Robert & Karin MacDowell

106 **Armand Marseille**
by Jürgen & Marianne Cieslik

109 **Googlies**
by Magda Byfield

110 **A Simon & Halbig Portfolio**
by Robert & Karin MacDowell

113 **One Fabulous Face**
by Magdalena Byfield

114 **Collecting German Character Dolls**
by Robert & Karin MacDowell

116 **Max and Maurice**
by Patricia N. Schoonmaker

119 **German Character Children**
by Jan Foulke

124 **The Song of the Lenci**
by Beverly Port

Continued....

Page 148

Page 165

Illustration 1. Antique Bye-Lo bisque doll. Handle carefully — eyes and celluloid hands are generally not repairable if damaged.

How To Buy An Antique Doll

BY ROBERT & KARIN MacDOWELL

Having spent a great deal of time and effort in building and refining a museum collection, trading, traveling, and being wholly involved in the interesting field of antique dolls, we have evolved an approach which has been helpful in acquiring dolls of institutional quality based on realistic terms. We suggest that anyone willing to make the required effort can build a sound antique doll collection, and we hope the ideas presented here might be of assistance to collectors at all levels.

Sources

The following are comments on sources which generally yield dolls for consideration.

Antique Shops: As a general rule, we find antique shops to be not very productive because the proprietor must offer such a wide range of merchandise, most of which is basic and easily understood. Therefore they are unable to devote the energy necessary to do a really thorough job in handling dolls. The inclination seems to be toward regarding any doll as something really special and, not really knowing how to price the item, setting the price much too high. (Very occasionally, for the

same reason, price may be too low, in which case *you* win.) Generally, you are on your own; you must know your subject thoroughly, and you will have to visit a large number of shops, spend a lot of time, and sort through much material to make a purchase.

Doll Dealers: Specialists in any field provide a much greater variety of the items you seek, plus useful knowledge concerning the condition and authenticity of each doll offered. Since dolls are "normal" merchandise to them, pricing is apt to be more realistic. Doll dealers also have experience in examining, general handling, repairing, costuming, shipping and other facets of the business which can be very helpful. You can expect an occasional bargain as dealers often have dolls in stock which they have had for too long, they had to buy as part of a large collection, or for other reasons, making them willing to sell at cost—sometimes even at a loss.

Doll Shows: We find these to be excellent sources for dolls, as there is usually a great variety of merchandise, and a number of dealers present. Shows have their pitfalls,

however. You may encounter poor lighting, large crowds, and other conditions which make it difficult to give your purchase the time and attention to detail you could otherwise afford. Most dealers doing shows are serious about the business, have gone through a lot of trouble and expense to participate, want your business, hope you will visit every show they do, and, therefore will do their best to be helpful.

Auctions: Alert! Know what you want, examine the merchandise at preview and decide the maximum price you will pay. Be iron-willed! You may get some really good buys, but many dolls will go to some collectors who will pay absurd prices to get what they want.

Private Sources: Sometimes the seller lacks concrete information about the dolls in question. The doll "probably belonged to grandmother, must be at least 100 years old." You have to know your subject. Often, you can show such persons the doll in a price guide to establish basis for negotiations.

Mail Order: If seller offers privilege of return within a short period if doll is not as represented, then

6

this source is worth trying. Some dealers are mail order specialists and have very high ethical standards.

Flea Markets and the Like: Often, "lean pickings."

Reference Materials

Fortunately, many people have taken pen to hand on the subject of dolls, and there is a wealth of good material easily available. A basic library of your own is mandatory if you are serious about building a good collection, and it should include several price guides, some specialty books covering subjects like Schoen—hut, Lenci and *The Collector's Encyclopedia of Dolls* by the Colemans, a monumental and carefully researched volume on the subject.

Don't be shy about using reference books in front of sellers while you shop for a doll. You may upset some sellers, but most will respect you for being thorough.

Use price guides as they are intended—as guides only. They are a great help, especially when one consults several guides to yield an average.

Special Cautions

When contemplating an expensive doll (a so-called "character," early French, and others which may be in vogue at the time), you must be careful to avoid reproductions, some of which are amazingly good, and also to avoid altered dolls. For example, it is common practice these days to carve a piece of cork to look like a French pate, cement this on a German doll, then call this put-together a "French Doll." Also, many closed-mouthed unmarked German dolls are sold as French.

Another current gambit seems to be: 1). Buy good reproduction doll. 2). Break or crack head. 3). Have damaged head restored. 4). Sell as "restored, rare French Bébé" or "German doll." 5). Restoration throws buyer off track. After all, who would bother to restore a reproduction? Some sellers will take parts from various dolls and put them together in the most fascinating ways! You can protect yourself by thorough study of the subject.

Methodical Examination

Having found a doll you wish to seriously consider, ask the seller for permission to take some, or all of the following steps after you have basically decided to buy the doll at an agreed price, subject to examination. If you damage the item or reduce its sales-appeal, you should willingly pay compensation if you elect not to purchase.

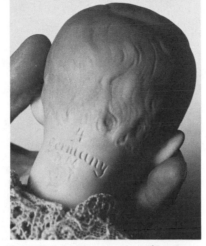

Illustration 2. Examination of head shows clear, sharp incised markings by Heubach which agree with published examples—good evidence of originality.

Head

Look for marks on the back of head, neck or shoulderplate and check reference books. If incised, see if clear and sharp; if not, head was cast in a worn mold or it could be a reproduction. Remove wig and pate. Try to determine if wig is original, a good human hair one or a cheap plastic version. Check pate to determine if new. If it is a cork pate, is it really old and original? Check bisque for missing flakes of material pulled away by old wig and glue. Carefully examine inside of head to determine if original sleep-eye mechanism is present and functional, and verify that cork pad is present to cushion weight of eye mechanism.

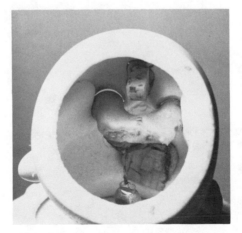

Illustration 3. View inside bisque doll head with sleep eyes shows cork pad which prevents eye weight from cracking chin and cork piece above eyes to limit closing movement.

See if eye plaster pieces are old or new, check eyes to determine if they have been removed, rewaxed, eyelashes replaced, etc. If eyes set sta-

tionary, are they original? If original stationary eyes have been removed and replaced, try to see why. Look carefully for paint or plaster of Paris painted inside head to cover up restoration or cracks. Check teeth, pieces of red paper and all other details for originality. Check hardware attaching head to body; try to determine whether original. Hold head up to bright light and observe light passing through the bisque. You may see dark areas which result from restoration and overpainting, and you also might detect hairline cracks.

Carefully examine all exterior features for even color and texture. Check delicate parts such as eyelids and earlobes for chips. Check glass eyes for scratches. If head is on

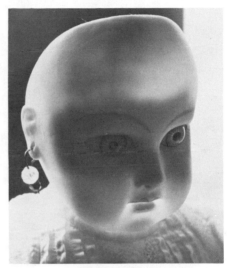

Illustration 4a.

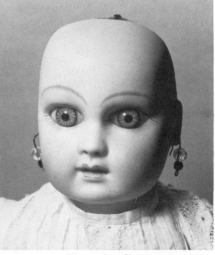

Illustration 4b.

Illustrations 4a & 4b. Portrait Jumeau head appears absolutely perfect when carefully examined in normal bright light. Concentrated bright light projected inside head reveals pair of cracks from right eye to crown. Dark area around eyes delineates original plaster of Paris which holds eyes.

composition body, pull head gently out of socket in body (if possible) and check neck for cracks, chips or other damage. Check the fit of neck into the body socket — it should be reasonably good; if not, you may have a put-together. At the same time, you should be able to determine whether the doll has been re-strung by looking at the elastic cord. Also see if stringing is firm, but not too tight.

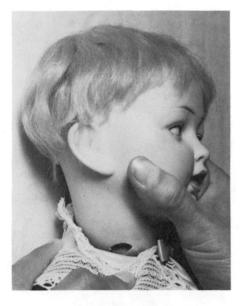

Illustration 5. Finding this concealed neck damage annoyed the seller but saved us $50.

Illustration 6. Desirable composition body marked Julius Steiner; head correspondingly marked.

Check body for marks which might correspond with those on head or shoulder.

If head is on kid, cloth or other type of body, check for fit—many heads are on wrong bodies.

Bisque Head on Composition Body: Undress doll completely (if practicable), double-check fit of head into socket at top of body. A very loose fit, or a head which will not fit into the socket would not be proper. Also, a head which fits too deeply into the body is suspicious—perhaps the socket has collapsed into the body, leaving a large hole. This often happens when dolls are restrung too tightly.

Carefully examine the hands, ball joints and arm sections. Gently pull the various sections apart slightly to ascertain if there is concealed damage inside the joints. At the same time, you should be able to see whether the arms have been re-strung, and if the tension is normal.

Likewise, check all components of legs; check feet. Look carefully to see whether all parts fit reasonably well. Examine hands and feet to see if they are a matching set; try to verify color matches other body parts. Many hands and lower arms have been repainted. Of course, the entire body might be repainted to disguise the fact that parts have been replaced or repaired. Replaced parts generally do not fit well and are fairly easy to spot. However, some of the French dolls exhibit rather poor body workmanship, and suspicious-looking parts may be original. German

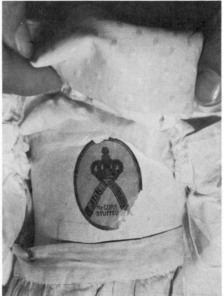

Illustration 7. Nicely marked Kestner kid body corresponds to marked celluloid head.

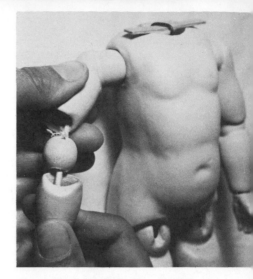

Illustration 8. Examination shows original parts in good condition; stringing is new.

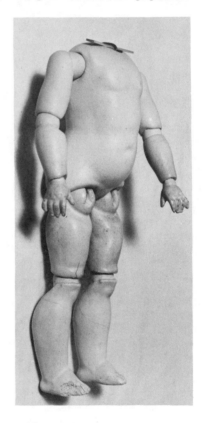

Illustration 9. Body shows its age, but is all-original and generally excellent. Note missing toes on right foot.

doll bodies usually were carefully made.

Bisque Head on Kid Body: Usually it will be obvious whether the shoulderplate fits the body by examining the joining of the two. Check for areas showing old cement, also for new cement. Search for marks on shoulder which may be covered by parts of the body, especially back of shoulder, and over the arms. Be careful not to tear the kid. Check to see if

Illustration 10. Photo shows the checking of lower arms on kid-bodied doll for size, color and general match.

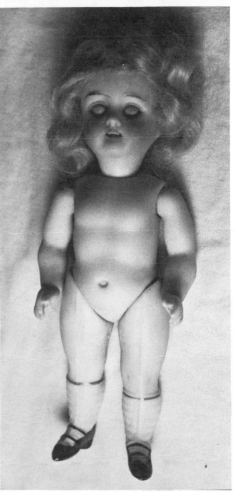

Illustration 11a.

bisque lower arms match each other; also determine if kid upper arms are original.

All Bisque: Undress and have a really good look to see if parts match and stringing adequate (or original). Replacement parts are easily available and very common. If you look at the hidden surfaces where the arms and legs meet the torso, you may be lucky enough to find incised numbers. If numbers on both arms and legs match, that would seem strong evidence they belong together. Check, of course, for good color match and proper fitting of parts.

Notes on Buying Damaged Dolls

By using good judgment, some of the best buys you can make will be damaged items. Also, many rare dolls are damaged, and you face the choice of buying "as-is" or doing without. Allowance for the damage should be reflected in the price. If you are considering dressing, buying a new quality wig or having professional restoration accomplished, bear in mind that all of these take time; supplies and services are somewhat expensive. It makes sense to invest in these services to upgrade an expensive or rare doll.

Black Light: An ultra-violet lamp

may be used in a dark room or closet to detect some restoration work, but that is not infallible— only an interesting analytical tool. We have a laboratory-quality instrument which we seldom use, having had more reliable results with good, bright incandescent or natural light.

Preservation

Generally, dolls seem to fare well if kept in conditions conducive to to human comfort. Avoid extremes of temperatures, humidity and light. If humidity is above 70%, we would suggest a dehumidifier, or an air conditioned environment. Bright light, especially fluorescent or sunlight will fade fabrics and cause physical damage. Be on the alert for insects— carpet beetles, moths and others —especially in newly acquired dolls. Have any suspicious items professionally examined and treated. Items clothed or decorated with natural furs and feathers need special caution and frequent examination; you may wish to keep such objects in glass cases or under glass domes with a few moth balls always present. You should keep any clothing or accessories acquired with the doll safely for future reference, or to pass along to subsequent owners.

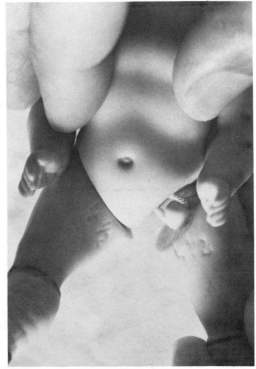

Illustration 11b.

Illustrations 11a & 11b. All-bisque German doll with sleep eyes found to be in excellent condition; closer look shows leg markings. In this particular case torso, both arms and back of head all marked 4½.

9

Why Bisque Heads?

DOROTHY & EVELYN JANE COLEMAN

Bisque head dolls are almost synonymous with collector's dolls. Generally doll collections today are comprised almost entirely of dolls with bisque heads. Dolls for sale at antique shows, auctions and on lists nearly all have bisque heads. There are infinite kinds of material from which dolls can be made. Therefore why this tremendous preference for bisque head dolls?

The reasons for the popularity of bisque heads are many. (1) They are available in large quantities. (2) They are familiar and what people associate with doll collecting. (3) They are relatively durable despite the fact that bisque is a breakable material. (4) They have a nostalgic appeal to the current generation. (5) Last, but not least, prices of old bisque dolls have been rising more rapidly than for almost any other type of dolls in recent years.

Bisque heads for dolls were made in tremendous quantities in the porcelain factories of Thüringia and its bordering areas in Germany from the 1870s to the 1930s, and probably as much as 90 percent of them came from this area. Raw materials were at hand, labor was cheap and molds could be used over and over again. Sometimes this industry was even subsidized. Thus the bisque heads were produced in astronomical quantities in Germany and supplied to children all around the world. During the

Illustration 1. Stone-bisque head doll with wig and painted eyes, on a cloth body with bisque arms and legs. It is dressed as a bride. 8in (20.3cm). *Coleman Collection.*

period of the bisque head production, social and economic conditions were such that a greater number of families could better afford dolls for their children than at any time prior to this. Bisque heads came in a variety of forms such as socket heads, shoulder heads, all-bisque dolls, wigged heads, molded hair heads, hatted heads and so forth. It was and is an endless variety from which to choose.

Present day doll collecting is almost entirely based on bisque head dolls. Although interest in both cloth and composition head dolls is rising, the vast majority of collector's dolls offered for sale and seen in collections are the bisque head dolls. Dealers at antique shows where dolls are sold offer largely bisque head dolls. Catalogs of doll auctions both here and abroad are predominately filled with bisque head dolls. Lists of antique dolls for sale seldom show anything but bisque head dolls. Although bisque heads were made in quantities as late as the 1930s, collectors usually think of them as being earlier and classify them as being antique. With so many bisque heads dolls shown everywhere there is no reason why collections, especially those formed in more recent times, should not be almost entirely made up of bisque head dolls.

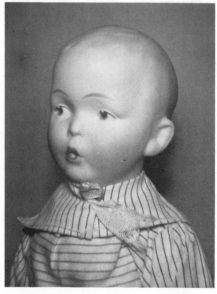

Illustration 3. *Whistling Jim* made by Gebruder Heubach has the square Heubach mark. The bisque head has molded hair and intaglio eyes. It is on a cloth body dressed as a boy of around 1912. 11in (27.9cm). *Sylvia Brockmon Collection.*

Bisque heads are breakable — there is no disputing this fact — but the care given to a collector's doll seldom puts the bisque head in jeopardy. Even cracked or chipped heads are still considered collectible and often their lower price is a great inducement especially to new collectors with limited purses. The years have been less kind to nearly all other materials than bisque and china heads.

LEFT: Illustration 2. Kestner doll with a bisque shoulder plate and swivel neck on a pink kid body with ball-jointed composition arms. It is dressed as a child of the 1890s. 17in (43.2cm). *Staten Island Historical Society Collection.*

From the December 1979/January 1980 Doll Reader.®

Illustration 4. Turned bisque shoulder head with a closed mouth, glass eyes and a wig, is on a cloth body with leather arms. It is dressed as a girl of the 1880s. 19in (48.3cm). *Alice Grinnings Collection.*

It has been pointed out that bisque head dolls are plentiful and durable — fine qualifications for collecting them but these attributes are not sufficient to entirely account for the vast number collected today. Forty or fifty years ago bisque head dolls were just as plentiful and durable as they are today but they were seldom seen in collections of that period. They were too recent and too inexpensive to be considered worthy of collecting. Originally bisque head dolls were less expensive than wax dolls, art cloth dolls and even most composition dolls. Gradually dealers and collectors began to realize

Illustration 5. Bru doll with a bisque shoulder plate and a swivel neck. It has glass eyes, closed mouth and a wig. The kid body with bisque arms is dressed as a lady in evening attire of the 1890s. 24in (61cm). *Brooklyn Museum Collection.*

Rubber and wax are extremely perishable. Paint peels off of metal and wood, but is almost always fired onto the bisque and cannot come off. Cloth soils quickly and is susceptible to bugs. Bisque can be easily washed and is impervious to pests. Composition heads, especially the early 20th century ones, peel easily and despite their "unbreakable" name, they will break and often they craze badly. For a collector a bisque or china head is the most durable and when washed it looks exactly as it did when new

Most of today's grandmothers played with bisque head dolls. Great grandmother's doll was apt to have also been of this material. Those prized family dolls are usually bisque head dolls. Even if dolls were not preserved in a family and passed down through the generations to treasure, one similar to the doll that grandmother played with has great appeal, especially if the grandmother herself collects dolls. She may be a real doll collector or she may only wish to have examples of the dolls that she loved in order to show to her children and grandchildren that they may share her appreciation and fondness for bisque head dolls.

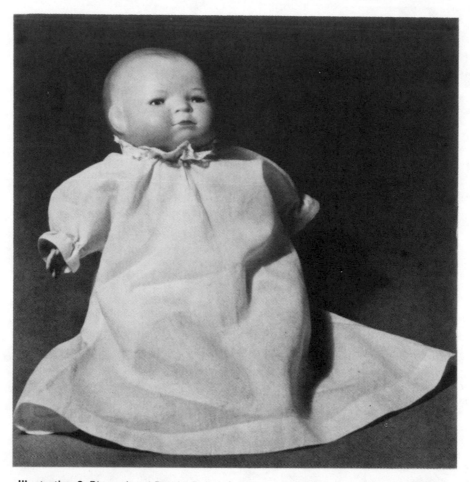

Illustration 6. Bisque head *Bye-Lo Baby* infant doll, designed by Grace Storey Putnam for George Borgfeldt & Co. It has painted hair, glass eyes, closed mouth, celluloid hands and a cloth body. 10in (25.4cm). *Newark Museum Collection.*

the profit potential and appeal in bisque head dolls and the market soared. Of course dealers are going to seek the dolls on which they can make the quickest and largest profit and the escalating price of bisque head dolls is one of the amazing phenomena of today's doll collecting. These rising prices have lured investors as well as collectors and the ever increasing demand only makes the prices rise even further. The big question is can these prices continue their rapid rise or will bisque head dolls be priced so high that the demand will diminish and collectors will turn to other types of dolls? At present bisque head dolls are so well entrenched among collectors that it would be difficult to change their preference.

Recently a new situation has arisen with the reduction of available petroleum products. Since modern vinyl dolls and their synthetic fabric clothes are both made from petroleum derivatives, their prices will probably have to rise the same as our gasoline. Already in the clothes market there is a noticeable return to natural fibers such as cotton and wool. Rumors

among doll manufacturers suggest that some of them may even be thinking of using bisque as an alternative to vinyl. Already modern dolls made primarily for collectors are usually of bisque. For generations little girls played with bisque dolls and a tremendous number of them survived. That is, both the little girls and the bisque dolls survived unharmed. During and immediately after World War I composition and cloth dolls replaced the missing bisque dolls for children. The war temporarily caused social and economic pressures that prevented the production of bisque head dolls. But with the return of bisque, when the *Bye-Lo Baby* was introduced in the mid 1920s, bisque head dolls once again became popular. The tremendous number of bisque head infant dolls attest to the popularity. Perhaps as prices of vinyl soar bisque dolls will once again reappear in the toy shops.

What the future holds no one knows but the artistic charm of many of the bisque head dolls should always be appreciated. □

The Womanly Ideal of the 19th Century and Her Dolls

by Estelle Johnston

The point has been reiterated elsewhere that the making of dolls has always been a commercial enterprise when done on a large scale. At the same time, the more handwork that goes into the making of a doll, the more of the maker is expressed in the creation. Dolls, on this scale, are made by adults and usually purchased by adults so, while the recipient may be a child, dolls have a way of saying a great deal about the tastes and values of the adults of their particular time. A study of the faces of dolls throughout the 19th century intended to represent women can tell us some interesting things about the changes in values and in the idealization of woman.

At the beginning of the century dolls were carved of wood and were likely to be individuals reflecting their carvers' flair for portraiture or even caricature. The excesses of style which preceded the French Revolution produced a pendulum swing to simplicity in the guise of classicism, and the peg-jointed wooden doll clearly evolved from the long slender look so fashionable in the first two decades. The court of Napoleon was the center of influence in this period of random borrowing from the Greeks and Romans of antiquity and, in its simplicity, clothing became democratic to a point where mistress and maid dressed alike.

Fine wooden dolls were costly and time-consuming to produce, and dolls of papier-mâché emerged in quantity as the romantic bourgeois flourished. Napoleon's day had ended. The classic line of long narrow white dresses had widened and puffed with multiple ruffles and full sleeves matched by hair styles of curls, braids and large combs until its zenith was reached and it collapsed into the rather tight and plain Jane Eyre look. The epitome of "the little woman" emerged: quiet, demure, often pale, large-eyed and gentle, and this ideal is most frequently seen in the papier-mâché dolls of the 1840s sometimes referred to as milliner's models. Occasionally, to be sure, one sees large papier-mâché dolls whose faces reflect the character and strength of the working women of their origins, Germany, but there seem to be many more of the insipid little romantics.

Has not woman always paid a price in loss of freedom and individuality for playing the romantic ideal?

Queen Victoria, as a young woman herself, represented to perfection this ideal, but the mother of nine children tends to lose a little in glamour. Victoria reigned over the increasing prosperity and wealth of England and was the undoubted leader of a prudish, even frumpish sense of values to which much of Europe paid lip service at the very least. This settled complacency and utter conviction of rightness, if not righteousness, is beautifully portrayed in the china dolls of the 1850s. No wild fashionable darlings these, but motherly homebodies, comfortable and pleasant-looking. Wax and papier-mâché dolls of the 1850s also mirrored the fashion for plumpness and crinolined bell skirts.

As Queen Victoria grew older and sadder, younger women con-

Illustration 1. 21in (53.3cm) carved wooden doll with pegged swivel joints; carved hair and ears with wire loops for earrings, dating from first decade.

Illustration 2. 7½in (19.1cm) papier-mâché doll; circa 1830; with kid body and wood lower limbs; brown painted hair with applied real hair curls; original pink dress with full sleeves and skirt.

tributed to the sense of style. The Prince of Wales' marriage to the Danish Princess Alexandra brought to England a tall slim lady with a flair for elegance while in "wicked Paris" Empress Eugenie had already preempted fashion attention and brought another change in the ideal as mirrored in dolls. The round faces of china dolls became longer and more slender, the hairdos more sophisticated. Parian dolls of the 1860s reflect much of the new elegance. Eugenie was never a real beauty but she had enormous style and, with the creative staging of Frederick Worth, introduced a new era in style; an era of conspicuous consumption and the culmination of intense Victorian materialism. No doll represents this era as succinctly as the cool fashion beauties of the 1870s with their richly trimmed and bustled dresses and their amazing array of accessories. The full docile-looking faces of the Rohmer and Huret dolls, as well as other early fashion dolls of the 1850s and 1860s, gave way to slimmer faces with a subtly knowing look - in some cases the doll known as "the smiler" actually seems to have a rather cruel, superior sneer. This was the period in fashion when wealthy women were literally loaded down with as much sumptuous clothing as their poor bodies could bear; a very effective way for a man to incapicitate his wife for any meaningful labor (or to hobble her from running away) and,

Illustration 4. 8in (20.3cm) china shoulder head doll; large painted brown eyes with lower lashes, stroked eyebrows; detailed modeling of features and tight curls around head.

Illustration 3. 12in (30.5cm) china shoulder head doll on jointed wood body with china lower arms and legs; circa 1840; molded and painted black hair with long ringlets; large painted brown eyes - very much of the romantic period.

Illustration 5. Group of china heads showing slender faces and sophisticated hairstyles. Left to right: 4in (10.2cm) china with shaded blonde hair, green snood and lustre scarf; 6in (15.2cm) china with brush-stroked hairline, molded bows and snood; 4½in (11.5cm) china with molded curls and chignon, large pierced ears; 8in (20.3cm) china with brush-stroked temples, molded comb with beads catching curls at lower back of head; 3in (7.6cm) china with brush strokes at ear level; low chignon.

Illustration 6. 18in (45.7cm) unmarked Huret shoulder head with painted blue eyes; original pale mohair wig; fully-jointed wood body.

at the same time, to have at his side a charming statement of his wealth and position. Wax dolls, too, changed with the times and the Pierrotti chubby child of the 1850s became the relatively slimmer lady of the 1870s with head turned aside in dreamy disdain.

In the 1880s lady dolls faded as the new and delectable bébés took center stage. Competition in the business of producing these new child dolls consumed the last two decades of the 19th century. While there were still some wax and wax-over-papier-mâché dolls produced and dressed as ladies, in bisque there was a definite hiatus in the modeling of mature female faces. One might speculate on the number of child dolls found dressed in original lady dresses of considerable style and richness of the 1880s and 1890s. Were women then to be deemed interchangeable with children? Ibsen would seem to corroborate this in his play *A Doll's House,* first published in 1879.

Illustration 7. 14in (35.6cm) parian doll with blonde hair molded in the Eugenie fashion; flat swivel neck; pierced ears; cloth body; bisque arms.

Illustration 8. 19in (48.3cm) unmarked fashion doll with cobalt blue glass eyes; pierced-in ears; original mohair wig; kid body; dress and hat of matching wool; silk and pale pink plush velvet.

Illustration 9. 20in (50.8cm) marked F.G. fashion doll with Gesland body; bisque lower arms and legs; the epitome of the 1870s in ivory wool dress trimmed with fine needlepoint lace, silk embroidery and bows, enamelled French buttons - not to mention lorgnette and silk parasol.

Illustration 10. 15in (38.1cm) wax-over-papier-mâché doll with large blue glass eyes; original brown crimped and curled mohair wig; cloth body with waxed composition lower limbs; dress of pink and green silk with matching wool cape of the 1880s trimmed with swansdown.

OPPOSITE PAGE: Illustration 11. Full length view of 20in (50.8cm) F.G. fashion doll shown in *Illustration 9.*

Finally, with the end of the century, lady dolls reappeared, true Edwardians owing something to the regality of Alexandra but a great deal more to the haughty mien of the famous idealizations of Charles Dana Gibson. A true 19th century man, he created with his pen an ideal aspired to by an expanding middle class busily climbing the social ladder. Few knew it in 1900, but the elegance and self-indulgence of the wealthy in the 19th century was coming to an end. The convulsions in the next decade of world war and revolution in Russia would herald the end of royalty in Europe, and with it the end of the high aristocratic life in the 19th century and the sumptuous dolls which reflected this life.

BELOW: 12in (30.5cm) tall Parian with molded blonde hair with beaded ribbon; very bright blue painted eyes, red eye liner, single stroke eyebrows; a tiny painted mouth; pierced ears; cloth body with leather arms and sewn-on leather boots. The yoke is nicely molded with ruffles around her neck and a necklace with the cross.

China &
Parian Dolls

Chinas, Parians and Molded Hair Dolls

A Photographic Essay
by Robert and Karin MacDowell

Photographs by Authors

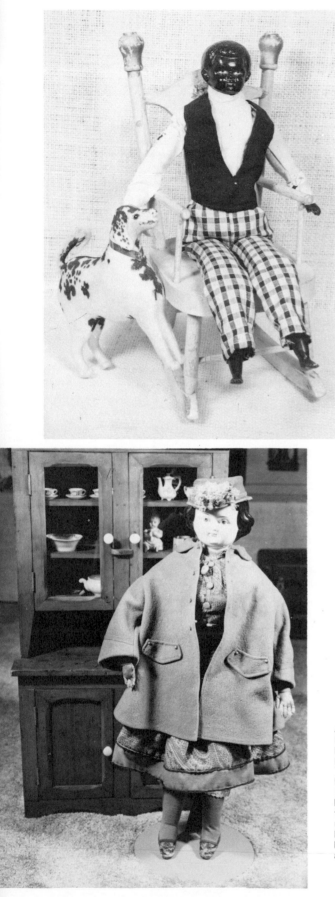

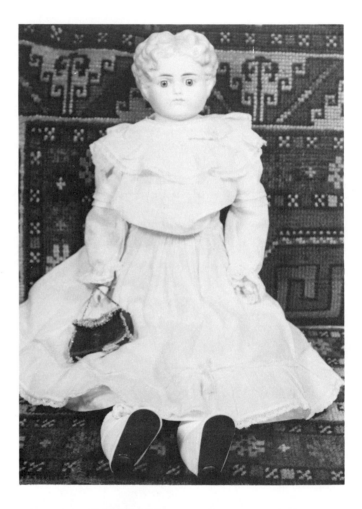

OPPOSITE PAGE: TOP LEFT: Illustration 5. This so-called "Highland Mary" is 12in (30.5cm) tall with short blonde molded hair with bangs. She has stationary blue eyes, feathered eyebrows and a closed mouth. She is on a replaced cloth body with bisque arms and legs. She holds a 7in (17.8cm) molded hair boy on a cloth body with bisque arms and legs. He wears his original leather suit.

LEFT: Illustration 2. This 12in (30.5cm) tall black china is a rare one. His hair is molded and his eyes are painted brown. He has very bright red lips but no cheek color. He is on a brown cloth body with china arms and legs. The feet and hands are very tiny. Butler Brothers in New York advertised him in 1899 as a Philippino.

ABOVE: Illustration 4. The molded hair doll is 20in (50.8cm) tall. She has short and curly blonde hair which leaves her ears exposed, stationary blue glass eyes, feathered eyebrows and a closed mouth. She is on a kid body with bisque arms. Her dress is believed to be original.

LEFT: Illustration 3. This is a stunning china. She measures 23in (58.4cm). Her china shoulder head is pink tinted. The eyes are painted brown with red eye liner and single stroke eyebrows. She has little dots for nostrils and a closed mouth. The head is attached to a cloth body with red leather arms. Her clothes are all original including a paisley dress, brown wool coat trimmed with brass buttons, red and brown felt hat, brown cotton stockings and black leather shoes. She stands in front of a pine hutch, American, circa 1860.

Illustration 1: ON PAGE 19. A group of chinas. Back row, left to right: 16in (40.6cm) glass eyed china with pink tint; 23in (58.4cm) brown eyed china with pink tint. Front row, left to right: 12in (30.5cm) spill curl china with blue painted eyes, a cloth body, china arms and legs; 10in (25.4cm) china with pink tint, blue painted eyes; seated 12in (30.5cm) black china.

Illustration 7.
Pair of Parians.
The little lady
is 15in (38.1cm).
She has blonde
molded hair with
a pink lustre
snood and scarf;
blue painted eyes
with white high-
lights, feathered
eyebrows, eye lashes
so fine they remind
you of a spider web;
a tiny painted mouth;
cloth body with leather
arms and sewn-on leather
boots. The gentleman is 17in
(43.2cm) tall; has molded hair
and a fancy yoke with blue and
gold tie; blue painted eyes with highlights,
single stroke eyebrows; a closed mouth; a cloth body with cloth arms
and singly stitched fingers.

Illustration 6. This molded hair 16½in (41.9cm) tall boy
has lovely modeling. His intaglio eyes are painted blue with
white highlights and single stroke eyebrows. He has exposed
ears and a closed mouth. His cheeks are very red. The blue
woolen suit trimmed with pink satin is all original.

Illustration 8. 4in (10.2cm) tall Parian shoulder head. She has
molded blonde hair with tiny roses; blue painted eyes, single
stroke eyebrows; closed mouth. Her yellow and gold necklace
is molded on the shoulders.

LEFT: **Illustration 9.** Doll house room with two 5½in (14.0cm) tall chinas. They are the so-called low brow chinas with china arms and legs and cloth bodies. The little boy doing his carefree somersaults on the bed is a 4in (10.2cm) long all bisque with molded hair.

BELOW: **Illustration 11.** This is a lovely so-called "Alice-in-Wonderland" 23in (58.4cm) tall doll. She has blonde painted and molded hair with a black ribbon; blue painted eyes with red eye liner; her tiny mouth indicates a smile; the head is attached to a cloth body with leather arms. She wears a blue taffeta dress with white organdy pinafore.

Illustration 10. 15in (38.1cm) china with pierced ears. She has blue painted eyes, molded eye lids, single stroke eyebrows; red nostril dots, closed mouth; cloth body with china arms and legs. Her boots are painted pink. She is dressed in pink with black trim.

Dolls' Christmas of Yesterday

by Elspeth

Featuring dolls from the Carroll County Historical Society

BELOW: Bisque head marked: "K Germany 14 / 171." Open mouth; brown sleeping eyes, composition body. Height 25in (63.5cm). Blonde mohair wig.

FOLLOWING PAGE (CLOCKWISE BEGINNING UPPER LEFT): (1) Left: Bisque head; open mouth; brown sleeping eyes; composition body. Height 25in (63.5cm). Blonde mohair wig. Right: Bisque head; open mouth; brown sleeping eyes with eyelashes; composition body. Height 25in (63.5cm). Brown mohair wig. (2) Unmarked bisque head; closed mouth; stationary brown glass eyes. Jointed composition body. Height 17in (43.2cm). (3) Left: Bisque head; marked with "7"; swivel neck; closed mouth; stationary blue glass eyes; pierced ears. Kid arms on cloth lady body. Height 20in (50.8cm). Right: All bisque child doll; marked "14"; open mouth; stationary grey-blue eyes. Height 10in (25.4cm). (4) Bisque head; open mouth; blue sleeping eyes; jointed composition body. Height 22½in (57.2cm). Baby: Open mouth; blue sleeping eyes; bent limb baby body of composition. Height 11in (27.9cm).

From the December 1981/January 1982 Doll Reader.®

Later Than You Think

by **Evelyn J. Coleman**

Illustration 1. 10in (25.4cm) so-called Queen Anne type doll, documented as of 1795. *Courtesy of the Wenham Museum.*

doll are original and what were added later. Even when we recognize the original clothes their exact date can be elusive. Alas, many of our dolls do not have any original clothes and yet we seek their dates. Most doll types were manufactured over a long period of time; often for 50 years or even more. In these cases no precise date can be given. We can say "after" a certain date which indicates the beginning of manufacture or we can give the time period over which the doll was made. The beginning of the manufacture of the doll type should NOT be given as the date of a particular doll.

Many collectors and some authors give dolls dates that were long before they were even made. This is particularly true of the early dolls. Collectors often refer to early wooden dolls as "Queen Anne" dolls. Queen Anne reigned from 1702 to 1714. None of the dolls of the type called "Queen Anne" were made as early as the reign of this Queen. Judging from documentation and original clothes most of the so-called Queen Anne dolls were made from about 1790 to 1840; thus going into the fifth generation after Queen Anne. See *Illustration 1* for a Queen Anne doll of 1795.

"Biedermeier" usually refers to an object made in the first half of the 19th century. The name "Bieder-

Illustration 2. 15½in (39.4cm) ball-head china (so-called Biedermeier) doll of the late 1860s. *Coleman Collection.*

"How old is my doll?" This question is asked almost as often as "Who made my doll?" The date when a doll was made seems to be very important to collectors. However, the age of a doll is a minor factor in determining its value. Most dolls on exhibit are dated. When a doll is entered in competition the date is often required. There is a certain satisfaction in being able to tell the age of our dolls when we show them to friends as well as when they are exhibited.

However, are we dating our dolls correctly? Or are they only guesses influenced by what we have read on the subject and perhaps not fully understood? Unfortunately not all dates seen in print are correct. Arriving at a true date is not easy and requires considerable study and knowledge. Of course the best basis for dating dolls is according to the date of their original clothes. Even if we have studied *The Collector's Book of Dolls Clothes,* it is not always easy to determine what clothes on our

meier'' is often used for bald china (glazed porcelain) head dolls that wear wigs. See *Illustration 2*. Because of the use of this name, Biedermeier, many collectors and some authors date these dolls before 1850. As a matter of fact I have seen a considerable number of these dolls and judging from documentation and/or original clothes all of these dolls date from after 1850. The majority are 1860 to 1880.

The dating of china-head dolls seems to be particularly erroneous. The wigged chinas or so-called Biedermeiers, are not the only ones that are often dated far too early. Many collectors believe that the hair style indicates the age. It is a known fact that many of the popular molded-hair types were produced over a long period of time. The collector has no idea whether a given head was made early or late in the period of its production unless the clothes provide a clue as to the time. Unfortunately original clothes are seldom found on china-headed dolls. The corkscrew-curl type of hairdo as seen in *Illustration 3* and *4* is sometimes attributed to the 1840s. Many

books indicate this date. However, the commercially-dressed doll wearing its original 1880s dress is seen in *Illustration 4*. Thus this popular type of doll was no doubt made from about 1840 to 1890. A particular doll of this type, without original clothes, could have been made at any time during these 50 years and a guess of 1840 as a date could be 50 years too early.

The commonest type of hairdo on china heads is shown in *Illustration 5*. These dolls are often dated 1880 when the style first appeared on the market. Kimport advertised china-head dolls with this hair style (but without the pet name molded blouse) during the 1930s. Once again it is a period of at least 50 years for their manufacture. A doll with a similar style hairdo but made of bisque instead of china was purchased new for a little girl in the 1950s.

China-head dolls are not the only dolls frequently dated too early. The Greiner dolls carry the date 1858 or 1872 but certainly not all Greiners were made in these two years. A Greiner dated 1858 could

BOTTOM LEFT: Illustration 3. 15½in (39.4cm) china head with molded corkscrew curls. Original dress indicates a date of 1850s or early 1860s. *Coleman Collection.*

ABOVE: Illustration 4. 7½in (19.1cm) china head with molded corkscrew curls, original commercial dress indicates a date of 1880s. *Coleman Collection.*

BOTTOM RIGHT: Illustration 5. 17in (43.2cm) china head with common hair style, also has pet name. The molds for the pet name dolls were owned by Butler Brothers and advertised from 1905 on. *Coleman Collection.*

Illustration 6. Historical series of 10in (25.4cm) bisque-head Jumeau dolls made in the 1940s. **Top row, left to right:** Empress Josephine, Queen Victoria, Empress Eugénie, Sarah Bernhardt; **bottom row, left to right:** Empress Marie Louise, Queen Marie Antoinette, Mme. de Pompadour and Mme. de Sévigné. Dolls sold by Franz Carl Weber stores.

have been made anywhere from 1858 up until 1872.

A doll with the type of composition head often referred to as "Pre-Greiner" with molded hair and glass eyes is documented, not before, but after the Greiners. This particular doll has wooden arms of the type found on the so-called milliner's model dolls. Both the head and arms bespeak of a much earlier doll; but it is commerically dressed in a Dutch costume and is documented as having been purchsed in "Amsterdam, Monday Nov. 7th, 1881" in an early holograph type of writing. A calendar check shows that in 1881 November 7th did fall on Monday. This does not prove that all dolls of this so-called Pre-Greiner type were made as late as 1881. No doubt most of them were made earlier judging from the hairdos. It simply shows that these dolls were made over a longer period than hitherto was believed possible.

Cloth dolls made by the Cocheco Manufacturing Company bear a mark dated 1827. This was the date for the beginning of this textile manufacturer. They probably did not make cloth printed with dolls that could be cut out and stuffed until 1889. Most people are aware of the true date for the beginning of these cut-out cloth dolls designed by Celia and Charity Smith, but occasionally the 1827 date is erroneously used. Although the production of these dolls started in 1889, they continued to be made for years. The best way of describing the date of these dolls is to say "beginning in 1889" or "from 1889 on."

Bisque dolls are not exempt from being dated far too early. Many of the Jumeaus are dated 1878 because they have "Medaille d'Or 1878" on their body and/or on their shoes. The date of the 1878 exhibition where the Jumeau firm won a gold medal has nothing to do with the date of a particular Jumeau doll. It is merely a form of advertising the fact that they had won a gold medal. It simply shows us that the doll was made after 1878. According to production figures Jumeau only made 85,000 bébés in 1881, then steadily increased their production. In 1897 they made three million dolls. The highest production figure available is seven million dolls in 1922, but this includes some smaller firms in the combined S.F.B.J. These statistics tell us that in 1878

Jumeau probably produced less than 100,000 dolls while 20 to 50 years later the Jumeaus numbered in the millions each year. Thus the probability of a Jumeau doll having been made in 1878 is very remote while the possibility of its having been made in the 20th century is more than likely. Jumeau dolls were produced even after World War II. Some of these are shown in *Illustration 6*. These dolls, 10in (25.4cm) tall, carry a round gold cardboard tag marked, "fabrication//Jumeau//Paris// Made In France." The reverse of the tag gives the name of the person represented by the costume on the doll. This historical series of Jumeau lady dolls are shown in *Illustration 6*. On the top row left to right are the Empress Josephine, Queen Victoria, Empress Eugenie, Sarah Bernhardt and on the bottom row are Empress Marie Louise, Queen Marie Antoinette, Mme. de Pompadour and Mme. de. Sévigne. In the Coleman collection there is Empress Marie Louise and Alberta Darby has Sarah Bernhardt. These two dolls were part of the stock of dolls sold in the 1940s by Franz Carl Weber, the famous chain of toy stores in Switzerland. These dolls have composition bodies and are jointed at the neck, shoulders and hips. Black slippers are painted on the feet, one of which has a hole to enable the stand to be inserted. The original Jumeau boxes contain a metal stand to be inserted in the hole provided for it. The dolls have bisque heads, stationary glass eyes, closed mouths and wigs. The faces all appear to be from the same mold and are incised "Unis France" and "221" over "3/o."

The November 1952 issue of *Doll News* has an advertisement of the Mme. de Pompadour doll, like one of the dolls shown in *Illustration 6*. With this doll is a larger child doll. The small doll is described as being a "French Historical" doll costing $15.00. The larger doll is "The New French Bru - 18 inches tall - Composition Body, Blue Glass Eyes - Bisque Head...$75.00 (Has voice of Ma and Pa)." The Bru appears to be a closed mouth judging from the picture. The face has an unmistakable Bru appearance. The ball-jointed composition body is jointed at the wrists. The clothes seem to be a 1950 version of an early French Bébé's attire. This

advertisement in *Doll News* also mentions 22 (14in [35.6cm]) dolls in various Swiss costumes. Presumably all the dolls in this advertisement were made after World War II. Collectors must realize that bisque-head Bru and Jumeau dolls were still being made as late as 1950; much later than you think.

The *Bye-Lo* babies were copyrighted in 1923 and generally are considered to be a 1920s doll. Yet, in the August 1952 doll catalog of Dolly Palmer this statement is made:

"Perhaps you are familiar with the fact that in the 1920s, also, in Germany there was manufactured a *By-Lo baby in all bisque,* with moving arms and legs. This By-Lo bore the Grace Putnam markings attached to the body of the doll, by means of a printed paper label. You may be interested to know, if you are not aware of the fact as yet, that about one year ago [1951] the manufacturer of the all-bisque baby By-Lo was begun once more in Germany, under the Putnam copyright. The first shipment of these was not large and sold out almost immediately. At present [1952] another shipment is expected momentarily. If you wish to purchase one of these modern marked Putnams of German manufacture, send your order at once. The dolls are in several sizes, the smallest of which is approximately 5½ inches long. In the previous shipment the price was under $4.00."

When we date our dolls considerably earlier than they really are, we only show our ignorance. Sometimes dolls are disqualified in competitions because they are actually later than the owner realizes. Fairly precise dates are almost impossible to ascertain unless there is valid documentation or the doll is in its original clothes than can be dated. The safest thing to say, when in doubt, is "after" a specified date or give the range of possible dates. The age of a doll has little effect on its value and almost none on our appreciation and enjoyment of the doll. So let us avoid wishful thinking and be honest in our dating even if it is later than you think. □

Dolls In Their Original Clothes

ROBERT & KARIN MacDOWELL
Photographs by the Authors

Among the numerous collecting specialties, original costuming commands quite a high level of interest. We are pleased to offer the following selection from the MacDowell Museum collection for your study and enjoyment.

One facet of doll collecting and research which particularly pleases us is the willingness shown by friends, visitors and colleagues to share their knowledge and data. We are especially grateful to Mrs. Anita Rae of Middleburg, Virginia, for her invaluable assistance with the descriptive information accompanying the illustrations.

Illustration 1. Edwardian Doll House Family. Mother: black cotton satin dress. Father: 5 in. (12.7cm) navy blue felt suit, cotton shirt, paper collar. Boy: Green knitted shorts with suspenders, white cotton shirt. Girl: Pale blue cotton skirt with tunic, pink and blue ribbon flowers at waist. Maid: Pink cotton two piece dress, white cotton apron.

Illustration 2. 18 in. (45.7cm) French Fashion. Swivel head. Cobalt blue eyes, closed mouth, pierced ears. Back of shoulders incised "B 4 S." Human hair wig, kid body. Lace stockings, cotton pantaloons, wool flannel petticoat, fine linen petticoat trimmed with handmade lace. Gray silk dress trimmed with blue silk and blue faille ribbon and gathered dickey. Blue velvet hat covered with silk veiling, white silk ribbons and exquisite glass beads.

Illustration 3. 11 in. (27.9cm) Minerva celluloid pair. Blue glass eyes, socket heads. Girl: Cotton teddy with crocheted trim, blue and white cotton dirndl trimmed with rickrack, red apron trimmed with embroidered tape. Cotton sox and leather shoes. Boy: White cotton shirt, black felt pants and suspenders with feather stitching, silk tie. Cotton leggings (calf warmers), leather shoes.

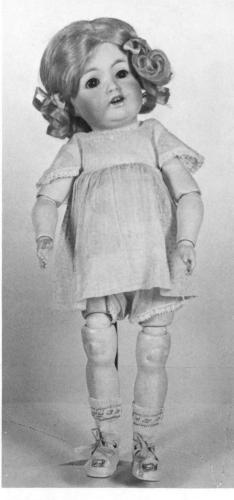

LEFT: Illustration 4. 13 in. (33cm) Kestner 260. Bisque head, brown sleep eyes, open mouth, blond mohair wig with blue satin bows. Fully jointed composition body with very long lower legs to accommodate short dress. Cotton panties, pink dotted swiss dress trimmed with cotton lace. Blue silk ribbons in hair match bows on shoes. Blue and white cotton sox, imitation leather shoes.

RIGHT: Illustration 5. 11 in. (27.9cm) French Belton. Paperweight brown eyes, closed mouth, goatskin wig with blue silk bow. Fully jointed composition body. Factory made chemise and pantalettes. Hand knitted leggings trimmed with buttons, hand crocheted blue and white coat dress trimmed with white buttons and silk bow. Hand crocheted hat trimmed with blue silk ribbon.

FAR LEFT: Illustration 6. 16. in. (40.6cm) molded hair Schoenhut girl with painted pink bow in back of hair. Cotton union suit, cotton sox, pink leather shoes. Original stand.

Illustration 7. 15 in. (38.1cm) German papier-mâché. So called "Milliner's Model." Papier-mâché head, wooden arms and legs. Kid body. Beautiful handsewn clothes. Plain white cotton pantaloons, gathered petticoat. Faded olive green corded organza dress. Faille sash.

Illustration 8. 4 in. (10.2cm) all bisque boy and girl. Solid domes. Stiff necks, arms and legs. Molded and painted boots and sox. Shoes painted lavender with black tassels. Faces painted in very fine detail. Girl: Brown silk ruffled dress with ecru lace and brown silk ribbons, silk and lace bonnet. Crude satin panties. Boy: Navy blue velvet suit and hat. Cotton embroidered shirt, white cotton collar, silk faille bow.

Illustration 9. 7 in. (17.8cm) German bisque head. Closed mouth, brown glass eyes, mohair wig, five piece composition body. White cotton blouse, lace collar, red wool skirt trimmed with green velvet. Metallic embroidered "Leibchen." Lace apron.

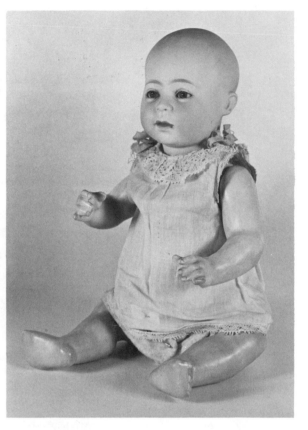

RIGHT: Illustration 11. 14 in. (35.6cm) "Lori." D. V. 4 Geschuetzt S & Co. Germany. Bisque head, molded and painted hair, blue sleep eyes, closed mouth. Bent limb composition body. Cotton flannel diaper, cotton chemise trimmed with cotton lace and pink ribbons.

ABOVE: Illustration 10. 18 in. (45.7cm) Lenci. Felt face, body, arms and legs. Painted features, mohair sewn in strips to make wig. Cotton teddy. Mauve felt coat dress and hat with matching shoes, cotton sox.

Illustration 12. 4 in. (10.2cm) all bisque boy and girl. Girl: Pupilless blue eyes, closed mouth, mohair wig. Movable arms and legs. Painted sox and shoes. Colorful cotton dirndl, white china beads, red felt hat. Buckram panties. Boy: Brown pupilless eyes, tiny blond mohair curls. Movable arms and legs. Painted sox and shoes. Cotton plaid tunic with white felt collar over white felt pants.

From the October/November 1980 Doll Reader.

RIGHT: Illustration 13. 20½ in. (52.1cm) hatted wax over papier-mâché. Cobalt blue eyes. Wooden arms and legs, cloth body with squeaker box. Fine linen underwear, blue chintz dress trimmed with beige gauze, fine lace and metal embroidery. Peau de soie sash.

FAR RIGHT: Illustration 14. 12 in. (30.5cm) papier-mâché shoulder head. Cobalt blue eyes, mohair wig with cotton ribbon. Composition arms and legs with painted shoes. Straw stuffed cloth body. Starched gauze chemise, batiste pantalettes with lace trim. Pink batiste dress trimmed with fine cotton lace.

RIGHT: Illustration 16. 11 in. (27.9cm) early composition shoulder head boy. Paperweight blue eyes, closed mouth, mohair wig. Bisque arms, cloth body. Fine linen shirtwaist, pointed collar, red challis vest with brass buttons, white faille jacket with brass buttons. Black velvet pants, white cotton stockings, black patent leather shoes.

Illustration 15. 5½ in. (14cm) all bisque German boy. Molded blond hair, painted eyes. Movable arms and legs. Painted sox and shoes. Navy blue wool pants and coat. Embroidered buttons, white linen collar, red bow.

LEFT: Illustration 17. 11 in. (27.9cm) papier-mâché shoulder head boy. Pupilless brown eyes, mohair curls. Composition arms and legs. Straw stuffed cloth body. Dark blue cotton suit trimmed with white cotton collar. Matching tam.

LEFT: Illustration 18. 17 in. (43.2cm) Käthe Kruse. Cloth doll. Oil painted face. Blond mohair inserted in tiny tufts into cloth scalp. Batiste combination underwear, printed linen dress, cotton sox, red felt shoes.

BELOW: Illustration 19. 13½ in. (34.3cm) early composition shoulder head. Paperweight blue eyes, closed mouth, blond mohair. Composition arms and legs with painted sox and shoes. Straw stuffed cloth body. Cotton chemise, cotton twill skirt and pantalettes trimmed with cotton lace. Dimity ribbon.

LEFT: Illustration 20. 7 in. (17.8cm) S & H bisque shoulder head. Brown glass eyes, closed mouth, mohair wig. Bisque arms and legs, cloth body. Cotton underwear, gauze slip. Faded green cotton and silk dress trimmed with corsage.

Dolls' House Dolls

by Magda Byfield

Small dolls have been used as inhabitants of miniature interiors since the dolls' house came into being. The first specimens were commissioned from craftsmen together with the fine furnishings and trappings and were exquisite miniatures of wax or wood, expertly dressed and elaborately wigged.

Early in the 19th century the commerical production of toy houses commenced together with every conceivable miniature item of furniture and paraphernalia — and of course, mass-produced dolls to scale. Throughout the second half of the 19th century manufacturers were making dolls' house dolls in a large variety of types.

The first commercially produced miniature dolls were the peg-woodens. In this type we find some of the tiniest jointed dolls ever made. The heads are ball-shaped, usually with a carved comb painted yellow and the head, shoulders and lower limbs are painted and varnished. Their hair and eyes are always painted black with gray spit curls at the temples. A more sophisticated version of this type has a gesso covered head with well modeled face and hair style and blue painted eyes.

Illustration 1. A pair of 5½in (14cm) peg-wooden dolls, the woman with carved yellow comb, black painted hair and gray spit curls. Dressed in black frock trimmed with lace and ribbon. Sleeves are spotted muslin and bonnet is lace. Man has painted hair in foreward-brushed style with grey side curls. Dressed in paper shirt, black waistcoat and wool suit. Both have spade-type hands with no thumbs. Circa 1850.

A more expensive line at this time was a 4½in (11.5cm) wax shoulder head doll with a sawdust filled cloth body and wax lower limbs, the molded boots elaborately painted green or brown with black laces. This type has painted or inserted hair and is usually found dressed in a short crinoline with pantaloons and a finely worked straw hat. Features are painted though occassionally eyes are tiny wax beads. So far only girl dolls are recorded (their fragility has caused few to survive) but one suspects, and it seems likely, that a boy version was made.

China heads became popular in the late 1850s and are found on various types of bodies: pegged through holes in the front and back of the shoulders to a wooden peg-jointed body or with china lower limbs. This latter type usually has a flesh-tinted head with black or brown molded hair and the right hand modeled closed with a holding-hole. More common are the china heads either sewn or glued to a cloth body with china lower limbs and molded ankle boots. Among these a fair number represent young men with windswept hair styles but the majority are models of women and girls. It is difficult to know what proportion of these dolls were commercially dressed in the first instance. Their relative durability lead to re-dressing as they passed from generation to generation in much the same way as their miniature homes were refurbished with changing fashions.

The exact purpose of the china Pillar Doll or Frozen Charlotte is now known exactly but they seem to have been connected with the Christmas season when they were used as cracker toys, trinkets to be cooked in the pudding and baubles hung on the Christmas tree. It seems they were also bath toys and certainly some must have been manufactured to fill the role of dolls' house babies. The most common type have painted hair and features and occasionally a specimen is found with a molded bonnet. They are entirely without articulation as their name implies and a few were modeled in a seated or semi-lying position. They all

represent children and, as is usual with dolls, the girls outnumber the boys. The tiniest were ideal for dressing as infants to occupy prams, cradles or the arms of a nanny doll.

In the late 1860s bisque became popular and at this point one finds china heads with bisque limbs and bisque heads with china limbs — a feature often wrongly thought to be a later marriage. Heads, too, combined both types of surface and some lovely hatted dolls were produced in the 1870s and 1880s with glazed trim and lustre adornments. For a time, too, a number of identical models were produced in both china and bisque. In eliminating the final coat of glazing a much crisper definition of features resulted and some finely detailed small dolls were made

Illustration 2. 6in (15.2cm) peg-jointed lady doll with gessoed head, the molded hair style with a bun at the back. Forearms and lower legs are painted, the feet with black flat slippers. Circa 1850.

From the February 1978 Doll Reader.®

Illustration 3. 1¼in (3.2cm) china seated Frozen Charlotte in original walnut shell hinged container lined with yellow silk. Probably intended to hang on a Christmas tree. Doll dressed in pink silk. Circa 1885.

Illustration 4. 3½in (8.9cm) pair of china shoulder head girl dolls on cloth bodies with bisque lower limbs, the legs with flat black ankle boots. Costumes of silk and lace with metal butterflies stitched to front. Circa 1870.

in this period. Blonde hair now predominated and the number of male dolls increased though they still represented boys rather than men. Height alone distinguished one from the other. Some bisque shoulder heads were made with mohair wigs and more rarely a glass-eyed specimen is found. Pierced ears are also seen in this small scale and a rare variant is a bisque shoulder head mounted on a peg-wooden body. In the 1880s dolls depicting men with moustaches and beards first appeared and factory dressed dolls

began to multiply. Though bisque now predominated, china and wooden dolls continued in production.

All-bisque dolls first appeared in the late 1860s and by the 1880s were being manufactured in a large range of sizes from 3/4in (2cm) upwards. Notably the majority were sold dressed — some in extremely sophisticated outfits. Many are thought to have been made in France as well as Germany, but few specimens are marked. The early ones were elastic strung from a bar inside the head giving mobility at the neck, shoulders and hips; high grade specimens having kid washers at their five points of articulation. A variant has additional mobility at the elbows and knees in the form of bisque ball joints. In very small sizes the neck was modeled with a loop to support the leg rubber (known as bell-necks). Among the many striking features of this type are glass eyes (stationary or sleeping), luxurious mohair wigs, excellent detail of modeling and decoration and well molded shoes or bare feet. All-bisque were also made with painted features and molded hair and bisque was used for some very fine Frozen Charlottes. Wire stringing was usual for the type where articulation was confined to the shoulders and hips only, and these are known to collectors as "stiff-necks." All-bisque dolls represented children (boys and girls as well as babies) but occasionally a ravishing adolescent is found superbly poised between innocence and elegance. The best of these were, of course, luxury dolls (often sold with extensive wardrobes) and

the 1880s produced some of the finest examples. Later they were mass-produced and the high grade bisque and sophisticated costumes gave way to lower standards. All-bisques continued in production well into the 1930s and have been found dressed as World War I munitions workers, nurses, soldiers and later designs in typical 30s fashions.

In the 1890s a realistic line of bisque shoulder head dolls' house inhabitants made their first appearance and scored a success which was as lasting as their hair fashions would allow. These dolls were modeled as portrait heads of boys and girls, men and women and notably, for the first time, an elderly couple representing grandparents. Their bodies were of pink cloth, the upper arm sections with inserted wire enabling them to be positioned in a variety of attitudes. Among this group were servants with hair styles that identified them as menials, though their costuming did not necessarily follow the social standing this indicated. Their clothing was simple but effective: machined wool, felt and linen with braid or paper trim and underwear of starched muslin. All had painted features and molded hair and among these we find the only dolls' house dolls with brown painted eyes. Many, of course, were re-dressed later but from the large numbers found in original factory outfits it seems likely that the majority were sold dressed.

Early in the 20th century a family of miniature half-bisque dolls were produced representing grandparents, parents and children. These were a combination of bisque and

Illustration 5. 1½in (3.8cm) bisque shoulder head girl doll with molded hair and inset glass eyes with painted upper and lower lashes. Circa 1880.

cloth but their design and construction was novel and was possibly a progression from the shoulder head doll with molded collar — a decorative type usually also with a molded hat or bonnet. Half-bisque dolls are bisque down to the waistline with molded jackets, shirts and blouses incorporating kerchiefs, bows and trim. The bisque forearms are surprisingly short and the stuffed cloth upper arm sections are glued into slits at the shoulders. Bisque lower legs are also short and the cloth upper leg and hip sections are glued inside the torso. Their costumes consist of sleeves and skirts or trousers concealing the stuffed cloth areas of pink or brown fabric. Molded shoes have slightly raised heels and are yellow or blue. There are eight models in all; four adults and four children with realistic character heads.

After World War I substances like rubber, celluloid and composition came into use for dolls' house dolls. Though Germany still produced the largest numbers, France, Japan and England had all come into the market. Bisque, china and wooden dolls were still made right up until 1939 after which the emergent plastics of the post-war period brought into play a series of factors which entirely changed the ideas and traditions of doll making.

The inhabitants of dolls' houses can be seen to have been many and varied. While some of the dolls are exquisite miniatures in their own right, their purpose was to be a part of a whole and we can best appreciate their charm by seeing them in related groups within a miniature setting. Part of their appeal today must surely be that they evoke an orderly and predictable society in which we can briefly lose ourselves. In opening a dolls' house we unlock a secret and enduring world whose delightful occupants predate us and will certainly outlast us.

List of dolls' house doll types from circa 1850 to circa 1939

1. All-wood with peg joints. Painted features. Carved hair and/or comb. Male or female.
2. Wood with gessoed head. Painted features and molded hair. Male or female.
3. Peg-wooden with china head and china lower limbs. Painted features and molded hair. Male or female.
4. Wax shoulder head and lower limbs on cloth body. Painted features and hair or wig. Only girls found.
5. Peg-wooden with bisque shoulder head. Secured by gluing to wooden dowel passing up through neck. Lower limbs painted but not varnished. Painted features and molded hair. Male or female.
6. China shoulder head and lower limbs on cloth body. Molded hair and painted features. Male or female.
7. Bisque shoulder head and lower limbs on cloth body. Painted features. Occasionally glass eyes. Some with pierced ears. Men, women, boys and girls.
8. Bisque hatted or bonnet dolls. Headdress molded in one with head. Cloth body and painted features. Occasionally molded and painted collar. Men, women, boys and girls.
9. Half-bisque dolls. Cloth upper limbs only. Painted features and molded hair. Men, women, boys and girls.
10. All-bisque dolls. Molded hair or wigs. Painted features or glass eyes. Sometimes molded clothing. Boys, girls and babies.
11. Frozen Charlottes. China, wax, bisque and celluloid. Molded hair or wigs. Sometimes molded clothes. Painted features. Boys, girls and babies.
12. Composition dolls. Molded hair and painted features. Men, women, boys, girls and babies.
13. Rubber dolls. Molded hair and painted features. No articulation. Boys, girls and babies.
14. Celluloid. Molded hair or wigs. Painted features. Boys, girls and babies.

The above list is a generalization of types. Anyone studying dolls will know there is always the excep-

BELOW: LEFT TO RIGHT: Illustration 6. 3¼in (8.3cm) bisque shoulder head girl doll on peg-jointed wooden body, the lower limbs painted but not varnished. Dressed in yellow silk and black top hat with veil in back. Circa 1880. **Illustration 7.** 3in (7.6cm) all-bisque girl doll with tightly curled mohair wig. Elastic strung from bell-type socket neck. Painted features and blue boots. Dressed in elaborate blue and brown silk dress and crochet hat. Circa 1885. **Illustration 8.** 6in (15.2cm) bisque shoulder head lady doll with painted features and molded hair style. Pink cloth body and bisque lower limbs, the legs with molded brown shoes and raised heels. Arms are wire-enforced. One of a group of eight models. Circa 1910.

Illustration 9. 4½in (11.3cm) hatted boy doll, the bisque shoulder head with molded sailor-type blouse. Cloth body with bisque lower limbs. Circa 1880.

Illustration 11. 5½in (14cm) composition man doll, elastic strung at shoulders and hips. Molded hair and painted features. Incised on back: "5599/1//Germany." Legs and arms each incised: "11." Circa 1930.

tion to the rule and new specimens continue to appear to confound our theories and sequencing patterns almost immediately after they have been compiled. Soon after this article was completed a collector produced an all-bisque *man* doll with molded moustache! Another reported a 5in (12.7cm) wax shoulder head *boy* with painted hair. I therefore emphasize that this article is based entirely on personal observations to date and readily concede that it is likely to be incomplete.

Illustration 10. 4½in (11.5cm) half-bisque boy doll, the head and body molded in one to the waist. Bisque forearms are exceptionally short. Plump legs have blue molded shoes with slightly raised heels. One of a group of eight models. Circa 1912.

THE MARGARET WOODBURY STRONG MUSEUM OPENS ON OCTOBER 12, 1982

A Preview of What is to Come

by
Margaret Whitton

Photographs by Harry Bickelhaupt

Illustration 1. A French composition doll. This composition is sometimes referred to as "carton moulé" or cardboard. Original costume. Pulling the string at the base activates the child in a rocking motion. France, circa 1815.

The long awaited opening of the Margaret Woodbury Strong Museum in Rochester, New York, will soon be here. October 12, 1982, is the official date, and doll collectors will have the pleasure of viewing some 12,000 to 15,000 dolls. Ninety-eight cases of dolls will be exhibited in the museum's study collections. A special exhibit entitled "Yesterday's Playthings" will feature 140 dolls, doll houses and toys from the past.

The dolls in "Yesterday's Playthings" will include rare and beautiful parian-types with elaborate molded collars, flowers and hair decorations; china head dolls will be seen with both painted and glass eyes, some with elaborate hair styles; 18th century wooden dolls will be represented as will dolls of wax, papier-mâché, fashions and French bébés.

The Thomas Edison phonograph doll and Emile Jumeau phonograph doll will also be on exhibition. Many times collectors confuse these two dolls in their minds, and this will give them an opportunity to study the differences in construction.

Also featured will be a collection of dolls in national costume. These dolls were exhibited at the New York World's Fair of 1939, having been submitted by various countries to show the beauty and quality of their native costumes.

The Spanish-American War is the inspiration for a display of bisque head portrait dolls representing William McKinley, president of the United States; George Dewey, commander of the Asiatic Squadron; and several other American navy officers. Also in the exhibit will be the toy ships representing the United States White Fleet of the Spanish-American War.

A very imposing group of boys' toys has been arranged for the public, featuring toys of wood, iron and tin. A Noah's Ark will be arranged with an impressive array of animals leaving the ark after the water had subsided, moving two by two down an incline. Live steam toys fired by alcohol burners, including an ocean liner, locomotive, machine shop and automobile, will also be on exhibit.

Doll houses and doll house furniture will be featured, with some of the rarest of the houses in the collection included in the exhibit.

Illustrations 2 and 3. Bisque shoulder head doll. When the opening in the back of the shoulder is held to a light, photographic scenes of Paris and religious figures can be seen through the glass jewels of the necklace. The head is signed Ed. Rocharde Brevete S.G.D.G. France. Patented 1867 and 1868.

Collectors of all types of children's toys will be pleased with the diversity of objects shown in the exhibit, "Yesterday's Playthings," and will find it well worth the trip to Rochester to see this amazing toy collection, much of which was assembled by the late Margaret Woodbury Strong.

Illustration 4. A bisque head doll with glass eyes, composition jointed body and bisque lower arms and hands. Original costume. The head is incised "A, Marque." France, 1916.

Illustration 3.

Illustration 5. A pair of French bébé's. The doll on the left has a bisque head stamped in red with a "7" and a check mark. The composition, jointed body is stamped "Jumeau Medaille d'Or Paris," and she wears her original costume. Manufactured by Emile Jumeau, Paris, France, 1875 to 1885. The black doll on the right has a bisque shoulder head, a swivel neck and is marked on the head with a dot and a circle. The body is kid and the lower arms and hands are bisque. She wears her original costume and was manufactured by Bru of Paris, France, 1879 to 1880.

Illustration 6. A fashion doll with a bisque shoulder head and kid body. The hair is set into a wax scalp. Patented by Josef Kubelka in France, Germany and Austria in 1884.

Illustration 7. A Hungarian woman and her children, designed and made by Marga. The face of the mother is molded felt and the children have composition heads. The costumes are hand embroidered. 1938 to 1939.

Illustration 8. A Queen Anne style doll. All wood with carved features and original costume. England, 1740.

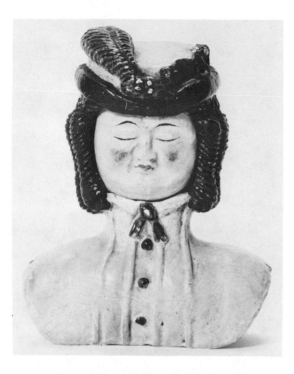

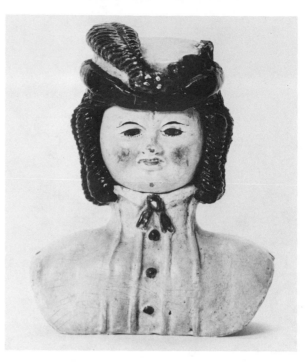

Illustrations 9, 10, 11 and 12. Revolving multi-face head, one sleeping, one smiling, one grinning and one scowling. Patented by Domenico Checkeni in 1866 and manufactured by Ozias Morse of West Acton, Massachusetts, 1866 to 1885.

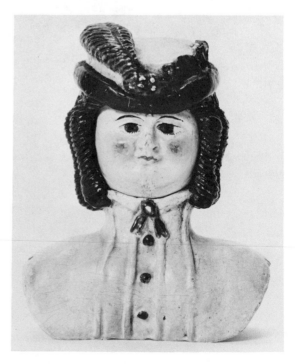

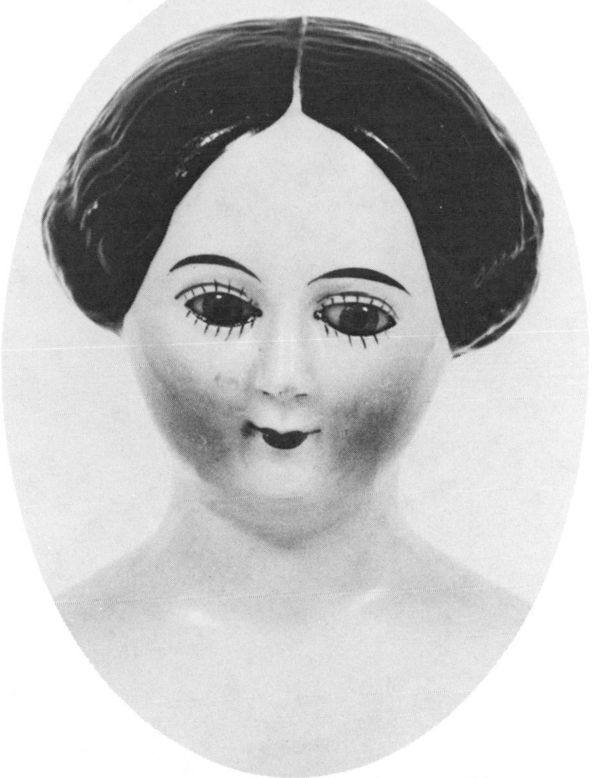

Illustration 13. China shoulder head with glass eyes. Molded black hair is drawn into a braided bun in back. The body is cloth with china lower arms and legs. Manufacturer unknown. Germany, circa 1850.

Illustration 14. "Burning Building." By pulling the cord at the base of the ladder, the fireman climbs the ladder, lifts a woman over the balcony and carries her down to safety. Manufactured by Francis Carpenter of Port Chester, New York, circa 1895. The horse drawn hose reel fire wagon was made by Kenton Hardware Company of Kenton, Ohio, circa 1920.

Illustration 15. "General Grant Smoker." Clockwork activates a piston that causes the figure to inhale smoke from a cigar and exhale the same when his hand moves the cigar away from his mouth. Manufactured by Ives, Blakeslee and Williams of Bridgeport, Connecticut, circa 1880.

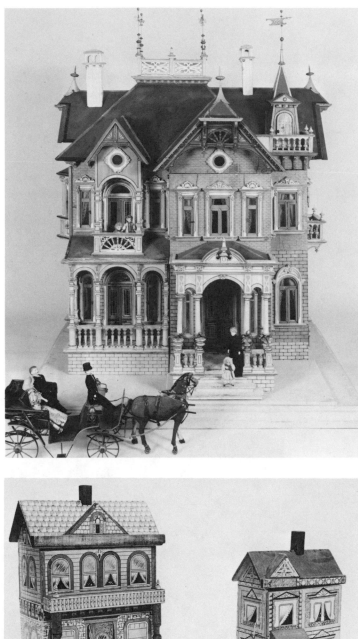

Illustration 16. Dolls' Mansion, lithographed paper on wood. Germany, circa 1890. This house was under the White House Christmas Tree, December, 1978.

ABOVE: Illustration 17. Two doll houses manufactured by R. Bliss Manufacturing Co. of Pawtucket, Rhode Island. The house on the left is lithographed paper on wood and is marked "R. Bliss" on the front door. The house on the right is also lithographed paper on wood and is marked "R. Bliss" over the door.

RIGHT: Illustration 18. Queen Anne style doll house, lithographed paper on wood. Marked "R. Bliss" in front on the second floor door and just under the peak of the roof. Manufactured by the R. Bliss Manufacturing Company of Pawtucket, Rhode Island.

English "Babies" of the 18th Century

by MARY HILLIER

Illustration 1. Portrait of Princess Charlotte with doll.

Shakespeare refers to them and in 1682 a lady was described as:

"Her petticoat of satin
Her gown of crimson tabby
Laced up before and spangled O'er
Just like a Bartholomew Baby."

Bartholomew fair was held in London annually in September and toys and dolls were peddled to the fun-loving crowds.

For an idea of these early dolls we have to rely on rare portraits or allusions in literature but in 1974 two dolls made history when, as widely reported in the press they were sold at Sotheby London for £16,000. They were bought by a Swiss collector but eventually, when the export licence was vetoed and the money raised by public subscription, they were bought for the Victoria and Albert Museum, London. For the first time dolls were recognised as a 'National Treasure.' The pair of 22in (55.9cm) large wooden dolls represented a lady and gentleman of the period which was calculated to be about 1695 on the evidence of the style and material of their clothes. They had passed down through one family and were traced to a relative of the diarist, Samuel Pepys. They had been called "Lord and Lady Clapham" as the family dwelt in this outlying area of London.

The fact which made this pair so exceptionally valuable was their fine condition and all original clothing. They even owned contemporary possessions which had survived: they sat in beautiful miniature chairs and both had ornamental shoes, spare sets of undress wear for night time. "Lord Clapham" carried a miniature sword and small money purse whilst his wife wore a gold wedding ring (attached to her wrist by a safety chain), had an embroidered foot

In 1585, when Sir Walter Raleigh led an expedition over the sea to America and a vast territory was named Virginia in honour of the Virgin Queen, Elizabeth I of England, some little dolls were handed out as gifts to the Roanoke Indians. It was recorded in a beautifully illustrated account of the expedition (now in the British Museum, London) that the children were delighted with the "puppets and babes brought from England." The word 'doll' was not adopted until the mid 18th century.

It is difficult to imagine what such children could have made of such little characters dressed with the tall hats and lace ruffs of the period but it proves to us that in Tudor times costumed dolls were already a speciality in London. Sadly, no examples seem to have survived but

Illustration 2. "Lord and Lady Clapham," 22in (55.9cm), 1695. *Photograph courtesy of Messrs. Sotheby, Bond St. London.*

LEFT: Illustration 3. Wooden with glass eyes (nun dress later), ca. 1700. *Photograph courtesy of Messrs. Sotheby, Bond St. London.*

RIGHT: Illustration 4. "Lady Clapham" showing details of features. *Photograph courtesy of Messrs. Sotheby, Bond St. London.*

stool and even a small black mask for carnival wear with an amber bead by which a lady would hold such a mask in place in her mouth.

The clothing and accoutrements are exceptional and in each case the finest quality material is used but the dolls themselves are also rare of their type and of fine workmanship; the finish and painting of the faces is especially good. The head and torso of this type of wooden doll was turned on an horizontal lathe much as a chair leg of the period might be fashioned. The roughly skittle-shaped body had accentuated 'hips' to which jointed wooden legs might be added by wooden pegs, arms were added with wire and fabric to hold wooden hands with cut fingers and the face was painted over a smooth enamelled surface after the features were carved. Human hair was used for the wig and then the 'baby' was costumed to hide the quite crude undecorated body.

It is very interesting to read an account of a Law court case which took place in 1733 in London when a doll maker (called William Higgs) accused two of his work team of having stolen some of his stock ("14 naked babies and two dozen dressed babies and one jointed baby") to resell. In evidence he declared that he was a turner by trade and chiefly made dolls and he would know his own work from anyone else's because of their type. The affair ended amicably but it is that last remark that is interesting since we can also

Illustration 5. Portrait of three young sisters, ca. 1620, showing the youngest holding a dressed doll. This shows beautifully the likeness of a Tudor doll and the sort of child owning it. The family and painter are unknown. It is very interesting to note how the middle girl wears a gold ring fastened to her wrist by a safety cord. This exactly resembles the ring and safety cord worn by "Lady Clapham." Presumably the little girl was already affianced as this took place widely with young boys and girls of noble families to ensure inheritance and the unification of two great houses. *Photograph courtesy of Messrs. Sotheby, Bond St. London.*

recognise among surviving dolls of the early 18th century outstanding characteristics which seem to suggest different makers.

"Lord and Lady Clapham" it is true were a *'de luxe'* pair, exceptional in their own day, but other dolls sold at the same time at Sotheby's and from the same family collection seem

to have been derived from the same workshop since there are similarities of body construction and carving, and an intriguing hint that the makers produced a range of different dolls to suit different purses. Some of these early "babies" even had heads moulded from papier-mâché and either painted eyes or inserted glass eyes

Illustration 6. Trade card of turner in fashionable London, ca. 1800.

Illustration 8. Mid 18th century wooden doll, 18in (45.7cm). *Photograph courtesy of Messrs. Sotheby, Bond St. London.*

and were 25in (63.5cm). In common with some of the others she also had the idiosyncracy of a system of hooks and staples on her legs which permitted the doll to sit with knees bent or to stand rigid. This is a feature I have never discovered on any wooden doll of the period. Others of the collection which are estimated to be of rather later date are all-wooden with glass eyes, very pretty features and fine clothing. One of them has been dressed incongruously by a later owner as a nun. A wooden doll of small size, 8¾in (22.3cm), seems to represent an infant and was perhaps used with "Lord and Lady Clapham" as their child.

I am often asked if children really liked these stiff curious 'babies' and did in fact play with them. We are sure they did since such artists as Hogarth pictured scenes where children were shown with the dolls and their miniature belongings: fine wooden furniture, silver coffee pots and pretty porcelain cups and saucers. They enacted the sort of life of the company in the grand houses where they lived. The dolls were expensive and obviously belonged to rich children who were themselves dressed in fine silks and brocades like miniature adults. In the Royal Palace at Schloss Friedrichshof in Kronberg, Germany, I found a delicious portrait by Sir Joshua Raynolds. It shows Charlotte, one of the daughters of George III, about 1770 when she would have been four or five years old. At her side is the stiff corseted wooden doll.

Most 18th century wooden dolls have been preserved in aristocratic

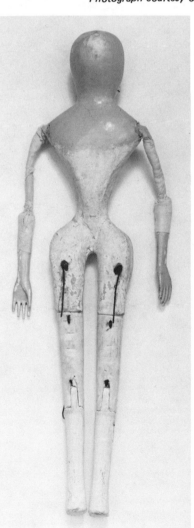

Illustration 7. Wire hook and staple construction.

family homes where they have been passed down through the years in line with all the other surviving treasures of a great house. The only example I possess, a very beautiful doll, dates from about 1736 (an established fact as she came to me complete with a needlework sampler with that date and the name embroidered of her child-owner, Elizabeth Tichborne). She was sold with costume from the family and the original owner told me she was "nearly put on the bonfire" as worthless. She was in a derelict state wearing a rough dress hacked out of an old 18th century gentleman's velvet waistcoat of cream and crimson pattern. Fortunately her original little green silk dress was with her and she is now restored and made respectable with a little extra hair on her head from my daughter which provided an uncanny match in colour and texture.

Early dolls should, of course, never be ruthlessly restored and it is not easy even to clean and repair existing costumes. A museum expert should always be consulted as there are fine new specialist techniques for conservation. I am always very fascinated in the family hisory of early wooden dolls who have stood as silent witnesses to what must have been intriguing scenes. Not the least among them would be the little emigrant dolls who found their way to American shores with the first settlers and founding fathers and are now revered in museums or historic houses as heirlooms from that famous past.

The finest wooden dolls were constructed over a relatively short

Illustration 9. Wooden infant doll, 8⅞in (22.3cm). *Photograph courtesy of Messrs. Sotheby, Bond St. London.*

Illustration 10. Papier-mache head with blue glass eyes, ca. 1700. *Photograph courtesy of Messrs. Sotheby, Bond St. London.*

period and were sold in fashionable London (see turner's trade card). By the end of the 18th century they had deteriorated. There were attempts to provide more novelty: sleeping eyes, turning neck and head, even a black doll and finally a method of reproducing features on a wooden head by a plaster mould (which was unsuccessful since the material cracked and broke). Finally, they were usurped by other types of dolls made of wax, composition and eventually porcelain so that wooden dolls were considered "old fashioned" and grotesque and they became unpopular. Only in modern times they have come once more into their own so that among collectors of antique dolls they are eagerly sought and highly valued. If we continue with careful research we may perhaps one day track down further information about their anonymous and skillful makers.

Illustration 11. Elizabeth Tichborne doll before restoration, 18in (45.7cm).

Illustration 12. Late type wooden doll with crude construction, 18in (45.7cm) ca. 1780. *Photograph courtesy of Messrs. Sotheby, Bond St. London.*

Illustrations 1 and 2. 9in (22.9cm) complete wooden doll with real braided hair looped around ears and back of head, painted features, wooden limbs, spoon hands and feet with flat, painted red slippers. She is dressed in a plum-red silk jacket with lace under-sleeves and a paisley bonnet with feather trim. The body is wrapped around from waist to ankle with hand-sewn felt and to this wrapping are attached the threads for securing the paper skirt. The top thread goes through each pleat, clearing the section which is pulled out to read the fortunes. The skirt comprises 100 coloured pleats in batches of each colour.

What Is Your Fortune, *My Pretty Maid?*

by BETTY CADBURY

Photographs by HUGH MILES

Thus says the old nursery rhyme. Today we should answer "My SKIRT is my fortune, Sir" she said! These fortune-telling dolls, comparatively rare, were made in the same tradition as the pedlars, probably having their origin in the age-old customs of the fairs, where pedlars sold their wares and fortune-tellers set up their booths for curious customers to peep into the future.

The wooden dolls used for the project were usually the finer, earlier types of the early 19th century and the three shown here are described in detail. Examination of the paper slips which form the skirts indicates that many must have been made and sold commercially, since each 'pleat' exactly matches the next - whereas, if they had been cut by hand there would have been variations on the cutting of the edges, scallops and so on. Also, many of the colours are similar in the different dolls.

The colours of the slips were important, as the 'pleats' were sometimes assembled in batches of one colour, the brighter the better. Vivid green, purple, orange, red, yellow and blue made up a gay design; the more slips which were incorporated, the wider the bottom of the skirt became, enabling the doll to stand unsupported.

Although the author has only seen commercially cut paper slips used for skirts, there is no reason why fortune-telling dolls could not have had hand-cut paper skirts and there are possibly many in existence. Some of the ladies' magazines of the last century which advised their readers on dress, cookery, manners and hobbies, gave instructions for making fortune-telling dolls. There is an opportunity here for further research.

The actual message, or fortune, always seems to have been hand-

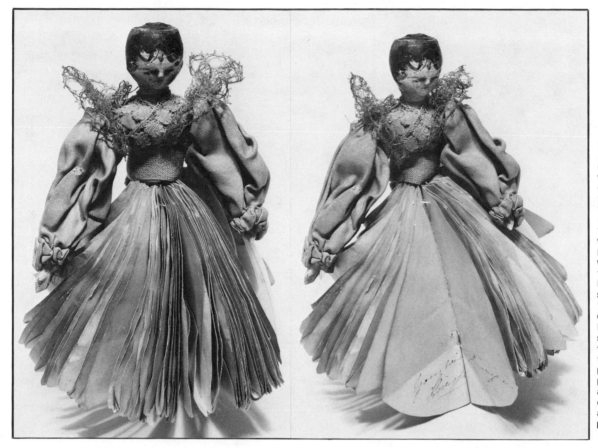

Illustrations 3 and 4. Another early wooden doll 6½in (16.5cm) with grey curls and delicate painted features. In this example, the whole doll is used and the skirt leaves the lower legs and feet with red painted slippers in view. Thus, it was never supported by the skirt and must have had a stand or been suspended. The doll is fully jointed and dressed in a pale fawn lace bodice with full, silk sleeves. The lightly fitting pantaloons are of fawn cotton. The paper pleats are cut from pastel coloured papers and fastened twice, once at the waist and again just above the pull-out section.

Illustrations 5 and 6. A wooden head and torso only, the doll being fully supported on the paper skirt and is 5½in (14.0cm) with the skirt. Her torso is 2½in (6.4cm). She has a fine head with grey curls beneath the black-painted crown with a yellow comb. Her wooden arms are jointed at shoulder and elbow. The upper body is dressed in dark red silk with lace trim at the neck and tiny ribbon bows at the shoulders. Gay, coloured paper pleats of 4½in (11.5cm) diameter form the skirt, cut in scallops, folded and are attached at the waist.

written. On many slips, the writing is thin, spidery, often indistinct with age and conveying the sentiments of a bygone age. Most were sentimental, relevant to lovers, marriage, children or estate in life. Not all messages were intended for the ladies; some of the quips and forecasts were meant for men:

"I will be Master of what is my own -
She is my goods, my house and my home."

"A maiden fair and fat and forty
Will grace your table very shortly."

And even for the ladies, not all fortunes were complimentary:

"It's want of wit as much as want of grace
That makes men see the monkey in your face."

But most held promise of future happiness or prosperity:

"A coach and four, what more could you require?
A footman grave to ride behind the Squire."

A Few warned of trouble ahead:

"How dare you Sir, go after another?
Must I bear it ill? I'll tell your mother."

"His gouty toes and old red-pimpled nose -
Will tell how he has lived, I do suppose!"

There were other fortune-telling dolls; one, owned by Queen Victoria as a child had the same method of combining paper pleats for the skirt, but had a china head. It would seem that the popularity of these dolls in the early years of the 19th century meant choosing the most suitable adult doll available and assembling the skirt with personally selected fortunes.

In her book, *Dolls and Doll-makers,* Mary Hillier mentions another rare fortune-telling doll which was called a 'Fate Lady' and directions for making it were described in *The Little Girl's Own Book* (Mrs. Child, 1847). This method of foretelling the future was very different. A wire mounted doll pointed to the fortune with a straw wand as she revolved around a flat card disc on which the fortunes were written.

What gentle fun they must have had! What did the future hold? No doubt the fortune-telling doll brought a blush to the cheek and a sparkle or tear to the eye. And, we hope, it also brought a copper or two for the owner of the doll, since the customer had to pass a coin, give a token or pay a forfeit before reading the message.

Some authorities suggest that this was one way of raising money for a charity, just as we hold coffee mornings today. Others think that it was a pastime for the ladies when they withdrew after dinner, leaving the men to finish their cigars and port.

For doll collectors, fortune-telling dolls make an unusual addition and the study of the fortunes gives a fascinating social commentary; for doll

makers they are a challenge, but the finished result would be a worthy antique of the future as well as delightful, personal family heirloom.

The pedlars, fortune-telling dolls and the 'old woman who lived in a shoe and had so many children, she didn't know what to do' - all these were surely family projects undertaken with help from parents, governess or elder sister. In many toy and doll museums there are examples of all these, some framed and glazed, preserved and restored for us to enjoy some 150 years later.

Old fortune-telling dolls seldom appear in the sale rooms, probably due to the fragility of the paper skirts. If you have a head and torso of an old wooden doll (ca. first half of the 19th century) maybe it was once a fortune-teller with a gay skirt? It could be again - with your help and imagination!

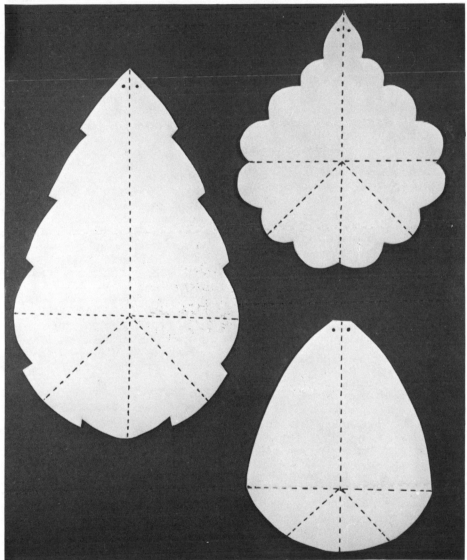

Illustration 7. Patterns for paper pleats of the three dolls illustrated. Dotted lines indicate folds. There were different shapes for the paper pleats, but the design was always cut so that the skirt would be narrow at the top and as full as possible at the bottom. LEFT: Doll in Illustrations 1 and 2. Measurements: Paper slips 7½in (19.1cm) in total length, giving a centre fold of 5in (12.7cm) when the bottom 2½in (6.4cm), on which the fortunes are written, are folded up inside the pleat. TOP RIGHT: Doll in Illustrations 5 and 6. Measurements: Paper slips 5in (12.7cm) in total length, giving a centre fold of 3in (7.6cm) when the bottom 2in (5.1cm), on which the fortunes are written, are folded up inside the pleat. LOWER RIGHT: Doll in Illustrations 3 and 4. Measurements: Paper slips 4½in (11.5cm) in total length, giving a centre fold of 3¼in (8.3cm) when the bottom 1¼in (3.2cm), on which the fortunes are written, are folded up inside the pleat. In all cases, a thread goes through the folded pleats at the waist, marked ●, and a second thread goes through the lower skirt just above the pull-out section on which the fortunes are written. All fortunes are hand-written below the horizontal dotted line. If you are assembling a fortune-telling doll (or restoring an old one), it is useful to cut a thin card template. The more intricate the folding at the bottom of the skirt, the fuller the lower circumference will be, and the better the finished doll will look and the firmer it will stand. The cutting of the template must be exact so that the vertically folded pleat matches edge to edge on both sides. All fortunes should be written with pen and ink and not with ball-point pens.

The "Model" Doll

by Mary Hillier

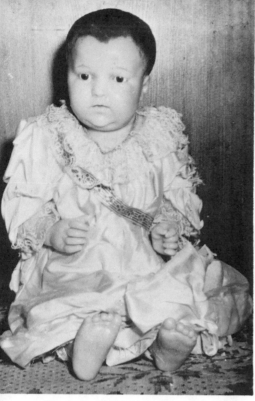

Illustration 1. "The Lost Dauphin." *Courtesy Nantucket Historical Society.*

Some years ago talking over various doll "mysteries," Dorothy Coleman asked me what I understood by the term "Model Doll" which collectors sometimes encounter in connection with wax dolls made in England during the last century.

I had to admit I did not quite know where it originated but I felt the operative word was probably DOLL. There was no lack of wax *model* making in England from the 16th century on and that they were lifelike, often life-size, and dressed in suitably fine regalia to complete the illusion, we have plenty of evidence from what was once called "the Ragged Regiment:" ancient effigies of kings and queens once carried at their funeral procession and now restored and displayed in Westminster Abbey, London, England. Perhaps the original model making began with the custom of taking a "death mask:" a plaster replica of features which could later be used for a completely reliable wax face. Many of the very skillful modelers in wax and plaster came from the continent of Europe and were French (Huguenot) or Italian in origin. Although wax models of children and royal princes or princesses were made, we are left with the question of who made the first wax model *doll?* One record is given that the very clever artist, Catherine Andras, from Bristol who was responsible for the lifelike model of Viscount Nelson after his death at Trafalgar (1805), made her early

living producing dolls but there is no evidence to prove this.

With life-sized effigies, the body was usually padded over a wooden frame and only the head, hands and feet were modeled in wax. With a doll it was necessary to have a soft fabric or stuffed body to make it acceptable to a child so the separate wax parts had to be sewn on through eyelet holes.

One of the most famous of wax modelers, Madame Tussaud, may perhaps have set the fashion for model baby dolls. Taught the craft of wax modeling by her uncle, John Curtius, she was in France at the time of the terrible French Revolution and actually had to undertake models and death masks of some of the aristocrats who were guillotined. We know she made "infants" as some were shown in her original wax work show set up in 1802 when she had fled to England. At that time she made a model of her own small son for the Duchess of York. Two very beautiful wax baby dolls or models have at times been accredited to her. In the Nantucket Museum they exhibit a life-size child who, tradition suggested, was the baby Dauphin of France, son of Marie Antoinette and Louis XVI: the so-called "lost Dauphin" who was said to have been transported to safety when his parents were killed. An old letter states this figure was brought back to America in 1796 by an old sea captain for his daughter, Priscilla Coffin, and passed down in the family. He was said to have bought it from a nunnery in Paris, France, and indisputably it is of first class workmanship. On the other hand, Madame Tussaud knew the royal family so well, having worked for them, and, indeed, she included a group of them in her exhibition in London. She recorded in her memoir: "The Dauphin was considered much to resemble his mother, having the same pure complexion beaming with all the freshness of childhood, a fine head of curling hair flowing on his shoulders, light blue eyes and a countenance which had much sweetness of expression." This wax model shows a rather stolid baby with brown eyes and dark hair.

Tradition has also attributed the second baby to Madame Tussaud and this time with possibly more likelihood as it was made for a family of Quakers who had definite connections with the French at the time of the Revolution and after to provide help. The infant, measuring 24in (61.0cm) has a stuffed body and legs and her wax head is quite bald. She is claimed by the family to be the first doll made by Madame Tussaud and represents Caroline Harris, born 22 November 1798. It is a lifelike model of a baby some month or so old with parted lips which reveal bare gums and just the indent where the first teeth should appear. Her original baby robes include a linen "pocket" with handkerchief. The present owner discovered when the doll head was removed that a little wire contraption in the head turned the pivot of the eyes and a delicately applied wax eyelid applied to the upper half of the blue eyes so the baby slept when a wire was pulled through the body (lever now missing). There was, in fact, no doubt that this was intended as a play doll and through successive generations of the family she had been a plaything.

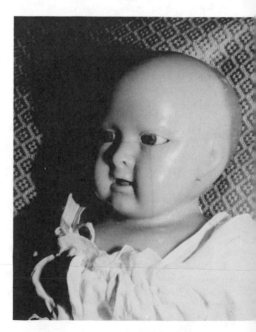

Illustration 2. Caroline Harris model. *Private Collection.*

From the November 1982 Doll Reader.®

The first actual mention of the term "Model" seems to have been used by Enrico Pierotti. Son of the first famous wax modeler of that name, Domenico, Enrico was born in 1809. He made very beautiful poured wax dolls and sometimes used his own family of children as models so we find them with a certain Italianate look and also possessed of the rare titian-colored hair which those children themselves had. He exhibited at the Crystal Palace when the Great Exhibition was staged in 1851 and shortly afterwards when he opened a toy shop at No. 108 Oxford Street, he called it The Gallery, Crystal Palace Bazaar. His advertisements included the claim "Inventor of the Royal Model Doll: Such beautiful dolls that will open their Eyes, You may wash, comb and dress them and not fear their cries." Unfortunately he did not mark his dolls and it is difficult to identify an actual example. A wax model of the Prince of Wales (Albert Edward, born 1841) dressed in tartan frock in the London Museum could be by Pierotti and represents a child of four to five years.

Besides Pierotti, other wax doll makers in London lay claim to having invented the royal model dolls. It is true that at the 1851 exhibition it was the dolls of Madame Augusta Montanari which were singled out for special mention and in this regard it was especially for their clothing. It was commented that they were expensive. "Undressed dolls sell from ten shillings to one hundred and five shillings. Dressed dolls are much more expensive." *Illustrations 4 and 5* both represent infant daughters of Queen Victoria. *Illustration 4*, from the Bethnal Green Museum, London, is said to show Princess Louise as a baby (born 1848) and *Illustration 5*, Princess Alice (born 1843). It is interesting to note that the dolls themselves seem to have been made from the same molds but the clothes are very different. It is very likely that the wax dolls were made by Madame Montanari's husband, Napoleon, who was skillful at all sorts of modeling and that she was responsible for the millinery. Queen Victoria's husband, Albert, died in 1861 and in the period of mourning that followed there were no more model royal dolls. Madame Montanari, herself, died of tuberculosis in 1864 and the later wax dolls produced by her son, Richard, were rather poor in quality compared with the early ones.

The doll in *Illustration 4* measures 14½in (36.9cm) and her clothes are of finest lawn and lace. The doll in *Illustration 5* is a little larger, 17in (43.2cm) and is said to be an exact replica of Princess Alice wearing a costume when she was about five as she drove out one day with Queen Victoria in her carriage. The tied bows on sleeves and shoulders are a mark of Madame Montanari style. The fringed taffeta frock is aquamarine and the lacy socks and shoes rose colored.

Other wax doll makers advertised that they would make model dolls and some specifically that they would use an actual child's hair to incorporate a good likeness. Meech was a name sometimes found who professed to be a doll maker to the royal family and Edwards made wax dolls on a large scale and of fine quality with expensive dress. However, it was especially the popularity of the large family of Queen Victoria who appealed to the public (she had nine children in all) and promoted the doll making just as later on fine models were made (in fabric, not wax) of Queen Elizabeth (Lillibet) and Princess Margaret Rose when they were children.

Illustration 3. Christmas tree wax fairy doll made by the Pierotti family for their own Christmas tree, (1905). *Miss Irene Pierotti Collection.*

It is inconceivable nowadays that we should commemorate a dead baby with a wax model but it was certainly sometimes done in the past, and there are some very beautiful models which appear to be a baby asleep on a cushion but in fact are memorials like those sad little stone effigies of early tombs. One of the finest is at Parham House, Sussex in England in the entrance hall. Similar in feeling and perhaps also a commemorative is *Illustration 6*. So beautifully designed, this little boy with his winsome look and embracing hands is a mystery without detail of maker or owner. His is not, of course, a doll but one wonders if he was made by a doll maker as an exhibition piece. The soft curling hair is unlikely for a statuette and this seems to represent a real child and perhaps, one hopes, a memory of a loved live child, not a dead child.

The skill and exercise of the old techniques of wax doll making is not dead. In fact, there is still in England some superlative modeling done. For my last illustrations I use examples by two present day artists. Myrtle Smith made 16in (40.6cm) *Pauline*, shown in *Illustration 8*. She was inspired by early dolls and studied examples to perfect the poured wax method herself. She has been making them from 1970 and specializes in child characters.

Illustration 4. Princess Louise baby by Montanari. *Bethnal Green Museum, London, England.*

Margaret Glover, who has won awards in the United States for her handmade dolls also restores some of the old treasures and then produces beautiful new treasures dressed by hand and representing various known characters. *Christopher Robin,* shown in *Illustration 9,* in the little English smock of the original illustrations to A. A. Milhe's books. *Illustration 10* shows the girl with the hoop borrowed from the very famous painting by the French artist, Renoir.

It only remains to be seen who will produce the first new royal model doll with a baby William!

Illustration 6. The entreating boy wax model, front view. *Private Collection.*

Illustration 7. The entreating boy wax model, back view. *Private Collection.*

Illustration 5. Princess Alice model attributed to Montanari. *Photograph Courtesy Sotheby's, London.*

Illustration 8. 16in (40.6cm) *Pauline,* a modern wax model doll by Myrtle Smith.

Illustration 10. *Girl with Hoop* after Renoir by Margaret Glover.

Illustration 9. *Christopher Robin* by Margaret Glover.

Illustration 1. The Toy Seller by John Thomas Smith (1766 to 1833).

The English Pedlar Doll
by Mary Hillier

The collector who can display a pedlar doll among her treasures nowadays is fortunate. They are among the most sought after of antique dolls and it is increasingly difficult to find a genuine example. The best and most complete models are usually those which have been handed down in a family and occupied some revered place on the mantelpiece or shelf with a glass dome to protect them. In the reminiscences of Laura Troubridge (*Life among the Troubridges, — John Murray: 1868*) she recollects a souvenir from her grandmother's home: "...sad to say we asked for some silly object of our childish imagination. I asked for a gipsy figure with a tray of tiny toys to sell, that lived under a glass case - I thought it rather like a doll..." Although there are few references in literature to pedlar dolls or how they first came to be made, there is plenty of lore attached to the actual pedlars on whom they were modeled.

> "Will you buy any tape
> Or lace for your cape
> My dainty duck, my dear-a?
> Any silk, any thread
> Any toys for your head
> Of the new'st and finest wear-a?"

So sung Shakespeare's Autolycus, the rascally pedlar in the *Winter's Tale*. In Elizabethan times and long before, stretching back to the Middle Ages, the pedlars trafficked their goods in remote country districts where people rarely had access to town shops. Their name was synonymous with roguery. Like Autolycus "a snapper up of unconsidered trifles" they were constantly accused of thieving and trickery although the punishment was very harsh if they were caught. There are records of savage whipping or of imprisonment in the wooden stocks. By law it was possible to take away the children of vagrants and it was essential for a pedlar to carry a license which registered his permanent place of dwelling.

Typically, Shakespeare's pedlar man, probaly based on a character he had met, carried all the little luxuries society loved: gloves, masks for carnival, bracelets, necklaces, perfume, hairpins and combs ("toys for your head"), ribbons and lace, even smocks and winding sheets for corpses. Especially he sold ballads and song sheets and one suspects not all were innocently worded. One of the early terms for a pedlar indeed was a "Bawdy-Basket" and he was the carrier of crude printed sheets with the latest sensational news of murders and disasters. Among themselves the pedlars even had a language of their own: pedlars'"cant" or "French" with slang words only *they* could understand.

The male pedlar carried stock in a case with straps on his back but the women more often had a basket on their arm and probably most of the recognized pedlars had a regular "run" with a base in their home town and there are records of the

Illustration 2. Man pedlar made by C. & H. White, Milton, Portsmouth, England, 1820 to 1830 period. (Note labeled bottle: pedlars carried a stock of "quack" medicine and ointments, cough remedies and liniments).

Illustration 3. Woman pedlar also with trade label of C. & H. White. (She includes household necessities such as bellows, lamp, candle and graters).

GIPSY CLOAK IN RED MERINO OR FLANNEL.

Bind the cloak all round with narrow sarsenet ribbon of the same colour. Put pleats along the straight part of the hood, and fasten it into the neck of the cloak, after lining it with white silk, cut a little smaller than the merino. Stitch it round with red sewing silk, according to the dotted line, to make a casing for the strings. Run these in, fastening them at the neck, and bringing the other ends out at the top of the hood, through an eyelet-hole, so as to draw the hood up. Bind the edges of the cloak and hood, round the neck, with a piece of ribbon, and sew on ribbons with which to tie on the cloak.

Hood.

Cloak.

CROCHET SHAWL IN SHETLAND WOOL.

Make a chian long enough to go round the doll's neck, with a fine bone crochet, in Shetland wool. 1st row: 2 treble stiches, 1 chain, miss 1 stitch of the foundation; repeat till you come to middle stitch, into which 2 treble, 1 chain, and 2 treble stiches must be worked; repeat 2 treble, chain, miss 1, again to the end of the row; turn back, and work the 2nd and all succeeding rows thus: 3 treble stitches in the space of 1 chain in the last row, 1 chain, 3 trebel in the next space; repeat till you come to the middle space, into which 3 treble, 1 chain, and 3 treble must be worked; then work as before to the end of the row. The shawl is to be worked thus, always increasing in the middle till it is large enough. End with a row of plain double crochet and a fringe made of lengths of wool 3 inches or so long, double and knotted in two strands, into every stitch of the row of double crochet. It is very pretty with the centre in white, and the border and fringe in scarlet, magenta, blue, &c.; in which case the last five or six rows would form the border.

ERMINE MUFF, IN FINE WHITE BERLIN OR ANDALUSIAN WOOL,—STEEL OR FINE BONE CROCHET.

Make a chain of 20 stitches rather tightly worked; join, and work about 12 rounds in plain double crochet; fasten off tightly and draw up the ends. Line the muff with cotton wadding and silk, and finish it with a rosette or bow of ribbon at the ends. Tie in ends of black wool at regular distances, over the muff, to represent ermine. It may be made also in shades, 2 rounds of each shade, or with a scarlet centre and 2 rounds on each side in white.

BROWN VELVET BONNET, TRIMMED WITH SCARLET.

Cut out the two pieces for the front and crown, in stiff paper or very thin cardboard. Cover them with the velvet, and sew the rounded part of the crown into the short side of the front piece. Line the front of the bonnet with white ribbon or silk. Put a piece of scarlet

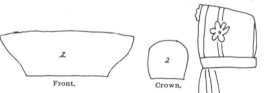

Front.   Crown.

velvet ribbon all round the neck for a curtain, and a narrower piece round the front and across the bonnet, a frill of lace inside for a cap, and a tiny sprig of flowers, or a bow or two of the narrow velvet ribbon, over the forehead.

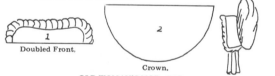

Doubled Front.   Crown.

OLD WOMAN'S MOB—CAP.

Fold the doubled part over the head for the front of the cap: the rounded part of the head-piece is gathered into the front, and the straight part drawn in round the neck.

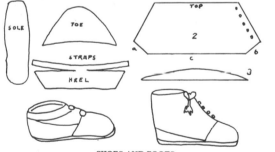

SHOES AND BOOTS

The shoes require no explanation: they look best made of morocco or kid, with soles of fine leather. For the boots, cut the toe-piece and sole the same as for the shoes in kid or leather. Then cut a piece of cloth or velvet to the shape of Fig. 2, join the short sides, marked a and b, to the toe-piece, and the long side c, to the sole round the heel. Cut a strip of kid Fig. 3, and put round the heel over the cloth. Sew up the front, and put small beads to represent buttons; or turn down and herringbone the edges, and lace them up with a piece of black silk or narrow braid: leave out short ends of the braid at top, and put tassels of black silk.

HATS

Are so constantly varying in shape that it seems useless to give patterns. They may be cut out in stiff paper or thin cardboard, and covered with black velvet, and trimmed with tiny feathers, ribbon, &c., to suit the prevailing fashion.

Illustration 5. Instruction pages from the *Home Book of Pleasure*, Mrs. R. Valentine, 1867; patterns for cloak, shawl, bonnet and mob cap.

Illustration 4. Pair of pedlars, man and wife with baskets of diary produce and garden plants, seeds, fruit and vegetables. C. & H. White, Milton, Portsmouth.

pedlar's "annual" visit as though folk knew when to expect them.

A delightful little pen and ink sketch with watercolor (6½in (16.5cm) x 7½in (19.1cm)) by John Thomas Smith shows an old pack man with his wicker basket containing little wooden toys, no doubt

Illustration 6. Pedlar doll from Gunnersbury Museum, London.

Illustration 7. Pedlar doll from Huddersfield Museum.

Illustration 9. The mirror stand doll, Abbot Hall Art Gallery, Kendal.

Illustration 8. Charity bazar doll, Bethnal Green, London, (Victoria & Albert Museum).

represents a local scene. This is a real pedlar with stout leather gaiters and a bundle on his back.

Some of the best facsimile pedlar dolls, nearest to reality in the goods they carry, were those made by C. & H. White, at Milton, Portsmouth, England. There are a number of examples usually mounted on a little square stand covered with marbled paper and bearing a trade label on the base. These are most often depicted as a pair and their goods complement each other. The man carries masculine requisites (*Illustration 2*) such as knives, braces, watches, gloves, straps and the woman (*Illustration 3*) ribbons, jewelry, buttons, needles and thread, scissors and toasting forks, or the man carries all sorts of vegetable and garden produce including seeds whilst she offers dairy goods such as eggs, chicken and butter packs (*Illustration 4*). They are so professional it has been suggested that such models were intended for shop windows to attract custom and to display the nature of the goods sold, but although an earlier writer (Alice K. Early, *English Dolls*, Effigies & Puppets, Batsford 1955) suggested that C. White had taken out a patent for pedlar dolls, I have not been able to trace it.

During the first quarter of the 19th century there seems to have been a vogue for creating pedlar dolls. C. & H. White seem to have worked during the 1820 to 1830 period but I do not think they were

homemade. They include animals, rattles and little pieces of doll furniture. Dating from the first quarter of 19th century, it shows the cottage interior with Granny, Mother and three excited young children. It belonged to the family of Sir John Swinburne of Capheaton Hall, Northumberland in England and perhaps

the first. Most English museums can exhibit an example which has been bequeathed from a local family and seems to indicate that it was a countrywide hobby. Was there somewhere a recipe published for making pedlar dolls, perhaps in a popular magazine such as the *Englishwoman's Domestic Magazine* which had a big following in upper-class homes? I believe there must have been but the earliest account I can find appears in the *Home Book of Pleasure and Instruction* by Mrs. R. Valentine (1867) much later than the earliest models. Here she includes a section by a Miss Dyson with details for dressing "an old market woman with a basket on her arm" or a gypsy (such a doll, she explains, could be converted into a "sewing companion" by stuffing the full skirt for a pincushion and filling her basket with cotton, thimble, tape and other items). The clothes represent standard wear of a pedlar woman: scarlet cloak and hood with mob cap and hard bonnet.

The author also gives a useful tip for breeches for male dolls which she found mentioned in a popular children's book of the period, *Poor Match* (a dog story): "pray don't use stiff shiny linen which refuses to adapt itself to the elegancies of the figure but use white kid glove fingers which are soft and plastic and there will be nothing left for you to desire in the way of tasteful results." I have since noticed one or two men pedlars with kid breeches made in this way (see *Illustration 11*) and little pedlar women with bound capes (see *Illustration 10*). However, these are earlier than the book so the method was already known and practiced. *Illustration 6* shows possibly the

Illustration 10. Grodenthal doll as pedlar, (Lilliput Museum, Isle of Wight).

Illustration 11. Eastwood Houst pedlars made by Mrs. Sugden 1820/30.

best example of a pedlar doll I have ever seen. It is so beautifully made and so very fully stocked with contemporary goodies. The full list contains nearly 50 different things and they reflect the owner's choice of articles rather than the typical goods of a pedlar. A miniature copy of the Bible and another of the Works of Shakespeare, a book of Fables and a tiny music book replace the scandal sheets. Tiny knitted socks and dainty gloves bear witness to the maker's skill. There are sets of knives and spoons, papers of pins, scissors and pincushions, woven reticules, cards of ribbon and laces for stays. In her right hand this useful character offers an assortment of meat skewers but also some folded paper fire screens. It was not thought genteel to have a cheek flushed by the heat of the flames.

The Museum at Gunnersbury Park, to whom this was given, also owns a fine small photograph of the lady who made this doll (dating from about the 1860 period). She is seated at a table with her workbox and appears to be a lady of some standing with fine features and a shawl about her shoulders. It is interesting to find that this doll is totally handmade with (so far as one can judge) a block wooden body, wired arms and a featured face of kid with embroidered eyes rather in the style of the C. & H. White dolls.

Another handmade doll from the same period is owned by Hud- dersfield Museum (see Illustration 7) but in this case the face seems to be made of modeled black wax, making her rather witch-like. In her basket she carries a beguiling selection of toys, ivory novelties and an assortment of little wicker baskets and trays and even a tiny cradle with a baby doll.

A little later in the 1840 to 1850 period it was more usual to use an actual doll dressed for the part of pedlar or even in some cases of the rather grander character who seemed to preside over a charity bazaar stall such as in *Illustration 8*. Here there is even greater scope for variety since goods are displayed on a nicely decorated table which is festooned with framed pictures and prints, embroidery and decorated felt. This doll has a composition head and wooden body, a typical German product of the time, and she is dressed rather smartly with an elaborate bonnet over her ringlets and a pretty lace collar to her beribboned gray frock. In England at this period there was much poverty because of the Industrial Revolution and hard times also for soldiers' families so the charity bazaar run by the local "Lady Bountiful" was familiar.

An even more elaborate booth of this sort belongs to a doll in the possession of Abbot Hall Gallery, Kendal (*Illustration 9*). In this case a fashionably dressed lady is seated by a three-tiered stand with a fan- tastic array of goods which are even further magnified by the fact that the stand has a mirror backing. The doll is a German china-headed type and a captivating small boy child doll dressed in black peaked cap and caped coat stands with his miniature hobby horse peering at the treasures.

In an interesting thesis on the subject of pedlar dolls, Miss Catharine Rorison (Catharine M..A. Rorison: Final year thesis for B A. (hons.) Department of History of Art, University of Manchester, 1977) traced the history of this doll. It is thought to have dated from about 1820 and took three years to make. Three sisters were involved in the project: Margaret, Eleanor and Ann Hutchinson, born 1798, 1799 and 1801, so that all were in their late teens when they planned and made the doll and her stall. The family called this model "The Shop" and it was housed under a fine glass dome (the sort used for displaying stuffed birds and animals) which kept it in pristine condition. Most of the goods from about 1820 and took three are skillfully handmade and their arbitrary choice reflects the life style of the family. Besides the usual selection of pins and millinery there is a mouse trap (with mouse), wooden clogs, and egg timer made of two hollow beads, cut glass decanters, ink wells and dressing table bottles made from fancy beads, mourning stationery (black edged note paper and envelopes), a miniature chess board and playing cards and even cigars. The handwork of sewn collars, crocheted and knitted garmets is exquisite and one can envisage the three girls engrossed in their task and occasionally adding some little bought treasure or toy. Passing down

Illustration 12. Market booth with cover and customers, Bethnal Green, London, (Victoria & Albert Museum).

Illustration 13. "The Old Woman who lived in a Shoe," prize given to a five-year-old girl for her needlework, 1860, (Saffron Walden Museum, Essex).

Illustration 14. "The Old Woman who lived in a Shoe" with a variety of doll children and a contemporary Nursery Rhyme book, 1860 period, (Mrs. Joy Robinson Museum, Warwick).

in the family, the doll was eventually inherited by a descendant of Margaret.

For simpler forms of pedlar dolls and perhaps better befitting her humble role, the cheap wooden dolls from Grodenthal were often used, the early "Dutch" doll or peg wooden. Structurally they were well-suited for dressing and mounting on a stand. *Illustration 10* shows one dressed very nearly to the recipe of Mrs. Valentine and she has a handwritten copy of Cottage Ballads and the laces, buttons and thread one might associate with a door-to-door traveler. One of the "tricks of the trade" was to buy a huge skein of cotton and wind small amounts on reels, so doubling the profit. This doll

is dated about 1830 and carries some 60 tiny objects.

The pair of dolls from Eastwood House display a similar stock *(Illustration 11)*. They were made in the 1820 to 1830 period by a Mrs. Sugden and are pictured with a painting of the house at Keighley, now demolished. Whilst this man and wife pair seem to represent traveling pedlars, the little scene depicted in the Bethnal Green Booth *(Illustration 12)* shows customers as well as market attendant. The booth is interesting as it has the draped covering which could be speedily pulled around in bad weather and was probably made of an oiled tarpaulin material. A mother in velvet cape and lace collar is shopping with her diminutive child in the frilly long pantaloons and full frock fashionable in the first quarter of the 19th century.

Tiny dolls were popular for model making especially among children. In Victorian days large families were the rule and not always welcome in a poor household. I was once shown a German novelty of a hollow wax potato with a set of tiny detailed wax dolls ranging in size from ½in (1.3cm) to 1in (2.5cm) all clothed and bonneted. Included was a little text (in German) which, translated, read: "After the Seventh, O Lord, Spare thy blessing." Perhaps this was a German version of the "Old Woman who Lived in a Shoe who had so many children she didn't know what to do!" The favorite nursery rhyme was often translated into a little

model in Victorian days sometimes using an actual pretty slipper or shoe or with a tiny shoe made for the purpose.

Guesses have been made to the original identity of the "Old Woman" and it has been suggested it might refer to Queen Caroline (wife of George II of England), 1683 to 1737, who had a very numerous family. The tiniest type of jointed wooden doll is often shown as one of the toys on a pedlar's tray and even very small girls could dress them up in scraps of lace and ribbon. *Illustration 13* shows a prize aptly awarded to a five-year-old school girl for needlework about 1860 and *Illustration 14* is a model of similar date from the collection of Mrs. Robinson of Warwick with an illustrated nursery rhyme book contemporary in style.

Nowadays the art of the miniature is again very popular and there is no reason why a collector should not assemble her own pedlar doll perhaps using an early doll and imitating the antique style with her own basket or tray of tiny treasures. A real challenge to ingenuity and a non-failing conversation piece in a collection.

Child doll. Bisque head, kid body. Pierced ears; closed mouth; stationary eyes. Marked on shoulder:

Left side: Bru
Right side: JNE 5
Beige satin, lace-trimmed dress and hat. Height 13in. (33cm). Blonde hair.

The "French" Selection
A Photographic Essay by Elspeth

The "French" Selection was prepared with the knowledge that many of our French dolls may be German ladies who traveled a bit before "getting it all together." Where no marks were evident, I have refrained from identifying the dolls, for even though I may think it is a Steiner...without marks one cannot make a positive statement.

The quotes are from the works of William Shakespeare. The dolls are graciously presented from the Marlene Collection.

Turn-of-the-century child doll. Bisque head with pierced ears; large stationary glass eyes. The head is marked
Deposé
11
L (red check mark)   Jumeau
The body is marked: Medaille d'Or
Paris
She is dressed in a white cotton and lace coat over a white dress. Height 24in. (61cm). Blonde hair.

"...Age, I do defy thee..."

Left:
Black child doll. Large stationary glass eyes; closed mouth; pierced ears. Mark on head:
8 L 121
She is dressed in a commercial dress of red, white and blue cotton. Height 14in. (35.6cm).

Right:
Large child doll of the early-twentieth century. Bisque head; stationary glass eyes; open mouth; pierced ears. Marked "14" on head. Composition body marked:
BÉBÉ
Jumeau
B^TE SGDG
Deposé
Contemporary white linen dress. Height 30in. (76.2cm). Brown hair.

Small doll with open mouth; pierced ears; brown blown eyes. Marked on head: Jumeau
1907
Marked on body: BÉBÉ
Jumeau
Pink satin and lace dress. Height 14in. (35.6cm). Brown hair.

Early-twentieth-century child doll in regional costume of red and purple. Closed mouth; stationary eyes. Marked "E.D." on head. Height 10in. (25.4cm). Blonde hair.

Left:
Turn-of-the-century doll in elaborate costume of cream and blue floral material with overskirt; trimmed with lace. Marked "F.G." on shoulder; "2/0" on head. Height 10in. (25.4cm). Brown hair.

Right:
The child doll in the blue sailor suit dates from around the turn-of-the-century. It has stationary blue eyes, closed mouth and pierced ears. The head is marked:
Deposé
Tête Jumeau
B^TE S.G.D.G.
7
The body is marked: Jumeau Medaille d'Or Paris
Height 17in. (43.1cm). Blonde hair.

"Princess Elizabeth" by Jumeau, around 1930. Bisque head, ball-jointed body. Closed mouth; stationary glass eyes; pierced ears. Marked on body;

BÉBÉ
Vrai Modèlle
Fabrication Jumeau

Dressed in smocked, pink, silk crepe dress with matching bloomers. Height 13in. (33cm). Dark brown hair.
The larger doll who is doing the ironing is interesting...and unmarked.

"...and thy eternal summer shall not fade....."

This turn-of-the-century child bears the shield containing the Schmitt mark on both head and body:

She has stationary eyes, closed mouth and pierced ears. She is dressed in a charming off-white floral print costume. She is 14in. (35.6cm) tall and has blonde hair.

Blonde lady doll. Pierced ears, stationary eyes, open/closed mouth. She is on a kid body with bisque hands. Mark obscured. Height 14 inches(35.5cm). Late 19th century.

Lady doll. Bisque head on jointed wooden body, similar to those shown in the Bru catalog of 1872. She has pierced ears, smiling closed mouth, and stationary glass eyes. Head is marked "4". Height 15"(38cm)

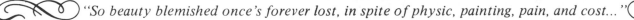

"So beauty blemished once's forever lost, in spite of physic, painting, pain, and cost..."

Early twentieth century child doll. Pierced ears, stationary blown eyes, open mouth. Head marked:

SFBJ
Paris
9

Composition body. Height 20 inches(50.8cm). Brown hair.

Turn of the century child doll. Marked with circle and dot on head. Pierced ears, stationary eyes, closed mouth. White cotton dress. Height 8 inches(20.3cm). Dark brown hair.

Mark

"Weary with toil, I haste me to my bed . . ."

Illustration 1. Some of the accessories of a well-dressed doll include: a parasol, straps for carrying a railway rug, tan leather gloves and a red leather purse. The hats were made by Huret and the bonnet is by Felix of Paris. This particular doll was sold about 1867 at the Maison Huret in Paris. Height of doll 16in (40.6cm). *Courtesy of the Museum of the City of New York.*

Dolls and Dolls' Accessories
Sold in Paris 1870-1871

BY DOROTHY & EVELYN JANE COLEMAN

*O*ne of the most famous doll shops in Paris was A la Poupée de Nuremberg located at 21 rue de Choiseul. This shop was operated by Mme. Lavallèe-Peronne who also provided the little girls of France as well as the entire world with the fascinating periodical *La Poupée Modèle* (The Fashionable Doll).

On the pink paper covers of some of the issues of *La Poupée Modèle* there is provided information on the various dolls and the types of accessories that were sold by Mme. Lavallèe-Peronne as well as the prices of the dolls, their clothes and accessories. These catalog listings not only give information about the items sold around 1870 but they also give a clearer picture of what a doll was expected to have in its wardrobe and accoutrements. Another account of what was available for dolls was given in the *English Woman's Domestic Magazine,*

in the December 1865 issue. This article entitled "Lilliput in Regent Street" discusses the offerings of Cremer Junior of 210 Regent Street.

In the December 1869 issue of *La Poupée Modèle* a separate dolls' head with a swivel neck cost 6 to 8 francs ($1.20 to 1.60). Apparently all too frequently the bisque dolls' heads were broken and thanks to Mme. Lavallèe-Peronne, the little mother could replace her dolly's head at the shop of the rue de Choiseul.

The standard-sized doll in 1870 appears to have been No. 4 which was 45cm (17-18in.) tall. In April 1870 a little girl could buy a doll No. 4 with a bisque head having a curly blonde wig and a kid body for 11 francs ($2.20). The clothes that this doll needed were as follows:

Un Costume de fantaisie
(a fancy dress outfit)...... 15 fr. ($3.00)
Un Chapeau (hat)............... 3 fr. ($ .60)

Un corsage blanc
(white waist)................... 2 fr. ($ .40)
Un jupon
(skirt or petticoat)......... 2 fr. ($. 40)
Un pantalon
(drawers)..... 1 fr. 50 centimes ($ .30)
Une chemise
(chemise).... 2 fr. 50 centimes ($ .50)
Des bas
(stockings)............ 75 centimes ($ .15)
Des bottines
(boots).......... 2 fr. 50 centimes ($ .50)

Thus the dressed doll amounted to 41 francs 25 centimes ($8.25), and the clothes cost nearly three times as much as the doll itself.

Apparently this was one of the cheapest of the No. 4 dolls. In May 1870 *La Poupée Modèle* lists doll No. 4 as costing from 11 francs ($2.20) to 30 francs ($6.00) depending on the articulation. It seems likely that the more expensive dolls may have had the fully articulated wooden bodies or kid

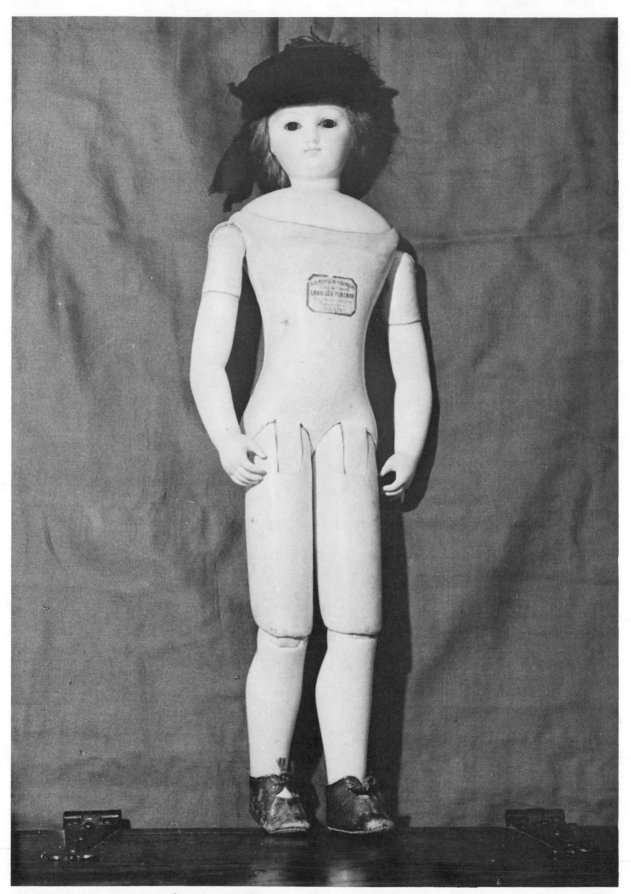

Illustration 2. Doll with the Lavallee-Peronne label on its chest (see *Illustration 3*). This picture is from Clara Fawcett's book, *Dolls, A New Guide for Collectors,* Charles T. Branford Co., page 43, where it states "Doll labelled *Nuremberg,* made in Germany for the French Trade." The name of the shop where this doll was purchased was "A la Poupée de Nuremberg" but this does not necessarily mean that the doll came from Nuremberg, Germany. There is considerable evidence that most of the bisque heads on dolls were produced in the Sonneberg or Waltershausen areas of Germany at the time that this doll was made. However, Nuremberg was a distribution center.

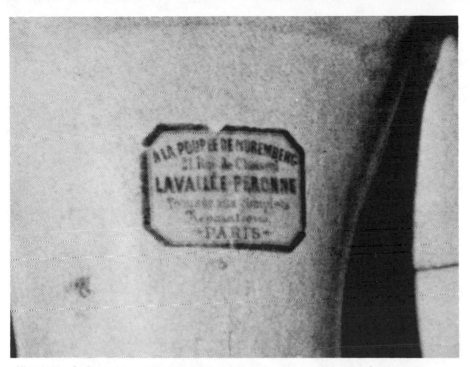

Illustration 3. Paper label found on the chest of dolls sold by Mme. Lavallèe-Peronne at her shop, "A la Poupée de Nuremberg," 21 rue de Choiseul in Paris. Besides the dolls, complete wardrobes were sold and this shop also repaired dolls.

over wood bodies (see *Illustration 2*).

Mme. Lavallèe-Peronne in June 1870 published a long list of all the accessories that a little girl would be tempted to buy for her dolly after she had obtained a dressed doll or made the clothes for her doll from the patterns provided by *La Poupée Modèle*.

First on this list are the "Album à photographie, pour poupées, prix 2.50 à 5.00." These were the Carte de Visite Albums for dolls priced at 50 cents to $1.00. No doubt they were similar to the albums distributed by rival shops such as Au Paradis des Enfants of Paris and William Cremer of London.

This list is as follows with the French translated in the parenthesis and the francs converted into the dollars of 1870.

Items With Prices

Album à photographies pour poupées
(Album with photographs
for dolls) .... 2.50 à 5.00 Fr.
(50cents to $1.00)

Boites à chapeaux
(Hatbox) .... 1.00 à 2.50 Fr.
(20 to 50cents)

Buvard (Blotting case
or writing case) .... 6.50 Fr.
($1.30)

Courroies pour châles et waterproofs
(Straps to carry shawls and waterproofs) .... 1.00 Fr.
(20cents)

Cerceau (Hoop) .... 1.50 a 2.00 Fr.
(30 to 40cents)

Cordes à sauter
(Jump rope) .... .50 à 1.00 Fr.
10 to 20cents)

Cartes de Toilette
(Social cards) .... 2.50 à 5.00 Fr.
(50cents to $1.00)

Cartes de bureau
(Business cards) .... 2.00 à 3.00 Fr.
(40 to 60cents)

Cravaches (Horse whip) .... 4.20 Fr.
(90cents)

Démêloirs (Large comb
for the hair) .... .50 à 2.50 Fr.
(10 to 50cents)

Dominos (Dominos) .... 1.00 à 1.50 Fr.
(20 to 30cents)

Damier (Draught-board) ..... 2.00 à 2.50 Fr.
(40 to 50cents)

Epingles à cheveux, la douzaine
(Hairpins, per dozen) .... .30 Fr.
(6cents)

Eventails (Fans) .... 2.50 à 5.00 Fr.
(50cents to $1.00)

Formes, tulle pour chapeaux
(Forms and tulle for hats) .... .50 Fr.
(10cents)

Hamac (Hammock) .... 5.00 à 12.00 Fr.
(1.00 to 2.40)

Jarretières (Garters) .... .50 Fr.
(10cents)

Gants peau et fil
(Leather gloves and string
gloves) .... 1.50 à 2.00 Fr.
(30 to 40cents)

Jeu de nain-jaune
(Card game called "Pope
Joan") .... 2.50 Fr.
(50cents)

Jeu de loto
(Game of Loto) .... 2.50 Fr.
(50cents)

Lunettes, lorgnons, binocles
(Eye glasses, lorgnette and opera
glasses) .... 1.50 à 2.00 Fr.
(30 to 40 cents)

Livre de messe
(Book for mass) .... 2.50 à 6.00 Fr.
(50cents to $1.20)

Mitaines (Mittens) .... .75 à 1.00 Fr.
(15 to 20cents)

Montres avec chaîne
(Watch and chain) .... 1.50 à 3.00 Fr.
(30 to 50cents)

Médaillon
(Locket or medallion) ...... 1.50 à 2.50 Fr.
(30 to 50cents)

Malles pour trousseaux
(Trunks for
trousseaux) .... 15.00 à 20.00 Fr.
($3.00 to 4.00)

Necessaires de toilette
(Toilette articles) .... 5.00 à 28.00 Fr.
($1.00 to 5.00)

Ombrelles et En-tou-cas
(Umbrellas and
parasols) .... 3.50 à 5.00 Fr.
(70cents to $1.00)

Pantoufles (Slippers) .... 1.00 à 3.00 Fr.
(20 to 60cents)

Peignes à chignons
(Combs with chignons) .... .75 à 5.00 Fr.
(15cents to $1.00)

Pied ou support pour
la poupée (Doll stand) .... 2.00 à 4.00 Fr.
(40 to 80 cents)

Papeterie (Stationery) .... 4.00 à 9.00 Fr.
(80cents to $1.80)

Peignes, brosses
(Combs and brushes) .... .50 à 1.00 Fr.
(10 to 20cents)

Paniers de voyage
(Baskets for travel) .... 7.00 à 30.00 Fr.
($1.40 to 6.00)

Resilles (Hairnet for a
Spanish headdress) .... .60 à 1.50 Fr.
(12 to 30cents)

Souliers (Shoes) .... .75 à 2.50 Fr.
(15 to 50cents)

Sacs à ouvrage
(Work bag) .... 1.50 à 3.00 Fr.
(30 to 60cents)

In August 1870 *La Poupée Modèle*, gave the sizes that corresponded to the various numbers at that period. Size 0 is 30cm (12in.); No. 2 is 36-40cm (14-16in.); No. 4 is 45 cm (17-18in.); No. 5 is 50cm (19-20in.) and No. 6 is 54cm (21-22in.). The article goes on to say that very few No.1 sizes were sold so they do not give its height but presumably it would be between 12-14in. (30-36cm) or about 13in. (33cm) tall. This suggests that No. 1 fashion-type dolls are probably rare. No mention at all is made of size No. 3, which is probably even rarer than size No. 1.

Due to the Franco-Prussian War, *La Poupée Modèle* was not published for the four issues between October 1870 and March 1871. Some of the effects of this war are reflected in the

Illustration 4. A photograph of a doll for sale at Au Paradise des Enfants in Paris about 1870. This picture is shown in a dolls' Carte de Visite Photograph Album, which was probably similar to the "Album with photographs for dolls" advertised by Mme. Lavallée-Peronne in 1870. The doll in this photograph appears to have bisque arms and carries a fan such as the one advertised in *La Poupée Modèle*. Source: *Album de la Poupée* which has been reproduced in facsimile by Evelyn Jane Coleman.

doll-related paper items offered for sale at the office of the magazine and listed in *La Poupée Modèle* in April 1870 and November 1871. More things were listed in 1870 than in 1871 but paper dolls were more in evidence in 1871. Some items rose in price and some fell during this period; a game of Sphinx cost 10 cents in 1870 and 15 cents in 1871; a music file-case and piano stool cost 5 cents in 1870 and 10 cents in 1871 while a Christmas Creche cost 30 cents in 1870 and only 25 cents in 1871. In both periods a table cost 10 cents, a chair 5 cents, an armchair 5 cents, a candelabre 5 cents, a mantle clock 5 cents, a mantle 10 cents and a piano cost 20 cents. All of these items were in paper form and probably many of them had appeared as parts of earlier issues of *La Poupée Modèle*.

One associates patterns for dolls' clothes with *La Poupée Modèle* but there are many other fascinating things such as paper furniture for dolls' houses. This furniture is colored and embossed. Many issues of *La Poupée Modèle* have colored paper dolls. There are theaters with various scenes and actors and actresses, zoos with buildings and animals of numerous kinds.

The December 1879 issue contains a Christmas tree with a wide range of trimmings. Many of the colored paper ornaments are designed so that two-dimensional objects can be converted into three-dimensional ornaments of traditional shape. Thus *La Poupée Modèle* and Mme. Lavallée-Peronne provided dolls with practically everything that human beings enjoyed having. How fortunate are the collectors of today in that although they cannot visit Mme. Lavallée-Peronne's shop, nevertheless they can read all about it. The patterns, furniture and many other items such as the photograph album can even be reproduced in facsimile so that dolls can once more have the clothes, accessories and accoutrements that they enjoyed over a century ago.

French Fashion Dolls
"As Pretty As Hummingbirds"
by SYBILL McFADDEN
Photographs by the Author

Illustration 1A. This 19in (48.3cm) French Fashion-type doll is sometimes known as "The Smiler" because of her tiny, enigmatic smile. Her original blonde mohair wig is done in crossed braids ending in one long braid over her shoulder. Her jeweled hair ornament is seen in the full-length illustration. Feathered eyebrows frame paperweight blue glass eyes with indented eyelids, eyelashes are painted around black-rimmed eyes. The mouth is two-toned. Antique gold-mounted ruby ear drops are in her pierced ears. She is circa 1860 and all original. *Sybill's Museum of Antique Dolls and Toys*

Illustration 1B. The 19in (48.3cm) "Smiler"-type Fashion wears her original dress with a 10in (25.4cm) train. The fitted gown is pale blue striped linen with a front closing. Bands of teal blue linen run vertically and horizontally around the dress and train. Teal blue bands show through the ecru lace collar and cuffs. Her head swivels on a bisque shoulder plate and is incised with a letter "C," and her shoulder with an "H." The bisque is very pale. Her body is gusseted kid with wired fingers. *Sybill's Museum of Antique Dolls and Toys.*

"As pretty as hummingbirds," said Madame Lavallee Peronne, mistress of a doll shop at 21 Rue de Choiseul, in Paris, in the 1860s. Her description referred to the lovely lady dolls of Paris sometimes known as "Parisiennes," "Poupée Modéles" or Fashion-type dolls" as our UFDC *Glossary* suggests.

"A rose by any other name," these dolls express the French elegance of their day. They have been treasured now for more than 120 years by child and adult alike, and if we dare a peek into the future, it seems very likely they may go on being collected, admired and increasingly treasured a hundred years hence!

Appearing in France in the late 1860s and 1870s, they followed on the delicate heels of the French china dolls introduced first by doll makers Mademoiselles Huret, Rohmen and Simonne, among others. These pink-tinted porcelain French china dolls wearing wigs, were sometimes equipped with lovely porcelain china arms, hands and feet. Their plump, sweet faces with painted or inset glass eyes, seemed to represent adolescents or younger-type girls than the French Fashion ladies with which this article deals. The bisque heads of the Fashion-types become just a bit slimmer, longer and more ladylike, and the paperweight glass eyes were larger and of great beauty.

Fashion-type ladies are found on gusseted kid bodies, articulated all-wood bodies or bodies of metal or wood, covered with stockinette, drilling, twill or leather. The most desirable are on wood, metal or unusual bodies, or have bisque hands and forearms and, less frequently, bisque legs and feet, or are marked.

Characterized by flair and a certain insouciance, they could only have been French. The German doctrine of thrift and organization, and the prim, proper and repressive quality of Victorian English and American life in the late 1860s precluded such frivolity or show of excess as pertained to little girls' dolls.

In France, Napoleon III was now Emperor. He was Louis Napoleon, nephew of Bonaparte. His Empress, Eugenie, exerted a strong influence on luxurious and extravagant styles, as she attempted to re-establish France's silk industry and its leadership in the world's markets. The new Fashion-type dolls reflected her opulence, taste and imagination.

Once launched in Paris, however, the dolls then traveled speedily to well-to-do children on both continents, for they were part and parcel of the rapidly changing world economy and the wealth of the coming industrial and mechanical revolutions. The new wealth demanded the best of everything in the way of heavily decorated houses, elaborate clothing and, of course, the finest and most expensive toys for their offspring. The new fashionable French lady-type dolls were truly elegant works of art, and European travelers brought them home to their daughters and granddaughters, while fancy shops in London and New York imported them for the "Carriage Trade."

That they were always expensive is well documented. That they were playthings for little girls is also well documented in small booklets or "fashion magazines" directed to the little mother by advertisers and makers of the dolls. The children were instructed to care for their dollies in exactly the same manner as their mama took care of them. The magazines were filled with advertisements for accessories for the dolls, and included patterns for dresses and embroidery which a child, with the aid of her nurse, perhaps, could construct, so that "Dolly" might be clothed in the same elegance to which she had become accustomed! Included also were bits of fashion gossip, just as in the grown-ups' magazines.

These miniature masterpieces with hand-colored pictures were thought to be the creations of the leading ladies of the "Maisons" or doll making establishments of Paris, among whom the best known were Mademoiselles Calixte Huret, Madame Leontine Rhomer, Madame Simonne and Madame Peronne to whom the children's fashion booklet, *La Poupée Modéle,* was attributed.

In these long-ago days before the phrase "liberated women" had ever been heard of, is it not somewhat surprising to find that the French chinas and their sisters, the French Fashion-types, were largely the brain-children of women? Records of their inventions and patents for the tailored, gusseted kid bodies, and articulated ball joints, swivel heads, shapely wooden bodies and an 1851 patent by Mademoiselle Huret for a molded gutta-percha doll, still exist. This is not to say that the well-known firms of Bru and Jumeau were not also making fashion-type dolls in the 1860s and 1870s. But these women,

Illustration 2A. An olive green satin and black lace hat with feather plumes tops an original blonde mohair wig on this large 22in (55.9cm) fashion-type lady. Her head swivels on a bisque shoulder plate. Indented eyelids and feathered eyelashes frame her unusually large and luminous brown paperweight glass eyes. Brown eyes are not often seen on French Fashion-type dolls. The mouth is two-toned, and she wears a gold rose on a black velvet neck-band. *Museum of Old Dolls and Toys, Winter Haven, Florida.*

whose savoir-faire combined business acumen with inventive genius, led the field, and ran their own Paris "Maisons" as outlets for these unequalled dolls of their own invention.

The interdependence which may have existed between all of the firms, and how much selling back and forth of heads and bodies, and of bodies and heads, is not well-known. The firm of Bru, established in 1866, seldom marked their lady dolls, but the so-called "Smiler," occasionally marked with letters rather than numerals, is sometimes attributed to this firm, and Jumeau fashion-type ladies, sometimes with marked bodies, have bisque heads with very large eyes, which are also occasionally marked. However, attributing these early lady dolls without definite markings, to either of these firms, is difficult and risky. Identification is further complicated by the trading of parts mentioned at the beginning of this paragraph, not only with French makers, but with German firms, as well. The "Parisiennes" most often marked are the ones incised, usually on the shoulder, with an "F.G.," thought to be the mark of Fernand Gaultier. He is known to have provided his marked heads to other doll makers who made bodies, so that a completed doll may have had two makers.

Illustration 2B. This regal 22in (55.9cm) French Fashion-type lady wears a rust-brown faille redingote fastened with large brass buttons. Intricate black beadwork decorates the shoulders and the center back of her peplum. Her skirt is olive green satin with a wide lace hem and she wears brown shoes with lace stockings. Her body is a shapely kid with long bisque arms reaching almost to the shoulder. She is unmarked. *Museum of Old Dolls and Toys, Winter Haven, Florida.*

Illustration 3A. An early 18in (45.7cm) French Fashion doll with a stiff neck on a bisque shoulder plate appears to be a Rohmer-type. She wears her original lilac checked taffeta dress, trimmed with bands of lavender taffeta. The skirt is overdraped with side panels. Her puffed sleeve blouse is of white voile. She is on a kid body with unusually long bisque arms and softly curled bisque hands. *Museum of Old Dolls and Toys, Winter Haven, Florida.*

Thus arguments as to whether the French Fashion-type dolls were children's playthings or adults' models, it is hoped might end with documented proof that they were at times, both — intended originally as dolls for little girls of the day, and used sometimes by adults interested in fashion, as couriers of the latest styles from the fashion capital of the world.

That these "Parisiennes" epitomized the elegance of bourgeoise luxury, there is no doubt. In the 1860s the sewing machine was not yet in general use in European countries. In America its first commercial use was the making of Civil War uniforms! Thus the early French dolls' dresses were all handmade and display the most astonishing miniature details of pleating, piping, tucking, beading and embroidery. By the 1870s the gowns show evidence of some machine stitching, but a lot of the detail was still done by hand. Today it is a rare occurrence to find a French Fashion-type doll in her more than 100-year-old original gown, and these are treasures indeed.

Some of these fabulous dolls came with trunks of additional clothes and luxurious accessories. At the height of their popularity in the 1870s there abounded in Paris, a whole area, we are told, devoted to making tiny accessories to fill these trunks.

A little shopper in Paris, were she so minded, could find almost anything her heart desired to furnish

It is documented that once exported from Paris, some of these dolls also became models for ladies' fashions in other countries. It stands to reason that since Paris, in the 1870s was the established leader of women's fashions, and since the "Parisiennes" were known to be dressed in the same fashions as the great ladies of the day, sometimes by their own couturiers, it should come as no surprise that dressmakers of other countries sent for the dolls to display in their shops. This is documented in the newspaper advertisement of a New England dressmaker in which she invited customers to come round to her shop to see, for a small fee, her imported French doll dressed in the latest Paris fashion, and for another additional sum, to rent it to take home for copying of the gown and perhaps hair style. (One shudders at the risk of this venture!)

Illustration 3B. This 18in (45.7cm) early Fashion lady has purple-blue eyes, black rimmed and framed with painted eyelashes. Her eyebrows are delicately feathered and the mouth is two-toned. Her bisque is very pale. Atop her brown mohair wig she wears a little bonnet of flowers and lace which is tied under her chin. Incised in the bisque is a slash mark and a lower-case "r." *Museum of Old Dolls and Toys, Winter Haven, Florida.*

Illustration 4B. This lovely 21in (53.3cm) lady boasts a straw chapeau decorated with pink taffeta and two ostrich plumes. Her paperweight blue glass eyes have indented eyelids and are rimmed in black. The ears are peirced, the mouth two-toned and she has a double chin. The neck swivels on a kidlined bisque shoulder plate and she wears a tiny cameo on a black velvet neck band. *Museum of Old Dolls and Toys, Winter Haven, Florida.*

Illustration 4A. A 21in (53.3cm) French lady wears a cream and pink flowered redingate over a vest and skirt of green taffeta lavishly overdraped with antique lace. She is on a gusseted kid body with bisque arms and delicate bisque hands. She is unmarked. *Museum of Old Dolls and Toys, Winter Haven, Florida.*

"Dolly's" wardrobe trunk and enhance her gentility and refinement. There were tiny parasols, reticules, kid gloves, toilette sets, opera glasses, embroidered handkerchiefs, corsets, monogrammed stationary, enameled watches, jewelry mounted with miniature precious stones, tea sets and the drollest of ironies, often a miniature all-bisque French doll for *her* doll, sometimes with a tiny wardrobe of its own!

In this day of inflation and the cost of *one* fine miniature, such opulence is hard to imagine, but it makes a delightful dream-fantasy, nevertheless, for us, today's collectors!

The doll makers of Paris, those talented leading ladies, Mesdames Huret and Rhomer, Simonne and Peronne, have long departed, but they left for collectors a precious legacy - - their dolls, which more than a century later remain, mais certainement, as pretty as humming-birds!

Illustration 5A. A light blonde original mohair wig is topped with a black feathered and beribboned chapeau decorated with pink velour roses on this 14in (35.6cm) dainty French Fashion-type doll. Her grey paperweight glass eyes are black rimmed. The ears are pierced with gold ear drops. The mouth is two-toned, and the head swivels on a bisque shoulder plate. *Museum of Old Dolls and Toys, Winter Haven, Florida.*

Illustration 5B. A petite madamoiselle is the 14in (35.6cm) French miss in a warm maroon gown with boat neck and bodice ending in pointed peplum. Her skirt boasts three wide pleated ruffles and her little gold cross suggests she may be on her way to church. She is on a kid body with bisque arms to elbows and is unmarked. *Museum of Old Dolls and Toys, Winter Haven, Florida.*

~Les Parisiennes~
Tres Jolie ~~ Tres Chic

A Photographic Essay
by Sybill McFadden

Ah, beautiful ladies of Paris, with what pretty insouciance you carry your more than 110 years! We mere mortals, pawns of Time, can only admire your pale and perfect porcelain, your youthful figures, your unlined brows, and wish with all our hearts that we could fathom your ageless secrets!

The French Fashion-type dolls we so cherish in collections today appeared in Paris in the 1860s and 1870s and became the treasured and admired playthings of well-to-do children on the continent and in America as well. As the dolls were dressed in miniature by specially trained seamstresses, following the styles which the great couturiers of the day designed for their aristocratic lady patrons, the beautifully gowned dolls also became models of the latest Paris fashions. Here, then, are seven presented for your enjoyment.

ABOVE: Illustration 1. Madamoiselle Francoise has a face typical of the fashion-type dolls marked with an "F.G." usually on the shoulder. She has delicately painted eyelashes and painted black eyeliner around her paperweight blue glass eyes which bulge in the French manner. The lip painting on the closed mouth is two-toned. Her original blonde mohair wig is upswept, secured with two tiny French braids circling the head. In the pierced ears are drop earrings of blue glass. Her chapeau of straw is decorated with blue cornflowers, white ruching and feathered blue ribbons.

RIGHT: Illustration 2. This 16in (40.6cm) French Fashion-type lady is marked " F.G." on her bisque shoulder plate, sometimes thought to be the mark of Fernand Gaultier, doll maker of Paris in the 1870s, and is on pristine white leather body. She wears a two-piece gown of electric blue taffeta trimmed with pale blue binding, with rolled French seaming at the shoulders. Her shoes are original of red leather with tiny gold buttons and French heels. Her dress has been replaced, but she wears her original undergarments.

From the April/May 1981 Doll Reader.®

Illustration 3. Madamoiselle Evette *is 21in (53.3cm) tall and is on a kid body with bisque Bru-type hands. She wears a teal blue taffeta two-piece gown. Cut steel buttons fasten the bodice, and lace medallions decorate it. The apron-type skirt has two ruffles with matching feathered-fringe. She carries French white kid gloves.*

Illustration 4. Evette's honey-blonde mohair wig is original. It is topped with a chapeau of feathers, beads, ribbons, lace and fruit. Real turquoise earrings in antique gold mountings are in her pierced ears. Her bisque is extremely pale. She has stationary blue threaded glass eyes with black lining the tops of the eyes and indented eyelids. The mouth is two-toned.

Illustration 5. Madamoiselle Camille *is 18½in (47.0cm) tall and is a wood-bodied French Fashion-type. Her all-wood body is fully articulated with beautifully hand-carved feet and toes. Her hands are wrist-jointed, also of wood. She wears a pink and gray two-piece taffeta gown with matching chapeau and carries a beaded bag.*

Illustration 6. Camille is a wood-bodied doll with a swivel head on a kid-lined bisque shoulder plate attached to the all-wood body with a wide strip of kid leather. She has protruding blue glass paper-weight eyes, black rimmed, with indented eyelids. Her lips are two-toned and the ears are pierced. Her original human hair wig is brown. Her bonnet of open-work straw is topped with pink and gray taffeta, satin ribbons and curling egret plumes.

Illustration 7. Madamoiselle Mimi *represents a young girl fashion-type doll. She is 15in (38.1cm) tall and on a pristine corded white leather body with separately wired fingers and toes. She is dressed in white batiste with a bodice of tucks and lace and three-quarter length sleeves. The skirt is also tucked and lace trimmed with a pale satin sash. She wears her original hand-knit stockings and brown high-button boots.*

Illustration 8. Mimi *wears her original blonde mohair wig in a long style befitting a young girl, and it is tied with its original pink silk ribbons. Her bisque head swivels on a kid-lined shoulder plate. The delicately feathered eyebrows frame her protruding pale blue paperweight glass eyes. Her mouth is two-toned and her pierced ears have real turquoise drop earrings in antique gold mountings which are also original.*

Illustration 10. Lisette *is an unusual lady with a pale bisque oval face, black rimmed paperweight blue glass eyes which bulge, and indented eyelids with deftly and delicately painted eyelashes around the eyes. Her slightly smiling mouth is two-toned, and the ears are pierced. Her original mohair blonde wig is upswept and crowned with coronet braids.*

She wears ruby earrings and a ruby choker, which all match exactly the ruby velvet of her gown.

Illustration 9. Madamoiselle Lisette *has a rare and unusual carton-moule body covered with a twill-like material called "drilling." Her wooden feet are articulated at the ankles, and mortise and tenon, as well as ball joints are both used and both covered with drilling. The beautiful bisque hands with bisque arms ending halfway up, are attached with drilling. She is 16in (40.6cm) tall, and was found in this ruby chiffon-velvet gown in two pieces with a cowl neck ending in a pointed bodice. The red velvet skirt is trimmed with white net ruffles as are the sleeves of the bodice. The dress was obviously designed for her, but while it is not unacceptable, it lacks the panache of a French-designed original.*

Illustration 11. Madamoiselle Simonne, *the Fashion lady on the cover of this issue, wears a two-piece green taffeta gown trimmed with black velvet bows and collar. She has a shapely white kid body with molded bosom, and bisque hands and forearms are dimpled and reach above the elbows. She is 17½in (44.5cm) tall and is unmarked but is entirely original.*

Illustration 12. *Simonne's pale bisque oval face is set off with lovely serene blue threaded paperweight glass eyes with black eyeliner and eyelashes painted on the top and bottom. Her upswept blonde mohair wig has a French twist held in place with the original turquoise and gold hair comb. The head swivels on a kid-lined shoulder plate. She is unmarked.*

See also color illustration on page 89.

Illustration 13. Madamoiselle Gabrille, *sometimes called* The Smiler French Fashion *because of her tiny Mona Lisa-type smile is on an all-kid body with separately wired fingers and toes. Her gray-blue paperweight eyes are black lined and have indented eyelids above which are delicately feathered eyebrows. Her human hair wig is original and is arranged in long blonde curls which fall down her back, and are caught with a black velvet ribbon. Her lace-edged gown is decolletage, and very likely she wore a piece of jewelry around her kid-lined neck, but if so, it is no longer with her. Her straw hat is decorated with orchid and pink ribbons and a large pink plume with curled edges.*

THE MARQUE DOLL

Close-up of A. Marque doll shown on the following page.

BY MILDRED SEELEY

From the February/March 1980 Doll Reader.®

Not everyone is familiar with the Marque dolls. This is not in the least unusual, as most doll collectors consider the Marques the rarest, most expensive, most coveted dolls of all dolldom. People who own them are sometimes afraid to say they do for fear of theft, so I will not list the owners that I know. There are not many, as less than 50 have actually been found in collections. Several pairs have been separated. For study, there is one in the Margaret Woodbury Strong Museum in Rochester, New York, two in the Museum of Old Dolls and Toys in Winter Haven, Florida, and one in the Wee Lassie Museum in Homestead, Florida.

The price on these dolls is dictated by the people who own them — there seems to be no limit. At the 1978 Denver Convention there was one for sale at $32,000 and the doll was either carried or held during sales hours. Two others were purchased a few years back for around $30,000 each. Rumor is that one recently sold for $35,000.

Six of these dolls were imported by the late Harriet Miller, owner of Whimsey Antiques of Arlington, Vermont, around 1939. The dolls were in pairs and dressed in regional costumes. This information came from Gaynell Denson, who, some 30 or 40 years ago, purchased many dolls, including a pair of Marques from Harriet Miller.

There are a few dolls being passed off as Marques that are not Marques. These dolls have a slight resemblance to the Marque, especially in pictures. There is even one mold on the market whose advertising carefully says that it is considered a Marque. The real Marque is easy to identify — it is signed. It also has unusual mold marks in unusual places. If you have your heart set on owning one, be careful.

The Marque dolls are 22 in. (55.9 cm) tall. They have the proportion of a tall, thin child. The hands and fingers are exquisitely modeled and are of porcelain bisque. The bisque lower arm is strung to a composition upper arm and composition body. The feet are long and thin.

The head is a masterpiece of modeling, the mold having been made in five pieces to avoid any undercuts. This modeling appears to be the work of an artist making a few of a kind, not a dollmaker preparing a doll for mass production. This may shed some light on why there are so few Marques. The Marques have faces that you cannot stop looking at. They are not quite sad — perhaps pensive — a little bit pixieish — like no other doll. Even the ears are different. It is no wonder people pay high prices for the Marques.

The eyes are paperweight, similar to Bru eyes. The rich brown brows are feathered, the lashes and eye rims are black. The eyelid line is a deep crease and the lashes have to skip, as they are painted over the crease. The mouth is closed and painted a deep pompadour red similar to the color used of F.G.'s (Gaultier). The tear ducts are painted light pompadour red and the nostrils are the same color.

The head is clearly incised with the signature, *A. Marque*. None of the usual size numbers or mold number appear. It is made of fine white translucent bisque.

From here on, all the Marques were different although apparently all were made from the same mold.

The Marque, called André, that I purchased is, I believe, the most interesting. He has red hair done in a Dutch boy bob. He has on his original clothes. The jacket label reads: Margaine Lacroix, 19 Boulevard Haussmann, Paris. The jacket is made of a fine green velvet lined in silk. His full short pants are a grey-green, held up by buttoned suspenders. His vest is ribbed raspberry-colored faille and decorated with bands of gold and blue braid. His shoes are Jumeau-like and tied, and his high leggings are glove leather hooked in the back. His big straw hat frames his face. The whole outfit looks like a late 19th century French country boy.

Marque hands are porcelain, carefully molded

The A. Marque is 22 in. (55.9 cm) tall.

Label from Marque jacket.

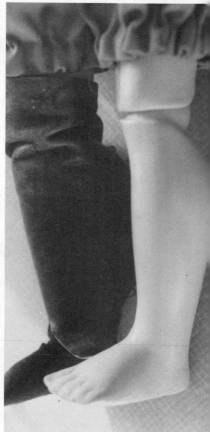

The feet are long and slender, like no other doll

On The Production Of Dolls' Biscuit Heads In France

by CLAIRE HENNIG

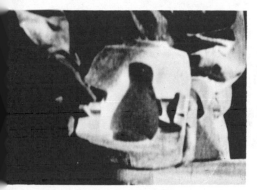

Illustration 1. We look into the empty mould for the back of the doll's head. It is one of the two pieces which will be put together for the casting of the bisque head. This half of the mould takes up almost three quarters of the full size. Both mould parts are T-shaped and form a socle and a base. A deep black shadow shows where the attached ears are spared out. Two additional round holes, as well as "lock and key" in the plaster are made for better tightening. The tighter the mould closes, the less work has to be done on the cast head. The full roundness of the pouring hole is situated in the lower socle.

Illustration 2. The two parts of the mould have been jointed and the whole form turned upside down. The pouring hole is now on top. A very uneven mould line is conspicious.

Illustration 3. A cord or wire holds the two parts together. The woman has a kind of garden watering can in her hands, ready to pour the slip into the mould. (At that period, the ceramic slip still had to be mixed on the spot in the factory. Today it is bought ready mixed.)

At a doll convention in Schloss Wilhelmsbad, in Hanau near Frankfurt, Germany, I reported on a French film which is about 60 years old. A worker shows the manufacture of a doll's head, then still called "porcellaine." The film was taken on a strip of 9.5 millimeters and cannot be reproduced as reproduction apparatus is not available anymore for this size. For this reason, I had a number of slides taken from this film and commented on them in my lecture. I should like to give a short summary which I derived from studying this material.

The film was probably meant to entertain the lay public. It has been taken in a French factory, the name of which unfortunately is not stated. The French words and explanations, intermingled with the actions, are partly outdated. *La barboutine* for the slip, *Thibet* for mohair, are just two examples.

For the sake of easy survey the same woman was shown at every step of the procedure, whereas we know that about 80 workers were engaged in the complicated production of the bisque heads.

A few facts, never shown in illustrations nor mentioned in the literature, can be seen in this film. Other points, still being debated, are clarified by the sequence of the film.

The first and still most informative description of the work in French doll factories (mainly with Jumeau) came from Leo Claretie (born in Paris, 1862) in his *Les Jouets, Histoire et Fabrication* (no date, but 1894 is now established). In 1894 it was published in English by C. M. Linington in the periodical *Silent Salesman,* and again 70 years later by Dorothy Coleman in *The Age of Dolls.* In *The Collector's Encyclopedia of Dolls,* page 405, Dorothy Coleman repeats these translations and adds some comments. She says: ". . .after baking. . .they (the heads) pass then to the cutting out which consists of making holes for the eyes which were blank as in ordinary busts. . ." She continues: "Some modern makers of ceramic dolls question whether Claretie could have seen the eyes cut out before rather than after baking." In her correspondence she says that she still thinks Claretie is confused.

The mistake, repeated in a German translation, occurred because of the misunderstanding of Claretie's word "alors" (page 146) which was correctly translated with "then." In this case the "alors" simply means: "then the next room." On his illustration on page 148 where he shows the cutting of the eyeholes, he gives the title: "Découpage *avant* cuisson," which means "cutting before the baking."

Claretie described his walk through the different rooms of the factory and gave a highly dramatic and spirited description of what he saw there. He never intended to give a documentation of the exact sequence of the procedure. It is said of him that his books are written "avec une facilité spirituelle et aimable."

Taken in the factory, my film proves the order in which doll's heads were produced. The film also shows the cutting of the eyeholes and mouth and the piercing of the neckhole which I never saw nor heard of before. (See Illustrations 10-12.) I have not been able to identify the name and shape of the tool used for piercing the neck. It consists of a wooden handle and a metal driller or corer which either takes out, or pushes inside, the clay which, of course, must still be moist. At the same time it shapes a beautifully rounded neckhole.

In his descriptions in *Les Jouets,* Claretie is particularly fascinated by the manufacture of the wigs. He tells of the "Thibet," imported from England, being carried inside the hairdressers' department in large bails. It was the hair of the goat, then only found in Asia, now called mohair. (England, at that period, was the only country which had the monopoly to trade with Tibet.) Claretie describes how these strands of hair were cut to size, dyed, curled in special gas-heated ovens and in a final stage turned into the hairstyles of the day.

Since the size of the film is outdated, it would be desirable to have a reproduction made according to present standards, to be able to show it in its full length and detail. This, however, is a costly affair which I shun for the moment.

Illustration 4. The slip is thick flowing and consistent.

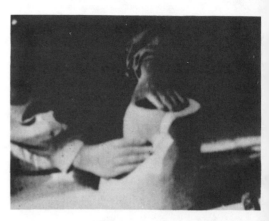

Illustration 8. The mould for the back of the head being set aside; the much more complicated face part with probable undercutting is yet to be loosened.

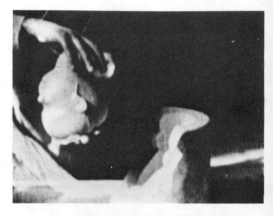

Illustration 5. After a waiting period of about 15 minutes, the mould is turned and emptied of the slip which has not yet set and is still liquid.

Illustration 9. The head is completely freed of the mould, turned neck up and held firmly between two hands. The mould line which is clearly visible runs along the outer edge of the attached ears. The interlocking has not been completely firm. There is still work to be done to scrape the clay off along the mould line.

Illustration 6. The upturned mould is placed on two wooden bars situated across a wooden barrel.

Illustration 10. On the right-hand side stands the emptied mould, neck downward, showing the rounded shape where the neck rested. The neckhole is still to be opened. This procedure I have never seen mentioned nor illustrated. To proceed, the woman has now taken a tool between her hands.

Illustration 7. The two mould shapes are separated slightly. The very uneven mould line, "lock and key," the round of the pouring hole within the thick top rim can all be seen very clearly.

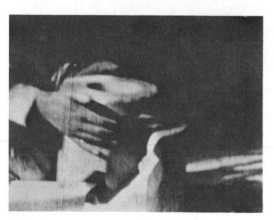

Illustration 11. This tool has been slightly inserted by a twisting or screwing movement. It consists of two, if not three parts: a wooden handle and a metal front with a slit. I examine many tool catalogs but found none this shape. It seems that the portions of clay removed by this tool fell right through the open crown. It is not likely that they were lifted and taken out on top, as only by a pushing-in movement could the beautifully shaped inward curve of the neck hole be achieved.

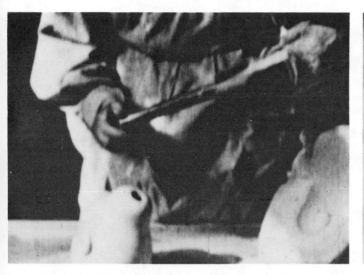

Illustration 12. A neat neckhole has resulted.

Illustration 15. Afterwards, they are arranged on refractoring round trays and baked for the first time in a kiln at a high temperature.

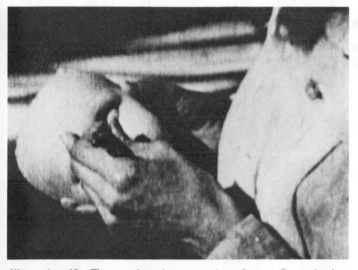

Illustration 13. The mouth and eyes remain to be cut. By resting her right hand against the head, the woman cuts the eye openings with a short knife.

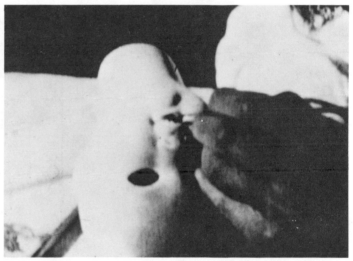

Illustration 16. By means of pincers the teeth are inserted singly into a prepared palate.

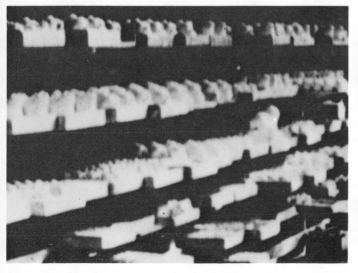

Illustration 14. On square trays, heads of different sizes are air-dried on several shelves.

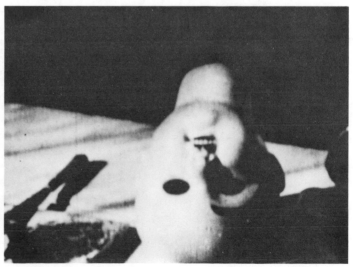

Illustration 17. As in Illustration 16, the open crown rests on the working table. The mouth and eyebrows are being painted, surprisingly in a downward movement.

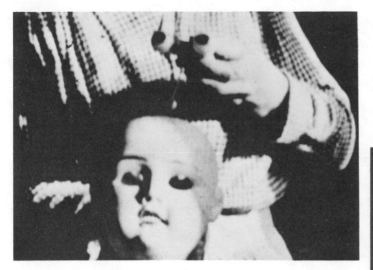

Illustration 18. The jointed pair of eyes in her hand, the woman holds the head upright and facing away from her.

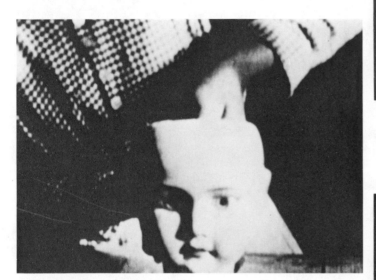

Illustration 19. Pressing slightly from the rear, she fixes the eyes provisionally in a prepared layer of wax.

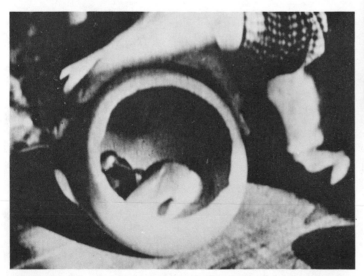

Illustration 20. We now look inside the head and see the final fixation of the eyes by means of plaster of Paris. We can also notice the rim at the crown, shaped inside the mould, where the ceramic slip is turned slightly inward underneath the broad socle which held the pouring opening.

Illustration 21. The eyelashes have been glued in.

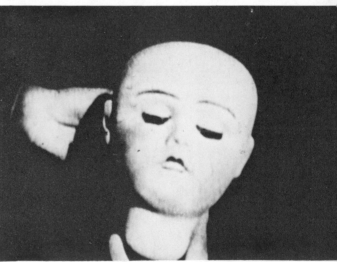

Illustration 22. The sleeping beauty has been created.

DOLLS IN EUROPE
GERMANY
by DOROTHY S. COLEMAN

Illustration 1. 14in (35.6cm) bisque-head baby doll with bent limb composition body. Purchased in Düsseldorf, Germany, in 1914.

After spending two exciting weeks in England, Jane and I flew to Düsseldorf, Germany, where my first bisque head doll had been purchased for me as a child in 1914 (see Illustration 1). Nearby in Jülich, Marianne and Jürgen Cieslik live in a large two family house. The occupants of the second floor are doll collectors as well. We had met the Ciesliks several years ago and are most impressed with their excellent research on German dolls. Just as we had anticipated, their home is a treasure house of early records: prints, catalogs and publications relating to dolls and manufacturers of dolls as well as toys. Their collection of dolls is small but very fine and diversified, which would also describe the collection of their upstairs neighbors, the Biermanns, who are both artists.

Reluctantly we had to tear ourselves away from the many fascinating books at the Ciesliks so that we could see some of the nearby sights. First we visited Aachen to see the church built by Charlemagne which contains Charlemagne's throne. While in Aachen we stopped at a toy shop and saw the new dolls which are being made from the old molds of Rheinische Gummi und Celluloid Fabrik Co. (Schildkröte). The material of which these dolls are made resembles celluloid but may be a plastic.

On another day we went to the museum in Kreis Viersen where the collection of dolls and toys of H. G. Klein are attractively displayed with excellent use of modern exhibit techniques. We first saw a slide program about the dolls, but unfortunately some of the commentary information was not accurate. Attached to each display case were two earphones that described the contents, one in German and the other in Dutch; alas there was none in English.

Next we visited the Niederrheinishes Museum fur Volkskunde und Kulturgeschichte in Kevelaer. The Director, Dr. Robert Plötz, escorted us and showed us some of the dolls from the Juliana Metzger collection which they were preparing for exhibit by November 1981. This well-known collection will be beautifully displayed from what we could see in late August. They have the largest Schlaggenwald china head with morning glories decorating the hair that I have ever seen.

The next day we visited the home of Frau Christiane Heede who specializes in German dolls. She has a marvelous Steiff doll dressed as a German soldier with all its accoutrements which Jürgen coveted as well as some unusual hairdo chinas which the Colemans coveted. Frau Heede has exhibited some of her dolls in German museums from time to time.

Regretfully we left Jülich but were happy to be accompanied by the Ciesliks. Jürgen drove us along the Rhine and crossed it by ferry so that we could look across the river at the finest part of the scenery. Near Frankfurt we stopped for lunch with Frau Stiegel, who has an interesting doll collection started by her mother. Frau Stiegel's father, a sea captain, brought back dolls from the Orient and elsewhere. Being a teacher, Frau Stiegel's interest in dolls includes their educational importance for children. One of her recent acquisitions was a Chinese Door of Hope doll.

In Bamberg we met Herr Meinhard Meisenbach, the publisher of *Das Spielzeug,* formerly *Deutsche Spielwaren Zeitung,* the German toy trade journal that is such a marvelous primary source for doll data. Herr Meisenbach has a few toys and dolls, among them one of the so-called Nürnberg dolls presumed to date from medieval times that were found in excavations.

After enjoying the famous Coburg sausages which are cooked and sold in the Coburg city square we went to Neustadt near Coburg a town that was in Thüringia until the 1920 plebicite altered the boundary and added that region to Bavaria. In 1970 I had visited the museum in Neustadt but now there are on view many more important dolls and items related to the history of dolls.

We were particularly impressed with the wooden dolls. There are several "Bébé Tout Bois" type all-wood dolls, both finished and unfinished, thus indicating that they had been made in this area, probably over a period of years. They were sold in Paris during the time when the German Fleischmann was head of the S.F.B.J. firm. We also saw similar dolls in other West German doll collections.

What amazed us even more was the presence in the Neustadt Museum of two wooden dolls having dates and a history. These had been found in the basement of this museum recently. These dolls of the so-called Queen Anne type with gessoed faces had belonged to local Fleischmann families. The mid 18th century dates given on these dolls corresponded with the 18th century clothes which the dolls wore. They wore printed cotton short gowns and skirts. There were no signs of any obvious repairs. One doll might have been imported but the presence of two of these dolls in this small wooden-doll producing area and having belonged to a doll manufacturing family made us wonder if some of our so-called English dolls could have come from this region of Germany.

Early the next morning we crossed the frontier into East Germany at nearby Eisfeld, Thüringia. The long succession of strong barriers and gates that we had to pass through were most impressive. Our passports were examined by at least four pairs of guards, one of them commented that only two other Americans and one New Zealander had been admitted through this checkpoint prior to us during the entire past year. However, the Ciesliks and many other Germans had come through this entry.

Our first destination in East Germany was, of course, Sonneberg and the Sonneberg Museum. This museum is closed on Monday, but we were privileged to see it on a Monday when the Director, Herr Hans Gauss, could escort us around the museum. Not all of the dolls on display were made in the Sonneberg area for they have cases full of Oriental dolls and dolls that had been

From the April/May 1982 Doll Reader.®

Illustration 2A and 2B. People of Thüringia in native costumes, 19th century.

made by American Indians. But they have an excellent German collection which is well displayed. We were particularly thrilled to see one of the Gullivers that was exhibited in Berlin in 1844/1845 and in London in 1851 as well as the Sonneberg Street Scene that was at the 1910 Brussels Exhibition. Gulliver is made of a rye flour and water substance, and the tiny Lilliputians are an amazing group of comical and expressive figures. The street scene is a life-size diorama filled with so many interesting characters that it is difficult to see and remember all of them after a single viewing. Most of the figures appear

to be made of some form of composition, but there are a few dolls with bisque heads. These are placed on a carrousel which still revolves. Other dolls are seen on a workman's bench.

Upstairs on the wall of the museum are some framed early catalog pages. One shows 12 dolls with the so-called Apollo knot hairdo. Placed on top of these representations of dolls are pieces of fabric with a variety of different printed designs. They appear to date from the late 1830s and early 1840s. At the waist of each doll a piece of ribbon forms the sash. The slippers are painted red, blue or yellow. These dolls are marked sizes 2, 1, 0, 2/0, 3/0, 4/0, 5/0, 6/0, 7/0, 8/0, 9/0 and 10/0 in descending order. Next to this is a page from a similar catalog showing dolls dressed in regional costumes including both men and women. They all wear black slippers. Herr Gauss showed us several early catalogs containing records of dolls but most, if not all, of this information has been published in a book by Dr. Manfred Bachmann.

Among the many interesting dolls that we saw at the Sonneberg Museum were a group of art fashion dolls of 1912 with bisque heads and limbs including accessories, made by Galluba & Hofmann of Ilmenau and a four-faced Carl Bergner doll made in 1908 having a black face, a brown face and two white faces. A papier-

mâché head with a wig on a doll with jointed wooden body of the mid 19th century or earlier, wore slippers with red high laces around its legs. This doll was reported as having been made in Sonneberg.

Other papier-mâché head dolls with Sonneberg provenances included a flirting-eye doll, a slit-head doll and a doll head with the so-called Gothic Victorian hair style. This doll had teeth. There were various styles of china heads and limbs on jointed wooden bodies. Many of the bisque-head dolls' house men had the wires in their boots or shoes to enable them to stand upright. Several dioramas, made in 1925, showed how dolls were made and a room was reconstructed to show how a doll making homeworker lived. Also displayed were some of the dolls that are being made in East Germany (D.D.R.) today.

The Sonneberg Museum has many modern dolls as well as antique dolls on display. Herr Gauss showed us some pouring molds for bisque socket heads that had recently been found when the walls of a building had been dismantled in the Sonneberg area. These molds had not as yet been put on display.

From Sonneberg we drove to Suhl where we stayed while in East Germany. Suhl has one of the Inter-

Illustration 3. The living room/work room of a family that made dolls' bodies in their home. Note the molds in the foreground and the finished bodies on the right.

Illustration 4. Mountains of Thüringia. Photograph taken in the 1890s.

hotels which caters to tourists from other countries. Our accommodations were not luxurious and the food was poor. The hot foods were generally served cold after waiting a long time for them. But we did have fresh flowers in our room. Some of the buildings, stores and streets in Suhl were obviously made to impress the tourists but behind these meager facades are the same decaying houses and unkept streets that are prevalent in East Germany. While there we did look into what they call a "Warehouse" and what we would refer to as a department store. We saw a poor selection of plastic dolls including representations of Max and Moritz and other toys that are being offered to the East German population.

Thüringia is a beautiful wooded mountainous region that is now used largely for vacation purposes. The mountains run roughly northwest by southeast with the highest peaks being almost in the middle. Sonneberg (literally Sunny Mountain) is at the southern edge of the mountains now lying chiefly in the plain beyond the hills, while Waltershausen occupies a similar situation on the northern edge where the hills disappear into the plains of Gotha. The steep sides of the mountains are covered with tall pine trees. There is very little traffic on the narrow roads that wind up and down over these mountains. Tiny villages occupy nearly every valley and despite the rugged terrain, trains seem to connect all the villages and towns of the region. Most of the houses are built with slate covering, both as siding and as roof. Sometimes the slate is painted which gives it a less dreary look. Some of the houses in Thüringia are the half-timber type which we associate with England.

In Sonneberg, which was rebuilt because of fire in the mid 19th century, many of the houses and factories were constructed of red brick. The houses of the great manufacturers like Armand Marseille, the Dressels, the Heubachs, and so forth were large Victorian mansions which showed the opulence of their era. The last doll making factory in private hands was taken over by the State several years ago. The main street in Sonneberg was called Jutta Street after a famous Countess Jutta who once lived in the vicinity. However, now the name of the street has been changed. The Jutta dolls of Cuno and Otto Dressel were named after this Countess. Sonneberg now includes Bettelhecken, Hüttensteinach, Köppelsdorf, Neuhaus, Oberlin and Wildenheid, where dolls and/or dolls' parts were once made. The old original part of Sonneberg

Illustration 5B. Sonneberg, looking towards the plain in 1981.

lies chiefly in a valley and through the years the town has spread out over the plain and occupies seven hills. The museum is located in the building that once housed the Industrial School where young people were taught to design and make dolls.

Besides Sonneberg and its environs we visited the Arnstadt Museum, Brattendorf; Catterfeld; Eisfeld including the museum containing the Kloster Veilsdorf artifacts; Friedrichroda; Georgenthal; Grossbreitenbach; Grümpen; the county of Hildburghausen; Ilmenau; Kätzhutte; Lichte; Plaue; Ohrdruf and its suburbs, Gräfenhain and Luisinthal; Rudolstadt; Schleusingen Museum with its Sonneberg material including another Gulliver; Suhl; Wallendorf and Waltershausen. All of these towns or places either had a doll related

Illustration 5A. Sonneberg, looking towards the mountains in the 1890s.

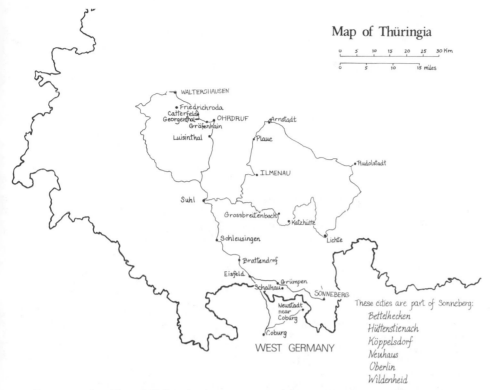

Map of Thüringia

0 5 10 15 20 25 30 Km

0   5   10   15 miles

WALTERSHAUSEN

Friedrichroda
Catterfeld   OHRDRUF
Georgenthal
             Gräfenhain
Luisinthal

Arnstadt

Plaue

ILMENAU

Rudolstadt

Suhl

Grossbreitenbach

Schleusingen   Katzhütte

Lichte

Brattendorf

Eisfeld

Schalkau   Grümpen

SONNEBERG

Neustadt
near
Coburg

Coburg

WEST GERMANY

These cities are part of Sonneberg:

Bettelhecken
Hüttenstienach
Köppelsdorf
Neuhaus
Oberlin
Wildenheid

Illustration 6. Map of Thüringia showing the towns visited by the Ciesliks and Colemans as well as the routes traveled by them in 1981.

museum and/or they had once been an area that made dolls.

At the Arnstadt Museum we saw the marvelous rooms created by the Duchess Auguste Dorothea of Schwarzburg-Arnstadt. She was born in 1666 and died in 1751. These 82 rooms with over 2700 objects, including many dolls, preserve for posterity the authentic furnishings, clothes amusements, occupations and way of life in the first half of the 18th century in Germany. This valuable document cost the Duchess all of her wealth, and she died in dire poverty without money even for her funeral. But thanks to her enterprise we can truly turn back the clock and see how some of our ancestors really lived. The dolls vary in size but most of them appeared to be about 1½in (3.8cm) to 1ft (30.5cm) or approximately 9in (22.9cm) tall, for the adults. Most of them were made of wax, but a few of them were made of wood. Some of the faces appeared to be portraits and several of the dolls are said to represent the Duchess herself.

Thüringia was formerly comprised of a large number of duchies and most of the museums are located in the local schloss or burg (castle). The Ohrdruf Museum which is in the castle as usual contains some of the most interesting objects that we found anywhere. Ohrdruf was a center for making porcelain. Here were located Kling, founded in 1834; Kestner & Co. which was the porcelain factory that Kestner took over in 1860; and

Bähr and Pröschild, founded in 1871. The museum contains some of the fabulous parian and china heads made by Kling and other concerns. Similar heads are shown in a framed picture dated 1934 which commemorated the 100th anniversary of Kling. A few

Illustration 7. Arnstadt in 1650, shortly before the Duchess was born.

Illustration 8. Ohrdruf, a porcelain making town as it appeared in the 1890s.

pincushion-type heads are also shown in this picture as well as a doll with china head and limbs on a jointed wooden body, thus showing the various types of dolls made by Kling during the 100 years of their existence prior to 1934. An original model and pouring mold for the doll known as "Gladdie" are among the museum's exhibits.

The Kley & Hahn factory, part of which is now a sawmill, is located on the outskirts of Ohrdruf. One of the buildings still has the remains of the Kley & Hahn name on its walls. In back of this factory Jane picked up a large group of shards including a doll's head probably for an all-bisque doll, parts of arms, legs and bits of ears, mouths and so forth. The shards included both china and bisque pieces. No evidence of a porcelain factory at this site has been found in the written records, but one cannot help questioning the origin of all these pieces of bisque and china picked up there in less than two hours. Many of the buildings in and around Ohrdruf contain walls built of discarded pouring (or pressing?) molds for dolls. Some of the old walls have molds for dolls with flat-top hairdos, corkscrew curl hairdos and bald heads.

Gräfenhain where the Simon & Halbig factory was located is only a

87

mile or so from Ohrdruf. This factory is now making cloth animals. We were unable to go into any of the factory buildings in East Germany, but we did find evidence that the kilns in which the dolls' heads were fired were similar to those we saw at the Gladstone Museum in Stoke-on-Trent, England. Nowhere in Ohrdruf or at the Simon & Halbig factory did we see evidence of any of these large kilns still in existence.

Next we went to Waltershausen and visited the Schloss Tennenburg where the museum is located. Here as in Sonneberg are dolls from Waltershausen and various other places including a socket head incised E.J. (Bébé Jumeau head). The museum also has some wax models for dolls and several books and papers that had belonged to the Kestner family and showed their business operations dating back to 1816. We were unable to locate the great Kestner and Kämmer & Reinhardt factories and presumed that they have all or partially disappeared. Jürgen did point out some buildings which he thought were part of the Kämmer & Reinhardt factory.

After nearly a week behind the iron curtain we returned to West Germany. The guards tore the car apart, but Jürgen was prepared for this and soon had it back together. As soon as we crossed the frontier Marianne phoned her mother to say that we were safely back in the West. We were lucky; there is considerable apprehension when going into and out of Thüringia.

Most of the museums in Thüringia and nearby Neustadt contain all-wood dolls similar to the ones collectors call the Grödner Tal type. We also

found this type in Berchtesgaden, our next stop after seeing the doll and toy collection in the Lydia Bayer Museum in Nürnberg. The all-wood dolls called "Docken (Dockin)" in German appear to have been made in the wooded mountain areas of Thüringia and the Tyrol. The ones in Sonneberg, Berchtesgaden, Oberammergau and the Grödner Tal all bear a close resemblance. Some experts claim they can identify the differences, but this would be very difficult to do. There certainly appears to have been some artistic influence that spread throughout these mountain areas where people spent their winters whittling wooden dolls. There is even evidence that the wooden dolls made in Russia had been under this same influence. The Thüringian jointed wooden dolls were more likely to have a composition or porcelain head than those of the Tyrolian areas. Dolls with these heads of other materials are sometimes considered to be later than the early carved or turned wooden heads. If this is so, the making of these dolls may have spread northward from the Grödner Tal.

In Berchtesgaden we visited the local folk art museum and saw some very interesting dolls which presumably were made in the Berchtesgaden area. An excellent diversified private collection of dolls is owned by a farm family living in the beautiful Ramsau valley near Berchtesgaden. We were privileged to spend several days with this family.

From Germany we went to Austria and Hungary. Our visits there will be recounted in the next issue of the **Doll Reader**. Unfortunately the East German Museums have few publications on dolls, and it would

Illustration 10. Wooden folk art dolls made in the Berchtesgaden area in the 1980s. These highly painted dolls include poupards (babies in swaddling clothes) shown in four sizes; three dolls that fit one inside the other; a lady doll that rattles when shaken and a bell doll. These dolls are currently available from Berchtesgadener Handwerckskunst, 824 Berchtesgaden, Schroffenbergallee 6, Schloss Adelsheim, West Germany.

be very difficult to obtain any of them.

While in East Germany (D.D.R.) we saw no shops selling any antiques. However, in one shop in West Germany we were informed by the owner that she had bought some of her dolls through the proper shops in East Berlin and had thus been able to obtain antique dolls from East Germany. Her prices were very high according to American standards.

Book purchased: Das Sonneberger Spielzeug Musterbuch, Spielwaren-Mustercharte, Von Johann Simon Lindner, copyrighted in Sonneberg by Manfred Bachmann, copyright 1979, printed in G.D.R.

Illustration 9. Waltershausen shown in a photograph taken in the 1890s.

Les Parisiennes

BELOW: French fashion lady wearing a two-piece green taffeta gown trimmed with black velvet bows and collar. She is 17½in (44.5cm) tall and is unmarked but entirely original.

See article on pages 73-76.

Emile Jumeau Doll with bisque socket head. Brown human hair wig over cork pate; blue paperweight eyes; open/closed mouth; pierced ears; jointed French composition body; original clothes. c.1890. Height 16½in (41.9cm).

Let's Look At

Heubach

A Photographic Essay by Shirley Buchholz

Illustration 1. "Percy," a 14¾in (37.6cm) shoulder head, and the bisque piano baby point out graphically the close relationship between the Heubach dolls and figurines. The smile on the baby is a bit broader and we can see two teeth while the little boy has closed his lips, but still smiles sweetly. The modeling of the two heads is almost identical. The boy has a kid body with bisque arms and Ne Plus Ultra joints at the hips. He is incised: "1//Square Mark//8724//Germany." The piano baby is incised with a "sunburst" on the back and "37" on the bottom. *Photograph by John Axe.*

Say "German bisque" and names of famous makers immediately come to mind: Armand Marseille, Simon and Halbig, Kestner and Heubach - - to name a few. Among them they produced millions of dolls for the world's markets during the period of the last two decades of the 19th century and the first two of the 20th century.

The typical dolly-face bisque was by far the most popular doll and most manufacturers allocated only a small percentage of their production to the so-called "characters," dolls modeled after real children. These tots resembled the little girls and boys who played with them instead of being an idealized version of a child with perfect features.

It would seem, however, that the factories of Gebrüder Heubach in Lichte, Thüringia, were an exception. Their dolls were mostly characters, many of which bear a close resemblance to the porcelain figurines for which that manufacturer was famous. The number of different models of Gebrüder Heubach heads is almost staggering. True, there may be only a slight variation, but they are not alike. In many cases we can almost see the same child grow from a baby through the toddler years and into childhood.

Gebrüder Heubach produced heads for various doll manufacturers who would then assemble them with bodies and either dress them or ship them nude to the distributors. The quality of the bodies varies from unbelievably bad to excellent. Many of the small heads are on the cheap plaster or cardboard bodies while some of the larger ones, especially the more conventional dolly-face types, are on fine ball-jointed composition toddler and child bodies.

Most Heubachs are fairly small dolls and this makes them particularly desirable to those collectors whose shelf space is limited. Indeed, there are in the author's collection

24 that are less than 15in (38.1cm), three are between 15in (38.1cm) and 19in (48.3cm) and three are over 20in (50.8cm).

Heubach used the intaglio eye more than any other manufacturer. The carved, enameled eyes with their white highlights have a far more realistic depth than can be attained by simply painting them. Schoenhut and Goebel were among the few others who used this type eye. Intaglio eyes are generally found on dolls with molded hair. The upper lids are usually molded with a black lid line and red corner dots, and no lashes. The brows are mainly painted brown with a single stroke. Dolls with glass sleep eyes are mostly found with feathered brows, molded lids without the black line but with upper and lower painted lashes.

Molded hair rather than wigs is predominant and some of the modeling is superb, on a par with the porcelain figurines. It would seem that when glass eyes were used it was easier to have an open crown to insert them, ergo the use of the wig or, as in the case of the glass-eyed Baby Stuart, the bonnet is removable.

Gebrüder Heubach dolls may be marked with the "sunburst," the "square mark," with a series of numbers or not at all. Marks may be found in the Colemans' The Collector's Encyclopedia of Dolls, in Gebrüder Heubach Dolls by Jan Foulke and in Carol Ann Stanton's Heubach's Little Characters.

In contrast with the dolls of other makers, it is the girls that are rarities among the Heubachs, especially those with intaglio eyes. Boy or girl, marked or not, the charming children of Gebrüder Heubach are among the most appealing dolls ever made.

From the June/July 1981 Doll Reader.®

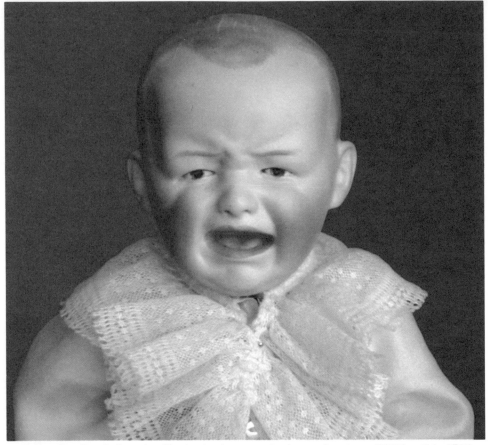

Illustration 2. A favorite Heubach character is the crying boy. "William" is 15½in (39.4cm) tall, a shoulder head on a kid body with bisque arms and Ne Plus Ultra joints at the hip. The open/closed mouth has a deep red outline on the inner lips and darker tongue. The intaglio eyes are blue and his brown hair is only slightly modeled. The numbers "7134" are incised on the back of the shoulder plate and a red paper label (printing unreadable) is on the chest. *Photograph by Jane Buchholz.*

PAGE 61: Illustration 4. "Eddie," a rare boy with prominent ears, is 16½in (41.9cm) tall. His body is ball-jointed composition with straight wrists. He has the typical blue intaglio eyes but the brows are heavier than usual. The lips of his open/closed mouth are pale red with a strong red outline at the bottom of the upper lip, the interior of the mouth is deeper red than the lips. He is marked: "stamped green figures//80 Square Mark 35// Germany." *Photograph by Jane Buchholz.*

BELOW: Illustration 3. The family resemblance is again apparent in this photograph of dolls and piano babies. Both dolls have good quality five-piece baby bodies. "George," the smaller, 9½in (24.2cm), is incised with what seems to be: "775 Sunburst 31// Germany." "Charles," the larger doll, 13in (33.0cm), has a beautifully modeled head with multi-stroke brows and is incised: "5//Sunburst//76 22// Germany." These dolls were originally purchased about 1915 and wear the clothes that were made for them at the time. The sitting baby with the shoe is 7½in (19.1cm) tall. His modeling is more clearly defined than on the creeping babies. The superimposed "G over H" is incised on the back. The 7½in (19.1cm) creeper has "Sunburst//over 3101" and the 4½in (11.5cm) one has a "sunburst and 1¼." *Photograph by Jane Buchholz.*

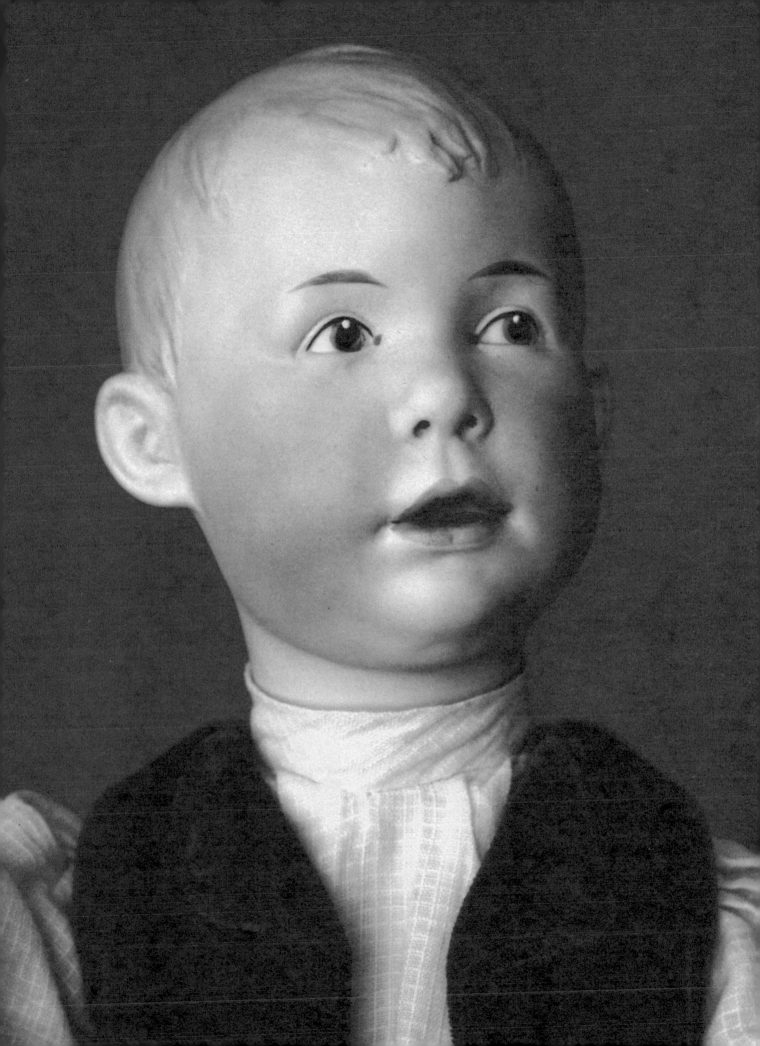

Illustration 6. These two little shoulder heads are on cloth bodies with bisque arms. "Josh," the smaller boy is 10in (25.4cm) tall. His body is pink and his lower legs are made to look like argyle sox. He has blue intaglio eyes and an open/closed mouth with two molded lower teeth. He is poorly incised on the back: "3//Sunburst//Germany" and numbers that seem to be "7124." His big brother, 14in (35.6cm) "Ralphie" has a white body and black lower legs, a Ne Plus Ultra hip joint. His smiling open/closed mouth painted darker red than usual has a molded tongue. He is incised: "2// 76 Sunburst 44//Germany." Both have slight modeling on the heads and painted hair. *Photograph by John Axe.*

Illustration 5. This little 13½in (34.3cm) boy with his bear has brown sleep eyes and an open mouth with teeth. His body is ball-jointed composition and he has a brown human hair wig. Incised: "8192//Germany// Gebruder Heubach//Sunburst//G 2/0 ½ H." *Joyce Kintner Collection. Photograph by John Axe.*

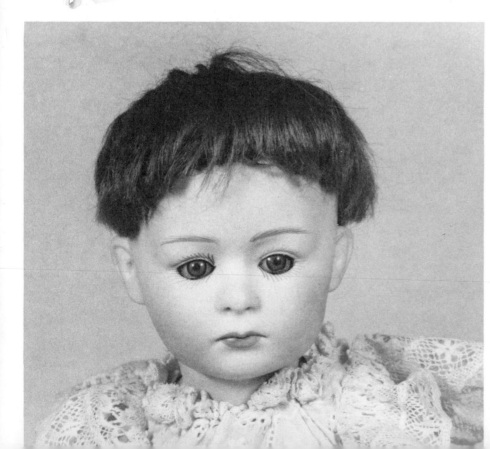

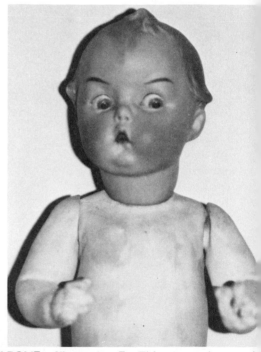

ABOVE: Illustration 7. This extremely rare, de 15in (38.1cm) tall, is a fantastic head on a rath common baby body. The bisque is fine, w modeled and well painted. The intaglio eyes ha such a high glaze they almost seem to be gla The head is incised: "7//85 Square Mark 56 *Ralph Griffith and Elmer Bell Collection* (owne of Ralph's Antique Doll Museum in Parkvil Missouri). *Photograph by Eva Langlois.*

Caption for Illustration 8 on page 95.

Illustration 9. 11in (27.9cm) "Carol Ann." Usually a little girl with intaglio eyes would have molded hair. This sober toddler with her double chin has an open crown and a light brown mohair wig hiding prominent ears. She has a very pink, cheap composition toddler body. The numbers "6970" are incised near the rim of the head. The back of the head is incised: "2 and green marks//Germany//Sunburst." *Photograph by John Axe.*

See color illustration on following page.

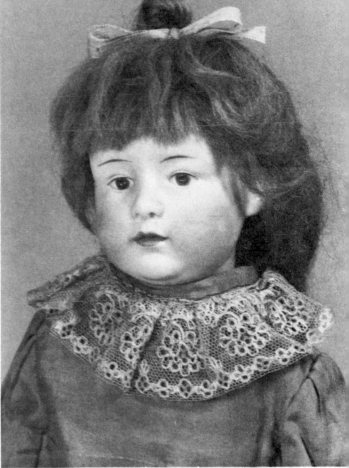

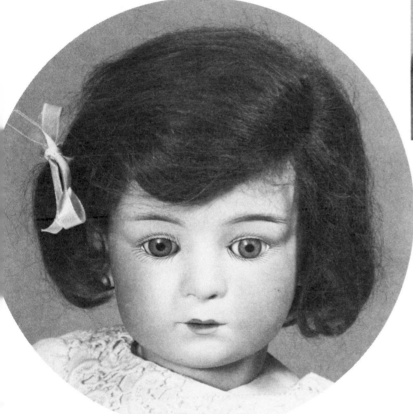

Illustration 10. "Heidi" is a 20in (50.8cm) little girl on a fine ball-jointed toddler body. Her sleep eyes are blue with painted lashes and feathered brows. The outer edges of her slightly parted lips are painted a deeper shade of red and four teeth are just visible. She is incised at the top of the head: "10532." Lower on the back of head is: "9//Square Mark//Germany." She seems to be an older version of model 6969. *Photograph by John Axe.*

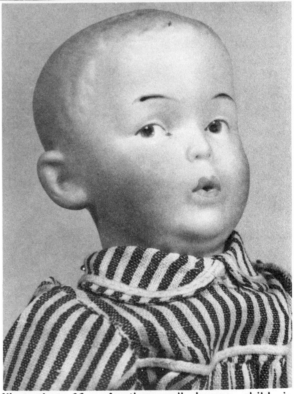

Illustration 11. Another well known child is *Whistling Jim,* a boy with prominent ears, blue intaglio eyes and an open mouth pursed to whistle. This head has a flange neck attached to a straw-stuffed body of pink drill that has a squeeker set into a cardboard inset. The three-quarter length arms are composition with cotton tops. They are attached with a wire through the body. The legs are of straw-stuffed pink felt, also attached with wire. He still wears his original black and white striped suit. The head is incised: "2//87 Square Mark 74//Germany." *Photograph by John Axe.*

Page 94 Illustration 8. "Paul," a very choice baby, is a 12in (30.5cm) sleep-eyed pouty with a brown mohair wig. The bisque is of excellent quality and well sculpted. He has blue glass eyes with painted upper and lower lashes and feathered brows. The body is a fair quality plaster-type composition jointed at the hips and shoulders. Incised: "6969//4//Sunburst//Germany." *Photograph by John Axe.*

BELOW: 14½in (36.9cm) Henry is another seldom-seen head on a ball-jointed toddler body of fair quality. He was originally spring-strung. The modeling on this head is exceptional, especially the hair. This rare little fellow is incised: "6(?)//Sunburst//77 60//Germany."

Heubach Dolls

Illustration 1. Black celluloid swivel head marked with a turtle in a diamond (for Rheinische Gummi und Celluloid Fabrik) over 32/34. The standing celluloid body is marked with a turtle in a diamond over T 34. Height of doll: 34.3cm (13½in). *Dorothy Annunziato Collection.*

Height Markings in Centimeters and Inches

by DOROTHY S. and EVELYN JANE COLEMAN

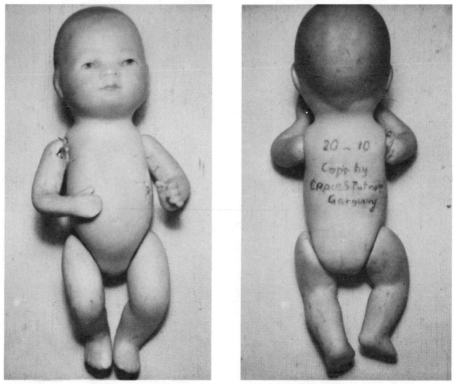

Illustrations 2A and 2B. All-bisque *Bye-Lo* Baby, the "10" on the back of the doll indicates that it is 10.2cm (4in) high. The height is also on the arms at the joints. *Jessica Norman Collection.*

Over 14 years ago when we wrote *The Collector's Encyclopedia of Dolls*, we stated in the Simon & Halbig entry (p. 572): "Most Simon & Halbig heads carry a size number as well as a mold number. Those made for Kämmer & Reinhardt seem to represent the height of the doll in centimeters." As we all know, Simon & Halbig made the bisque heads for Kämmer & Reinhardt. Unfortunately, judging by the many queries that we receive, this bit of information about the centimeter heights has become lost in the vastness of the Encyclopedia and its importance overlooked. Numerous people have reported a large K ★ R with a dolly face marked "100" that is totally different from the usual K ★ R "Baby" mold number 100. Of course, the 100 on the large

doll shows that it is 100cm (39½in) tall and has nothing to do with the mold number 100.

The recognition of the number on the K ★ R doll's head as being its

height in centimeters is extremely important, if the doll is on a ball-jointed composition body or if the head represents a baby and it is on a bent-limb body. If the number does not roughly agree with the centimeter height, one can be suspicious that the body is not original or that it is even a reproduction. When the head is on a bent-limb baby body or a toddler type body, the height is sometimes less than the incised centimeter number. When toddler bodies became popular, K ★ R recognized this problem by using a double number, especially on the celluloid dolls; for example, 43/46 indicated that on a bent-limb baby body the height would be 43.2cm (17in) but probably on a straight leg body it would be 46.0cm (18-1/8in). Dolls with kid bodies can also show variation from the height marked on the head.

Kämmer & Reinhardt used the centimeter heights on their bisque, celluloid and rubber heads. Moreover they were not the only company who put the height in centimeters on their dolls. This seems to have been a feature used especially by celluloid factories and porcelain factories in the

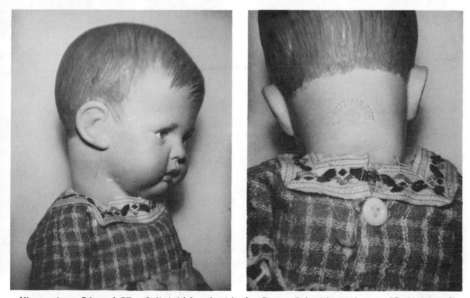

Illustrations 3A and 3B. Celluloid head with the Bruno Schmidt mark over 28. Height of doll: 28.2cm (11-1/8in). *Edith Meggers Collection.*

From the June/July 1982 Doll Reader®

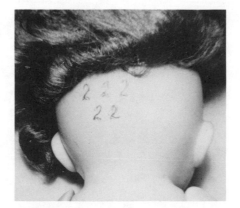

Illustrations 4A and 4B. All-bisque *Our Fairy* is marked:

222
22

signifying that it is 22.3cm (8¾in) tall. *Dorothy Annunziato Collection.*

Ohrdruf area of Germany. When both head and body were made by one company, as for example all-bisque or all-celluloid dolls, or when the head and body were made by two companies under a single control, such as K ★ R and Simon & Halbig, we are apt to find the height in centimeters on the doll. Other companies that put centimeter heights on some of their dolls included Kestner, which occasionally used a double number like K ★ R, Catterfelder Puppenfabrik, Adolf Hülss, Bruno Schmidt, who also made celluloid dolls and Franz Schmidt. Those who made and/or produced celluloid heads with the centimeter size designated included Rheinische Gummi und Celluloid Fabrik, which also occasionally used the double number, Buschow & Beck and the French Société Industrielle de Celluloid. Why Kestner sometimes used a size code and sometimes the height in centimeters is one of the many unsolved mysteries.

Unfortunately American collectors are not used to recognizing centimeter measurements, but they should learn to identify the height of the doll when it is actually marked on the head. These centimeter heights are usually near the bottom of a socket-type head and often hidden by the top of the body. Collectors have become very much interested in the mold numbers and their significance, but so far have nearly always ignored these centimeter height marks. All of the numbers and letters on our dolls would provide us with information if we only knew what they meant. Please look on your dolls and see if you can find more companies that

marked the centimeter height on their dolls. Thus far it seems that these marks were used chiefly in Germany after about 1900, but we need more evidence to be certain of this.

If the height of your doll is not precisely the same as the marked centimeter, do not be concerned. Some small variation must be expected but where there are several centimeters difference on a small or medium-sized doll that cannot be explained by the body type, you should seek to know the cause of this variation. Large dolls may have a proportionately larger variation without indicating a problem.

Sometimes it is difficult to decipher the marks on our dolls. Numbers can be confusing when partially obliterated in the making. The German 7 is not familiar to everyone. Occasionally an extraneous scratch mark appears. But since the actual height can be easily determined, we have a built-in clue as to what we are looking for in these height marks. Some of the dolls on which we have found centimeter height marks are all-bisque *Bye-Lo* babies, *Bonnie Babe,* K & K dolls, *Our Fairy* and *Wide Awake.* The *Wide Awake* height is on the bottom of its feet. Emil Pfeiffer put the height in centimeters on his composition bodies. The *Shirley Temple* doll often has its height in inches marked on the back of its body. A celluloid shoulder head with molded hair, marked on the back of the shoulders "Marks Bros. Co.//Boston Mass// U.S.A. 6." measures exactly 6in (15.2cm) in height.

The all-bisque *Bye-Lo* babies have the height in centimeters on their limbs at the joints as well as on the back of the doll. Rheinische Gummi und Celluloid Fabrik often put the centimeter height on each of

the parts of its all-celluloid dolls, that is on the head, torso, arms and legs. On some Kestner all-bisque dolls the mold number has been found on the limbs at the joints as well as on the head. When the various parts of a doll carry identical numbers, it almost guarantees complete originality.

Not all dolls have these numbers marked but we should know when and where to look for them. If you find that the numbers on the various parts of your doll do not agree, there can be several reasons for it. The person who originally assembled the doll could have made a mistake. There is always the possibility of human error, especially when we realize the tremendous number of dolls that workers assembled in a day and the fact that mere children often did this work. The part could have been replaced long ago or only yesterday. This can sometimes be determined by a knowledge of the history of the doll. If it is known to have come down to you directly from the original owner, the replacement was probably made years ago.

Our advice is to get a centimeter measure and check the height marks on your dolls. A little investigative work may reward you with some valuable information. The placement and method of making these height marks may even help to identify when and by whom your doll was actually made.

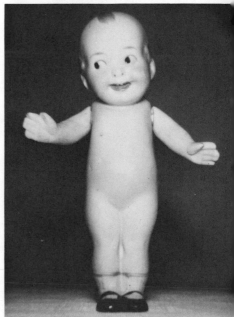

Illustration 5. All-bisque *Wide Awake* with the number "12" on the bottom of its feet. Height: 12.2cm (4¾in).

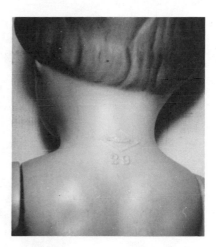

Illustrations 6A and 6B. An all-celluloid doll marked on the back of its neck with a turtle in a diamond over 29 (For Rheinische Gummi und Celluloid Fabrik). It has its arms marked "29" and the left leg is marked "29L" while the right leg is marked "29R." All marks are raised. Height: 29.2cm (11½in).

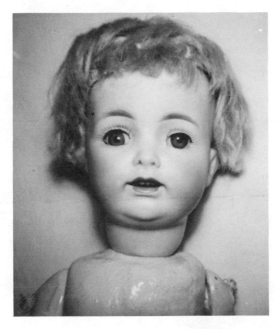
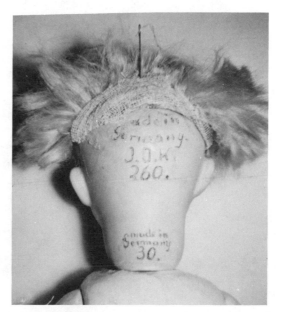

Illustrations 7A and 7B. Kestner (J.D.K.) bisque-head mold 260 has "30" denoting a 30.5cm (12in) height. The head is on a replaced body. *Alberta Darby Collection.*

The Collector's Mini-Digest on Kestner Dolls,

Part I
by ROBERT & KARIN MacDOWELL
Photographs by the Authors

During the period circa 1860 to 1925, the German firm J. D. Kestner, Jr., produced an extremely fine and diversified line of dolls featuring bisque heads and bodies of composition or kid.

This series of photo-essays provides an accurate presentation of construction details including, where possible, un-retouched photographs of the actual maker's marks. The format follows that used in our full-length book, *The Collector's Digest on German Character Dolls*. Installments appeared in *Doll Reader* April/May 1982 through December 1982/January 1983.

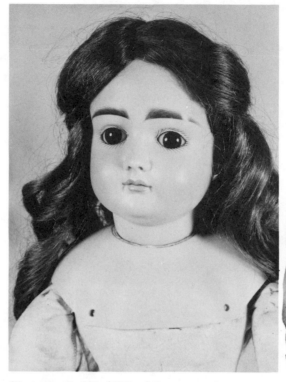

Illustration 2. 19in (48.3cm) Kestner.
Head incised: XII
Bisque shoulder head with swivel neck (kid lined) replaced wig; brown sleep eyes, feathered eyebrows; closed mouth; kid body with lower arms and legs of composition (a very unusual body).

Illustration 4. 19in (48.3cm) Kestner XII shown with combination kid and composition body.

Illustration 1. 19in (48.3cm) Kestner XII shown in her original dress of blue organdy with ecru lace; imitation leather shoes in blue and lace stockings.

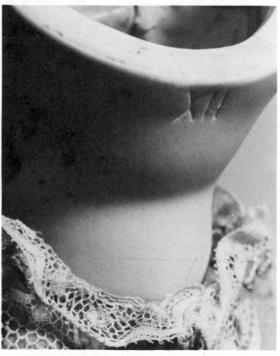

Illustration 3. 19in (48.3cm) Kestner XII mark.

From the April/May 1982 Doll Reader.

Part II

Illustration 1. 13in (33.0cm) Kestner. Head incised:

> 4
> A made in Germany 4

Bisque shoulder head, original plaster pate with mohair wig; blue sleep eyes, feathered eyebrows; open mouth with upper molded teeth; kid body with lower bisque arms. *Anita Rae Collection.*

Illustration 2. 13in (33.0cm) Kestner 4 shoulder head mark. Note plaster pate. *Anita Rae Collection.*

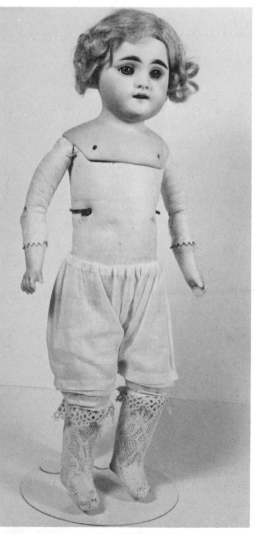

Illustration 3. 13in (33.0cm) Kestner 4 shoulder head dressed in blue organdy with white lace and matching bonnet. *Anita Rae Collection.*

Illustration 4. 13in (33.0cm) Kestner 4 shown undressed. *Anita Rae Collection.*

Part III

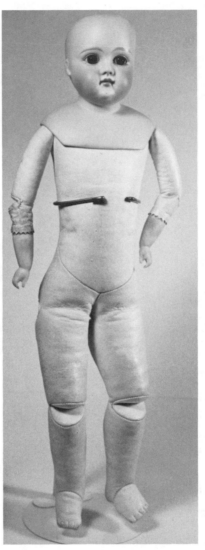

Illustration 1. 18in (45.7cm) Kestner. Head incised: 7. Bisque shoulder head, original plaster pate with blonde mohair wig; stationary brown eyes, feathered eyebrows; closed mouth, dimple in chin; kid body with lower bisque arms.

ABOVE: **Illustration 3.** 18in (45.7cm) Kestner 7 shown undressed.

LEFT: **Illustration 2.** 18in (45.7cm) Kestner 7 mark.

Illustration 4. 18in (45.7cm) Kestner 7 shown dressed in a white blouse and pink and blue print skirt with pink silk sash, straw hat with matching pink flowers, cotton sox and black leather shoes.

Part IV

Illustration 1. 22in (55.9cm) Kestner. Head incised: made in K Germany 14. Bisque socket head, original plaster pate with light blonde mohair wig; blue sleep eyes, feathered eyebrows; open mouth; composition body with straight wrists. The bisque is very pale and of fine quality.

ABOVE: **Illustration 2.** 22in (55.9cm) Kestner mark.

RIGHT: **Illustration 3.** 22in (55.9cm) Kestner shown undressed. Note solid wrists.

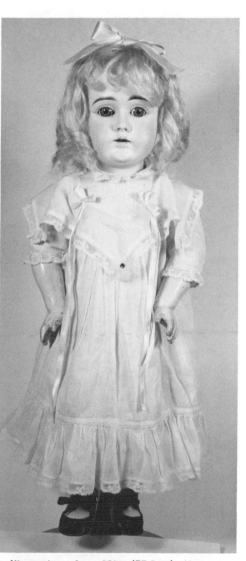

Illustration 4. 22in (55.9cm) Kestner dressed in an antique white lawn dress, trimmed with lace and pink ribbons; old cotton sox and replaced patent leather shoes.

Part V

Illustration 1. 19in (48.3cm) Kestner Head incised: 7¾. 154. Dep. Bisque shoulder head, original plaster pate with blonde mohair wig; blue sleep eyes, feathered eyebrows; open mouth with upper teeth; kid body with composition arms.

Illustration 2. 19in (48.3cm) Kestner 154 mark.

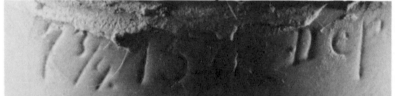

BELOW: Illustration 3. 19in (48.3cm) Kestner 154 shown on kid body with composition arms.

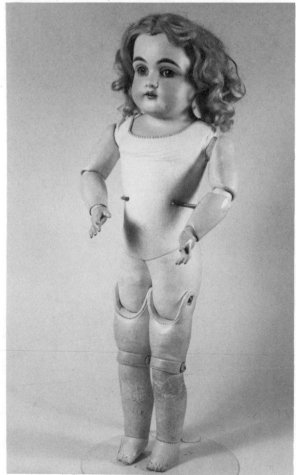

Illustration 4. 19in (48.3cm) Kestner 154 dressed in white cotton dress with yellow flowers, black sox and shoes.

Part VI

Illustration 2. 20in (50.8cm) Kestner 162 mark.

Illustration 1. 20in (50.8cm) Kestner Head incised:

made in
F Germany. 10
162.

Bisque socket head, original plaster pate with blonde mohair wig; blue sleep eyes, feathered eyebrows; open mouth with teeth, dimple in chin; composition lady body with straight wrists. Her body is stamped in red "2½."

RIGHT: Illustration 3. 20in (50.8cm) Kestner 162 shown undressed on her lady body. **Her** body is stamped in red "2½."

During the period circa 1860 to 1925, the German firm J. D. Kestner, Jr., produced an extremely fine and diversified line of dolls featuring bisque heads and bodies of composition or kid.

This series of photo-essays provides an accurate presentation of construction details including, where possible, un-retouched photographs of the actual maker's marks. The format follows that used in our full-length book, *The Collector's Digest on German Character Dolls*, recently released by Hobby House Press, Inc.

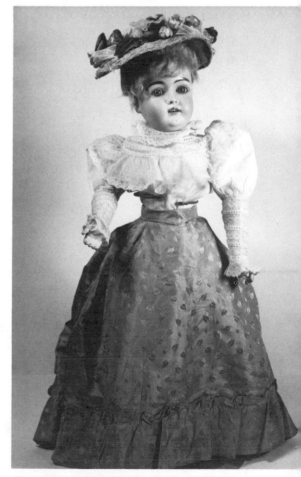

Illustration 4. 20in (50.8cm) Kestner 162. She wears a lawn and lace blouse, a pale green silk skirt with matching green leather high button shoes and a straw hat with flowers.

((Armand Marseille))

by JÜRGEN & MARIANNE CIESLIK

Illustration 1. Armand Marseille, founder of the porcelain manufactory in 1885. Born: May 19, 1856, St. Petersburg, Russia. Died: April 23, 1925, Köppelsdorf, Germany.

Illustration 2. Hermann Marseille, son of successor to Armand Marseille. Born: August 25, 1885. Died: October 4, 1971, Lichtenfels near Coburg, Germany.

Armand Marseille - - a magic name and concept to doll collectors. Millions of bisque doll heads bear his name or his initials "A. M.," yet, until recently, little was known about the factory owner, manufacturer and the private gentleman. After much research it is finally possible to cast some light on the previous obscurity of his life. Conversations with people who had known him and correspondence with his daughter-in-law, who is still alive today, yielded a new and fuller picture.

Armand Marseille was born May 19, 1856, in St. Petersburg, Russia. His father was a well-known architect of Huguenot extraction. As a young man he traveled around Europe visiting each country in turn, since he was fortunate to have enough money to live his own pace. He was originally drawn to Coburg, and later to Sonneberg, by the growth of the toy industry and its worldwide connections.

In 1884 he bought a toy factory, M. Lambert, and a year later, in 1885, a porcelain manufactory, Liebermann & Wegescher, producing porcelain jugs and pipe heads. The young factory owner had useful commercial experience but had not had any dealings with the toy or porcelain industry. He gathered reliable skilled toy workers together, enlarged the numbers of the existing porcelain workers, increased business through new customers and began to experiment with the production of bisque doll heads which had come into fashion.

In 1890 Armand Marseille put his first bisque heads into production and he had such success that he had to reorganize his whole works. In three years the firm was employing 550 workers to turn out doll heads and bathing dolls full-time. One of the first registered (dep=deponiert) heads he made in 1892 was for Cuno & Otto Dressel, Sonneberg, marked "C.O.D. 93 Dep," in sizes from 0 to 10.

Marseille benefited from his good knowledge of languages and from business contacts which he had made personally and kept up. He refused to resort to advertising. In a few years he had become a giant in the business. He was a father figure to everyone he employed with his strict principles. He turned down the title of Kommerzienrat, councillor of commerce, well demanded in this time and bestowed by the Duc of Sax-Meiningen, with the words: "I am Armand Marseille - not a Kommerzienrat."

In 1905 he expanded his production range with electric porcelain in a newly built factory in Neuhaus not far away from Köppelsdorf. In 1910

Illustration 3. Close-up of Armand Marseille's mansion from the 25th Jubille document.

Illustration 5. Close-up of Armand Marseille in his driving outfit from the 25th Jubilee document.

LEFT: Illustration 4. A document correcting a date in the history of dolls: 1885 to 1910, 25th jubilee of the factory of Armand Marseille given to the founder from the staff ". . . as a sign of reverence and gratitude and the deep wish that the prosperity of the manufactory will go on and give employment for many busy hands." At the top is Armand Marseille and under his picture is his mansion. At the bottom left is the manufactory of doll heads, while on the right is the electric porcelain manufactory Neuhaus.

he celebrated the 25th Jubilee of his business. In memory of this important day the staff presented him with an exciting document, designed by Professor Möller, director of the Industry School in Sonneberg. Marseille was an enthusiastic automobile fan and was one of the first owners in Sonneberg. The document shows him in his special outfit. His mansion was well-known and is still to be seen. The small building shown is the factory which produced doll heads in Köppelsdorf and the larger one is the electric porcelain factory in Neuhaus.

After a stroke Armand Marseille withdrew from active business life. His son, Hermann, took over as head of the enterprise. Before retiring, Armand Marseille crowned his life's work by achieving a merger with the procelain factory of Ernst Heubach which had similarly been established since 1886 in Köppelsdorf. From 1919 the company was known as United Köppelsdorfer Porcelain-Factory, formerly Armand Marseille and Ernst Heubach. The union had familial effects: his daughter, Beatrix, married Ernst Heubach's son. This merger was ill-fated and in 1928 it was dissolved. (Directories list the name

Illustration 6. Close-up of the doll head factory from the 25th Jubilee document.

Illustration 7. Close-up of the electric porcelain factory from the 25th Jubilie document.

"United Köppelsdorfer Porcelain-Factories" until 1949.) The factory expanded from a small cottage in 1885, to a great building with eight kilns in 1927. Armand Marseille did not survive these ups and downs of his company as he died on April 23, 1925, from a heart attack.

The factory produced special composition doll heads under the direction of Hermann Marseille until 1948. We can still find Armand Marseille's mansion and just opposite, the building of the porcelain manufactory. Often, when visiting Thüringia, we find fresh flowers on his tombstone. Armand Marseille is not forgotten.

Illustration 8. Tombstone of Armand Marseille at Köppelsdorf cemetery.

Googlies
by **Magda Byfield**

The term "Googley-Eyed" doll immediately conjures up for today's collector the pert, plump children made by most early 20th century French and German doll makers. The origin of their title is probably taken from the German: "Guck Augen," meaning eyes ogling to one side. The Googley doll is ALL EYES. While often somewhat caricatured in concept, the majority were created with a true understanding of the faces of the very young.

These roguish children made their triumphant entry on the stage of doll making along with the naturalistically observed "character dolls" with their truthful, often irregular features, which first entered the market with deferential stealth in the first decade of the 20th century. To the surprise of the toy trade their popularity was immediate and overwhelming. It seems likely that the appeal of character dolls was a revolt after a long run of idealized decorative child dolls and stylish lady dolls with ivory profiles. How tame, if lovely, the traditional detached types must have seemed to the changing vision of childhood that prevailed at this time. Dolls have always to some extent recorded successive developments in nursery standards, and in the "characters" we see reflected at acceptance of youthful exuberance for its own sake. Gone was the abstract purity of the inscrutable doll-faced-doll with its controlled stillness so reflective of acceptable 19th century nursery behavior. Toy shops found themselves selling character dolls as fast as manufacturers could supply them. Their breathless vitality and intelligent faces caught the hearts and imagination of the doll-buying public, though clearly some were not good sellers — as evinced by the scarcity of many known models. By this yardstick we can measure the emotive appeal of the Googley of which countless types in a large variety of size and quality remain.

Googlies capture the fleeting expression of a moment; nature has been simplified and rearranged into snub-nosed, rounded faces with alert eyes and laughing dimples. The dolls display a joyous urgency of life. They are small comedians of a rollicking nursery, reflecting the mood and spirit of their time. Their wide eyes have a humorous sparkle and their faces a certain rounded vulgarity. They are a far cry from the sensitive and fragile child dolls that had captured the markets of previous decades.

Googlies are presented as babies, chubby toddlers and children. They were manufactured from about 1912 right up to 1939. Today's collectors find them as irresistible as did the public for whom they were originally made. Their charming spontaneity of expression makes their appeal self-explanatory. Less pretty and less refined than many of their "character" contemporaries, their youthful exuberance enlarged the vision of childhood, breaking through the barriers which more reticent eras of doll making had so tenaciously perpetuated.

Illustration 1. Max.

Illustration 2. Moritz.

A Simon & Halbig Portfolio

by ROBERT & KARIN MacDOWELL

Photographs by the authors

The German firm of Simon & Halbig made porcelain objects and doll heads from circa 1870 to 1925. May we present some examples of this company's outstanding work.

Illustration 1. 11in (27.9cm) Simon & Halbig. Head marked:
S & H 1079
DEP
2½
Germany
Bisque socket head, replaced wig; very large stationary brown eyes, feathered eyebrows; open mouth with upper molded teeth; pierced ears. She comes on a fully-jointed French body. French firms very often used Simon & Halbig heads and joined them to French-made bodies. The bisque is very pale and smooth.

ABOVE: Illustration 2. 11in (27.9cm) Simon & Halbig. Head marked:
S & H
939
Bisque shoulder head with swivel neck, original blonde human hair wig; beautiful stationary eyes, feathered eyebrows; closed mouth; pierced ears. She also has a dimple in the chin like so many of the Simon & Halbig dolls. She has a kid body with bisque arms.

LEFT: Illustration 3. 15in (38.1cm) Simon & Halbig. Head marked:
S & H
Heinrich
Handwerck
This little sweet-faced doll has a bisque socket head, original sparse wig; blue sleep eyes, feathered eyebrows; open mouth with teeth; and pierced ears. She is on a fully-jointed composition body.

From the August/September 1981 Doll Reader.®

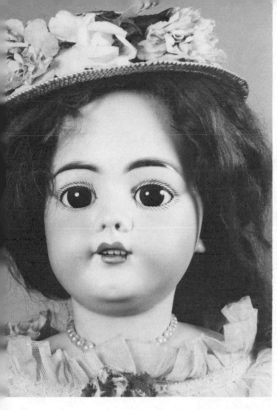

Illustration 4A. 28½in (72.4cm) Simon & Halbig. Head marked:

S & H 1079
13
DEP

The front of the shoulder plate is marked:

S H 1041 13

A much harder to find combination. The bisque head and the shoulder plate are completely original to each other despite the different mold numbers. The head swivels in the kid-lined shoulder plate socket. She has a very alert look with her brown sleep eyes, feathered eyebrows and open mouth with upper molded teeth. The ears are pierced. She comes on a kid body with bisque arms.

Illustration 4B. 28½in (72.4cm) Simon & Halbig 1079 shown dressed in an old beige silk dress with green sprigs of flowers. A straw hat with flowers completes the costume.

Illustration 5. 14in (35.6cm) Simon & Halbig. Head marked:

S & H 1249 — 4
DEP
Germany

Bisque shoulder head with swivel neck, human hair wig; stationary brown eyes, feathered eyebrows; open mouth with upper teeth; pierced ears. This one is a bit different from most dolls in that she has a kid body with composition arms. She wears a pale silk dress trimmed with lace, a matching bonnet, silk stockings and leather shoes.

Illustration 6. 11in (27.9cm) Simon & Halbig. Head marked:

S & H 1269
Dep
2
Germany

Bisque socket head, replaced wig; brown sleep eyes, feathered eyebrows; open mouth; pierced ears. She comes on a jointed composition body and wears her original clothes.

Illustration 7. 7in (17.8cm) Simon & Halbig. Head marked:
1079
Halbig
S & H
Germany
4/0
Bisque socket head, original blonde mohair wig in two braids; blue sleep eyes, single stroke eyebrows; open mouth with upper teeth; ears are not pierced on this little one. The head is attached to a five-piece composition body with painted sox and shoes. She is dressed in a white lawn dress with lots of tucks and lace and a matching bonnet. She is the smallest Simon & Halbig 1079 the authors have seen.

Illustration 8. 10in (25.4cm) Simon & Halbig. Head marked:
S H
950
7
Bisque shoulder head, original blonde curly wig; stationary brown eyes, feathered eyebrows; closed mouth; pierced ears. He is on a cloth body with bisque arms. He wears his original clothes which consist of a red wool vest with brass buttons, cotton collar and black silk tie; brown velvet pants and a light brown felt coat with brass buttons. A black felt hat, black cotton sox and imitation leather shoes complement the outfit.

LEFT: **Illustration 9.** 11½in (29.2cm) Simon & Halbig. Head marked:

S & H
1079
DEP
Germany

Bisque socket head, original wig; huge blue sleep eyes with feathered eyebrows, lower painted eye lashes only; open mouth with upper molded teeth, dimple in chin; pierced ears. She has a composition body with straight wrists. She looks a bit sad and is dressed in her original clothes: a fine lawn dress with lace, silk stockings and imitation leather shoes. The bonnet may have been added.

RIGHT: **Illustration 10.** 10in (25.4cm) Simon & Halbig. Shoulder plate marked:

S & H 1160—2/o

A lovely lady doll with a bisque shoulder head; stationary brown eyes, single stroke eyebrows; closed mouth; and pierced ears. She comes on a cloth body with parian legs, which have blue painted garters and black boots, and bisque arms. She wears an old straw hat with flowers, a dark green silk overskirt over lace underskirt. The dress is trimmed with silk embroidery and lace.

112

One Fabulous Face

by Magdalena Byfield

Illustration 1. Simon & Halbig, mold number 1469, shown "as found" in clothes wrapped in tissue paper in an old shoe box.

We have all come across outstandingly beautiful dolls by known doll makers with a rare mold number. The immediate question that such a doll brings into the collector's mind is why was this exquisite specimen not *mass-produced*? Of all the many puzzles of doll researching, this surely must be one of the most baffling. Allowing that tastes have changed, many of these fabulous-faced rare

dolls have, nonetheless, what must be dispassionately regarded as classical looks that would have been appealing almost throughout Western history. In truth, we shall probably never know why established firms produced limited editions of these dolls of striking loveliness. We can only make vague guesses such as production cessation due to outside circumstances or for whatever reasons, it was the firm's intention at the outset to produce limited numbers.

Bisque-headed dolls representing young ladies are, in any case, less frequently found than the jointed child doll and bent-limb baby doll. Today there is a reversal of this trend and the teen-age doll is the most profusely made type. Children's tastes, it seems, have changed somewhat in the last 50 years. In the first 30 years of this century the adult doll was less popular and we base this conclusion on the numbers remaining relative to other types.

The fabulous-faced lady doll I have selected to illustrate this article is by Simon & Halbig and is their mold number 1469, an undeniably svelte creature by any standards. Although this doll should be classified as a "character" for her sheer individuality, the face is so doll-like in its perfection that the type falls somewhere halfway between the two. If the live girl from whom this face was modeled was as intensely beautiful as the resultant doll, then hers was indeed a face to make the gods envious. The head is perfect from every angle and in complete balance with the lissome adult-type body which has small dainty hands and tapering elegant feet.

Clearly this exquisite creature has received the reverence quite rightly due to so lovely a doll, for her condition is absolutely mint. Her golden brown mohair wig is perfectly intact as is her lace-trimmed muslin underwear, black stockings and high heeled shoes with ribbon bows. Her dress, while being contemporary, is unlikely to be original as the hemline is above that of the stockings. But she is "dressed as found" when she came to light in 1981 wrapped in tissue in an old shoe box. Her original rubber stringing is now so loose that the doll cannot be supported on a stand and has been photographed supine. She

Illustration 3. Close-up of the face of the Simon & Halbig, mold number 1469.

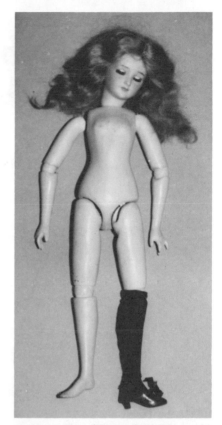

Illustration 2. Simon & Halbig, mold number 1469, shown undressed.

has blue sleep eyes with waxed lids and hair eyelashes, a closed mouth and pierced ears. The socket head is of the finest quality bisque as so often found on Simon & Halbig dolls. The crown is open with a cardboard pate. On the neck is incised "1469//Simon & Halbig//2." The composition body is articulated at the shoulders and hips and with ball joints at the elbows and knees.

What could possibly account for the comparative rarity of such an alluring doll is indeed hard to comprehend. If there existed a "Miss (Doll) World" contest, I venture to suggest this this model would very likely win the crown!

Illustration 4. Side view of the Simon & Halbig, mold number 1469.

From the October 1982 Doll Reader.®

Collecting German Character Dolls

ROBERT & KARIN MacDOWELL

Photographs by the Authors

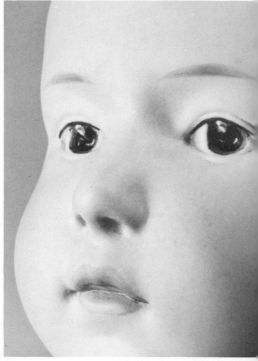

Illustration 46.

Considering conditions which influence today's doll collectors, the antique German Character Doll (circa 1909 to 1925+) continues to provide interesting material for study, pleasure and sensible investment.

Factors to consider are:

1. Availability - there are sufficient numbers in the marketplace to provide material for most serious collectors.
2. Prices - these dolls, generally, have not reached the price levels which place them out of reach of the average collector. A good antique example can be had for the price of an expensive reproduction or 'original,' making a much wiser investment.
3. Quality - workmanship and detail are usually much higher than can be easily reproduced.

Careful study of genuine dolls is most important; details such as body types and construction, size ratios, maker's marks and detailing of facial features, all contribute to an overall appreciation of this type of doll.

One major problem in studying any doll is that of having important identifying features covered or obscured by clothing, wigs and other accessories.

We have had unusual opportunities to closely examine many German Character Dolls in the course of building the museum collection, and also in executing restoration work for our many clients. Having the material available, we were able to photographically document a number of really fine examples in unusual detail. In every case possible, the dolls were photographed to show:

1. Close-up of face.
2. Close-up of maker's mark(s).
3. Complete doll, undressed.
4. Complete doll, costumed.
5. Special shots of unusual details.
6. Color transparencies, where appropriate.

A good example of the depth of photographic study possible is the following sequence taken from our book, *The Collector's Digest on German Character Dolls,* published by Hobby House Press, Inc. The photographs are from Illustrations 46 through 52.

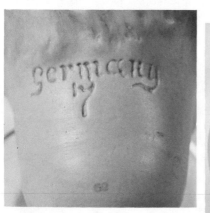

Illustration 47.

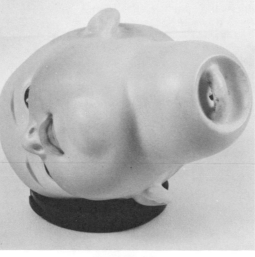

Illustration 51.

Illustration 48.

The Gebrüder Heubach analyzed would be most difficult to reproduce; a put-together of parts from different dolls should also be easy to spot. Details worthy of special mention are:

ILLUSTRATION	DETAIL
46	Overall excellent workmanship; balance.
47	Crisp, sharply defined incised maker's mark (detail usually lost in molds made for reproduction).
48	Unusual detail of intaglio eyes. Iris is concave; the white highlight stands out from the top of the iris - most likely added as a separate manufacturing procedure with white slip or clay.
49	Style, size and excellent fit of body parts.
50	Better than average modeling of hand features.
51	Very unusual method of attaching head to body.
52	The overall costumed doll as presently displayed in the museum.

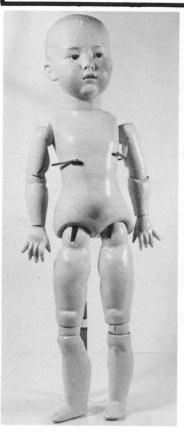

Illustration 49.

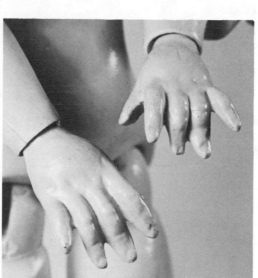

Illustration 50.

Illustration 52.

Max and Maurice

PATRICIA N. SCHOONMAKER

Illustration 1. (Far Left) Marked #123//Simon Halbig//K star R, doll has flirting eyes of brown, painted lashes only and dark painted brows. Original identity is "Max" of the book *Max and Maurice*. *Pat Schoonmaker Collection.*

Illustration 2. (Left) So-called "Funny Face Girl" shown on the cover of *Research on Kämmer and Reinhardt Dolls* by Pat Schoonmaker. Original identity is that of "Maurice," the storybook character. *Pat Schoonmaker Collection.*

Editor's Note: The spelling of the names "Maurice" and "Moritz" are used interchangeably to refer to the same character.

We have been waiting for several years for "proof-positive" that the highly desired and sought-after Kammer and Reinhardt dolls, model #123 and #124 were indeed "Max" and "Maurice." Finally an original catalog has come to Dorothy Coleman, our foremost researcher, depicting these famous German characters.

Drawn by Wilhelm Busch, the humorist, they are classics of children's literature. The book was published in English in 1962, translated by Walter Roome and published by Braun and Schneider (Munich). There are seven pranks related, with the boys finally meeting a dreadful end. The story is an object lesson using fear to influence children to be obedient. The original artwork is rather crude; Max is overly fat-faced and Maurice (for contrast) is thinner with a very pointy chin.

Our own examples of these Kämmer and Reinhardt dolls are eons away in contrast from the original artwork. The unknown artist of the bisque ball-jointed pair created expressions of such charm and basic appeal as to brighten the day of anyone viewing them. One can imagine them to be mischievous, but never participating in the cruel tricks of the book characters. We had no background on them when we acquired these models in the late 1950s or early 1960s, but called them "Funny Faces" for lack of a more specific identity. It was fascinating to finally learn that they were derived from the comics, or "funnies" (if in book form). However, in actuality, they are two boys—not a boy and a girl. Our own pair had no original clothes when they came to us, and

were so attractively costumed by my late mother, Hilda Bewley, that they will not be changed. The "Funny Face Girl" has established such an identity for herself, having appeared in hobby shows, art museums and exhibits that she will not revert to the original "Maurice" identity. If put on display in the future, the doll will bear an identifying card with background information. Anyone having original clothes should certainly preserve them and present the dolls with their true identity as *boy* storybook characters.

Max and Maurice artist creator, Wilhelm Busch (1832-1908), is credited with a big part in starting the American "funnies." Artist Rudolf Dirks joined the staff of "The New York Journal" in 1897. Coulton Waugh in "The Comics," published by Macmillan in 1947, comments:

> "It was the very moment for a comic immortal to appear. The 'American Humorist' was in full swing. Rudoph Block, then comic editor, suggested that Dirks create a feature based on 'Max und Moritz.' The 'Katzenjammer Kids' with their demoniac pranks were derived from the earlier German pair."

This funny paper version inspired "Mama Katzenjammer" as well as the "Kids" fashioned as iron toys shown in 1907 as printed-on cloth designs.

There are other Max and Maurice dolls that we did not have available to photograph for this article, including

Illustration 3. English edition of the book *Max and Maurice* by Wilhelm Busch, translated in 1962 by Walter Roome. Size is 5-1/2 x 8-1/4in. (14 x 20.7cm). In color by Braun and Schneider, Munich, Germany.

the Schoenhut set. There are a pair of all-bisque with molded clothes as well as a miniature bisque with jointed arms and legs. Some have been dressed as girls.

The boy pair are very popular in Germany to this day. We own a pair of Steiff miniatures, 4in. (10.2cm) tall Moritz and 3-5/8in. (9.4cm) tall Max. Here is a contradiction to the button-in-ear rule! With no ears, the button was carefully attached around the ankle, denoting: "Made in Germany, original Steiff." The heads are either rubber or bendable plastic as are the arms and legs. The bottom of the black shoes are marked IN//D//AUSL-Pat. Moritz has reddish-blonde hair and dark eyes and a green felt jacket with blue and white cotton trousers. His name tag has an outer red edge with the words: Steiff//Original Marke and the symbol of a teddy bear on the third line. Max is most proud of his original label as well. His hair is black with pronounced comb marks. His all-felt clothing consists of a red shirt, blue coat with thread buttons, tan trousers and a bit of sock above the shoe. His markings are the same.

Another pair of much cheaper quality but still interesting, are Moritz, 5-1/2in. (14cm) tall, and Max, 5in. (12.7cm) tall, due to the former doll's ascending forelock of hair. The head is of a type that seems more like celluloid but is most likely plastic. These are twistables or "flexies" on fine wire. We could find no identification as to maker. Of better quality is a Max doll, 5-1/2in. (14cm) tall, by Schleich Flexies. Made in Western Germany, it was purchased a few years ago for $1.89. The doll was encased in a plastic bag with the slogan, "Twistable Figures—Hours of Fun" printed on cardboard at top. Also, his right foot reads: "Made in West Germany// IN & AUSL-PAT." The left foot is marked: "Schleich//Biegeguren" with a symbol of the bendable figure in an oval on the third line. He has a painted-on red suit with yellow bow on chest, black hair and shoes and very blue eyes. His date is unknown, but he is a toy of much amusement for a child.

The smallest miniature of all is Maurice or Moritz of hand-carved wood. He is 2-1/4in. (5.7cm) tall and

most likely the oldest of all. His hair is brown; his eyes are black. His painted-on clothing consists of a blue tie, a green coat over white shirt, yellow trousers and brown shoes.

Illustration 6. Miniature Moritz of hand-carved wood, probably the oldest example in this article. Height is 2-1/4in. (5.7cm) tall. Tiny doll is propped against a thimble. Doll is strung on wires.

Other toys in our collection are a hand puppet of Maurice with a blue and white garment, green felt scarf and tan felt hands or mitts. The head is firm vinyl with orange-red hair and lips. The eyes are very black with one highlight.

Illustration 4. (Left) Fully-marked Steiff miniatures. Moritz is 4in. (10.2cm) tall and Max is 3-5/8in. (9.2cm) tall.

Illustration 5. Matched pair, 5-1/2in. (14cm) and 5in. (12.7cm) tall; probably a take-off on the Steiff pair. The twistables are on fine wire, with noses painted red like clown. Heads are of a type of plastic which seems more like celluloid but actually isn't. Doll on right of soft vinyl, 5-1/2in. (14cm) tall.

Illustration 7. Hand puppet 11in. (27.9cm) tall with vinyl head; wooden pantin 18in. (45.7cm) tall with carrot red hair, brown eyes and green coat. Doll on right is Maurice "Roly-Poly" toy with weighted bottom, height 7in. (17.8cm) and marked on bottom: "Made in Western Germany."

One of the most interestingly marked of these characters is an 18in. (20.3 cm) wooden pantin (middle, *Illustration 7*) who kicks his arms and legs up and down when the string is activated. On his unpainted back is the symbol of a toy ark and MERTENS KUNST (TOY)//HH//Moritz//Morris//Maurice (three translations of the storybook character's name)//Made in Western Germany//Copyright 1967 by Alfred Mertens, Pfullingen. If only all makers took as much pride in marking toys and dolls. Another form of Maurice is a Roly-Poly toy with a weighted bottom marked "Made in Western Germany" (right, *Illustration 7*). Another doll that did not get photographed before some children broke into the dollhouse of the late Sara Barrett's to play and wandered off with him, depicted Max in rubber holding a chicken by the neck behind his back. This was an earlier example and we have never seen another.

A wooden wall placque 6in (15.2cm) tall and 4in (10.2cm) wide was brought to me by a dealer from a shop in Mexico, where it had hung for years. It has a gold label, darkened with age, bearing a sketch of the bust of a man, and the word "ACHATIT" beneath, as well as "Handwork, Made in Germany," is legible. The figures are plaster sanded smooth and decorated. Maurice is blonde; Max is brunette.

Still another item is a wall hanging for a child's room which appears to be

from the 1920s. It is possibly constructed from a child's handkerchief, for the picture is bordered by a glossy green rayon ribbon with narrow red and gold stripes, and silk cord for hanging. This is the last scene in the first prank with Max and Maurice added in looking over the wall. They gloat as the poor widow brings in her dead chickens they have killed.

Illustration 9. Cloth wall hanging bordered in rayon silk ribbon. It depicts the last scene of the first prank in the book *Max and Maurice*, only the pictures of Max and Maurice have been added in. The lower left corner is a child's decorative pin of ivory-like material. Here Maurice is blonde with orange top and green trousers, and Max, a brunette, has blue jacket with red lapels and brown trousers. There is no safety catch on the pin's back.

Illustration 10. German "Scrap" of Max and Moritz. Embossed heads marked "L & B., 30649, Printed in Germany." Moritz is blonde with blue eyes and has a very long upper lip and upturned nose. Max is broad-faced and has brown hair in this artwork.

Illustration 8 (Left) Wooden wall placque 6in. (15.2cm) tall with painted plaster half-heads of Max and Maurice. Maurice has yellow hair; Max has black hair. On the back of the placque is a gold label which is only partially readable. The bust of a man is shown with "ACHATIT" beneath it, as well as "Handwork" and "Made in Germany."

Illustration 11. (Right) Antique postcard with divided back. Green background with greeting "with Best Love." Max has black hair flying in space and wears beige tunic over knickers. Moritz is blonde with exaggerated hair style and light jacket, green velvet vest and breeches with brown leggings. Both have dark eyes. Embossed.

German Character Children

by Jan Foulke

The creation of the character dolls -- dolls which were modeled after real children -- was an innovative development of the German doll industry, a refreshing and new doll concept after so many years of following in the footsteps of the French doll makers. The character doll movement began in Munich in 1908 with a group of artist-designers who conceived the idea of making dolls which were more real-looking and childlike than the pretty "dolly faces" which represented an idealized rather than a real child. Gebrüder Heubach and Kämmer & Reinhardt were among the first firms to produce these character dolls with bisque heads, but within a very short time other progressive firms had joined in.

Because of their artistic qualities and general appeal, these German character children are very desirable and quite sought-after by doll collectors. For some unexplained reason (perhaps economic, as these new dolls were not an immediate success with the general public) most companies went into rather heavy production of the character babies instead of the children, which causes the latter to be even more rare and desirable today.

No detailed descriptions have been given for these dolls, as the photographs speak for themselves, showing dolls which are superb examples of this period in the German doll industry; truly these character children are its crowning achievement.

Illustration 2. The Kley & Hahn factory also produced this boy with mold number 169; he is on a composition ball-jointed toddler body. *Richard Wright Collection.*

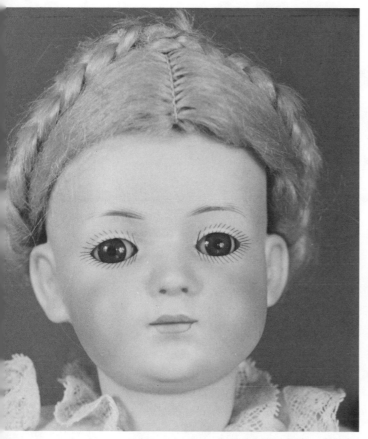

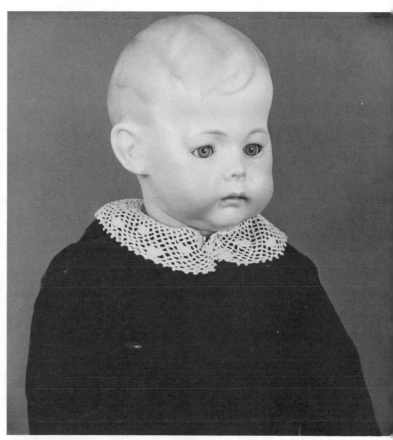

Illustration 1. A product of the Kley & Hahn factory in Ohrdruf, Thüringia, Germany, this 15in (38.1cm) character girl from mold number 546 has glass eyes and her original blonde mohair wig. She is on a composition ball-jointed body. *Jane Alton Collection.*

Illustration 3. This child with blonde molded hair is from the Armand Marseille factory in Köpplesdorf, Thüringia. He is "Fany," mold number 230 and is on a composition ball-jointed toddler body with unjointed wrists. *Richard Wright Collection.*

119

From the August/September 1982 Doll Reader.

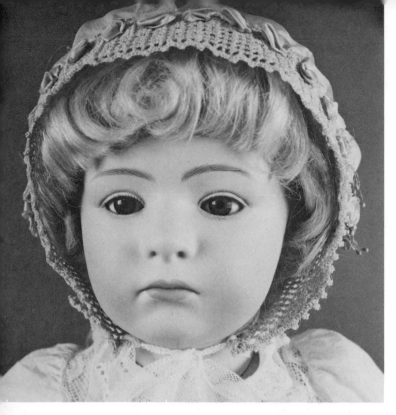

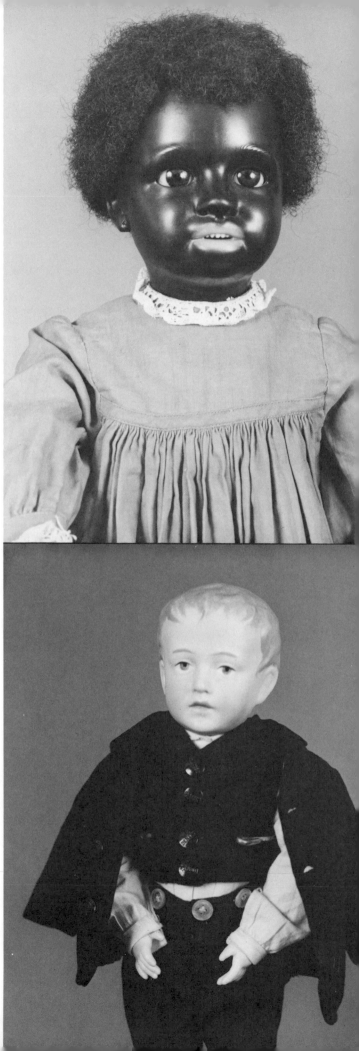

ABOVE: Illustration 4. The Gebrüder Heubach factory in Lichte, Thüringia, made the head of this 27in (68.6cm) pouty girl, mold number 6969. She has beautiful feathered blonde eyebrows and a decidedly down-turned mouth. She is on a composition ball-jointed body. *Richard Wright Collection.*

ABOVE RIGHT: Illustration 5. The Simon & Halbig factory also produced this very black character child with Negroid features, mold number 1358. She is on a black composition ball-jointed body. *Richard Wright Collection.*

BELOW: Illustration 6. A very rare doll from the Armand Marseille factory is this 16½in (41.9cm) girl with gray intaglio eyes and very full lips; she has no mold number. *Richard Wright Collection.*

BELOW RIGHT: Illustration 7. This 19in (48.3cm) boy is another doll from the Simon & Halbig factory; his long face, full lips and sharp nose are distinctive characteristics. His mold number is 150. *Richard Wright Collection.*

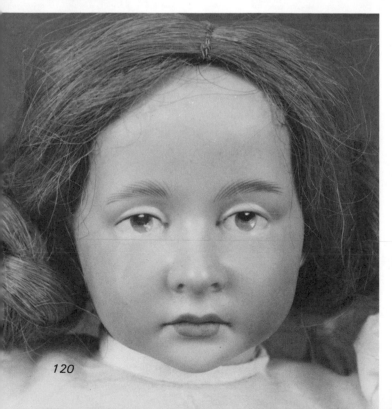

BELOW: 27in (68.6cm) K★R 117 Character Girl. *Jan Foulke Collection. Photograph by Howard Foulke.*

Color Illustration 1. From the factory of J. D. Kestner in Waltershausen and Ohrdruf comes this 16in (40.6cm) girl from mold number 189 with dimples, glass eyes and her original blonde mohair wig with coiled braids. She is on a pink composition ball-jointed body with the red "Germany" stamp used by Kestner and also has a paper label from G. A. Schwarz toy store in Philadelphia, Pennsylvania. *Richard Wright Collection.*

Color Illustration 2. This 19in (48.3cm) boy is another doll from the Simon & Halbig factory; his long face, full lips and sharp nose are distinctive characteristics. His mold number is 150. *Richard Wright Collection.*

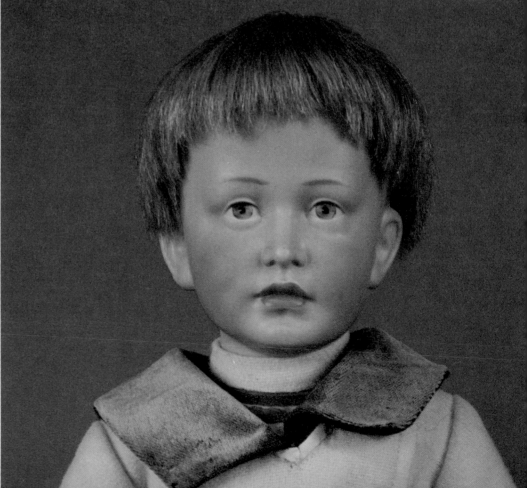

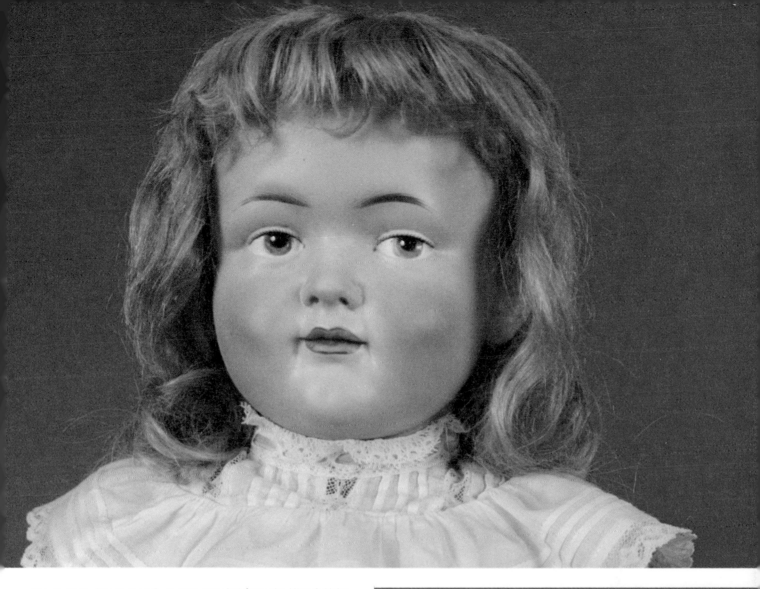

Above: Color Illustration 3. A very rare doll from the Kley & Hahn factory is this 21in (53.3cm) girl with gray intaglio eyes looking to the side; very tiny upper lashes are painted across her eyelid. With incredible detail in the modeling, she is from mold number 549. *Richard Wright Collection.*

Right: Color Illustration 4. Another doll produced by Kämmer & Reinhardt with a head made by Simon & Halbig is this 12in (30.5cm) boy from mold number 107. He is on a composition ball-jointed body and is wearing his original clothes. *Richard Wright Collection.*

The Song of The Lenci

By Beverly Port

The song of the Lenci echoes, lingers and softly wafts down through the many years since the creative mind of Elena Scavini first conceived the beautiful felt doll-children, so sought after by collectors of this era. She designed and created a myriad of styles--faces--color combinations unending.

Do you have a specialty in collecting? Madame Lenci had a felt doll to fit most categories. She made not only the adorable children, but googlies, pouties and other characters. Her lovely fashion ladies are wonderful additions to any collection, as are her portrait and celebrity dolls.

A colorful array of these lovable or unusual dolls is presented here for your enjoyment, and as a possible aid to identification of a "mystery doll" in your collection. Here is hoping it leaves you humming "The Song of The Lenci." All dolls in original clothing. All photographs by author unless otherwise credited.

Illustration 2. 20in (50.8cm) mischievous Lenci girl with rare glass flirty eyes of brown shown on the cover; her eyes move from side to side giving her much expression; black mohair is sewn in strips to her head and at her hairline tiny clumps of mohair are sewn in separately; her coral pink mouth is molded open with a pale pink lower lip, her eyebrows are molded as well as painted; her head, arms and legs are felt, the body is muslin. She has the round silver cardboard label reading: "Lenci//Torino//Made in Italy." On the back, written in pencil is: "Palentari 11." The cloth label reads: "Lenci//Made in Italy." In addition, she has a rectangular cardboard label with the word "Fobello," flanked by pink and green flowers with a green border. Her felt skirt of red and black has a cotton overskirt ornately embroidered in red, blue, yellow and green wool; high black felt boots are also ornately embroidered; wool pom-pons, with the same colors as the embroidery, are on each shoulder and two on each boot; she wears a white cotton blouse, waist, half-slip and pantalets. With her on the cover is a jack-o'-lantern for Halloween and a turkey for Thanksgiving. The turkey is a large candy container marked, "Made in Germany" and is of papier-mache construction with metal feet and glass eyes. His head and the front of his body come off revealing a hollow body for treats.

Illustration 1. 21½in (54.6cm) lovable, hugable Lenci girl of the 500 series, all pink and frilly, as if she was dressed for a special party. She has brown mohair in long curls matching her brown eyes; her head, arms and legs are felt, body is muslin; felt brim on her hat has organdy ruffles and a rose on front, back of hat is gathered organdy with more roses; rows of ruffles with picot edges form the skirt of the high-yoked, rose-trimmed dress with an attached half-slip of many more ruffles; a pink organdy teddy, frilly bloomers and pink felt shoes with quilted soles complete her outfit. She also has a short felt bolero with scalloped band around the edges, but does not like to wear it as it wrinkles her dress.

From the October 1982 Doll Reader.®

124

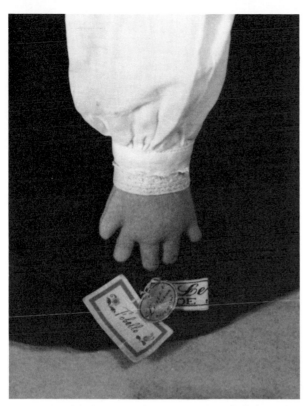

Illustration 2B. Close-up of the three original labels on the rare glass-eyed Lenci on the cover. Note hand detail--all fingers are separate. Label on left reads: "Fobello." Round one in center reads: "Lenci//Torino//Made In Italy," and has writing in pencil on back reading: "Palentari 11." The folded one on the right reads: "Lenci//Made in Italy."

Lenci
MADE in ITALY

Illustration 2C.

Illustration 2D.

Lenci   TURIN
        (ITALY)
DI E. SCAVINI
MADE IN ITALY
PAT. SEPT. 8, 1921 PAT. N. 142433
BRE SGDG.X 87395. BREVETTO 501.178

Illustration 2E.

Illustration 3. 22½in (57.2cm) Lenci boy from the 500 series; circa 1927 to 1928; extremely curly blonde mohair, brown eyes; head, arms and legs are felt, body is muslin; felt outfit of blue, trimmed with darker blue, has matching shoes with quilted soles; also wears a teddy. His name, "Tom," is embroidered in red on his brown button-on apron. Inside its pocket a piece of brown paper reads: "Italian Paper Boy. Notice the hat of Italian newspaper." Perhaps the extra large pocket *was* to hold miniature newspapers -- but -- the paper hat upon his blonde head was *not* a newspaper. It was an old Lenci advertisement! Carefully unfolded and translated it extols the virtues of the Lenci doll. Certainly an unusual "find." It is printed for you in this article.

Illustration 2F. Close-up of embroidered boots of rare glass-eyed Lenci on **Doll Reader** cover. Note pom-pons on boot tops.

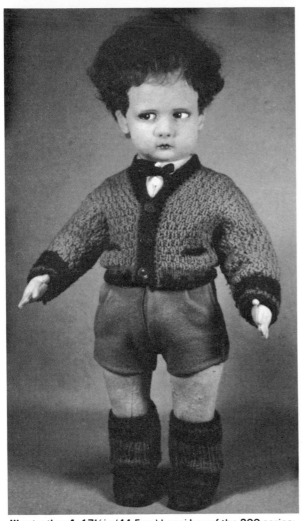

Illustration 4. 17½in (44.5cm) Lenci boy of the 300 series; brown mohair is sewn into the head in small clumps and is wavy with some curls; brown eyes; body of all-felt construction with hollow torso; felt shirt is cream with tiny black tie at collar, short pants are brown, wool knit sweater of green trimmed with light and dark brown has three brown buttons and two tiny pockets; knit socks match his sweater; brown leather shoes with leather ties. The brown soles and heels of the shoes are heavy cardboard with tiny nails around the outer edges.

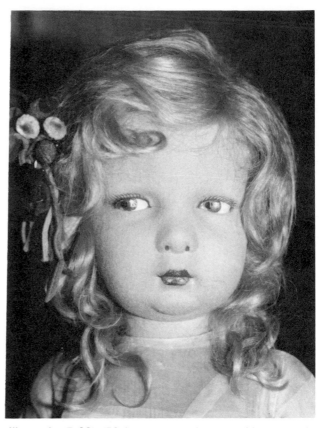

Illustration 5. 23in (58.4cm) Lenci girl from the 109 series; soft blonde mohair is sewn to her head in strips and sewn directly into head in tiny clumps around her hairline; brown eyes have two highlights, as does her lower lip; all-felt body with hollow torso; pale yellow organdy ruffled dress trimmed with green; slip, pantalets and teddy; green felt shoes with quilted soles; marked "Lenci" on bottoms of both feet. Original colorful Lenci box, with "Lenci" name in design.

Inno Della "Lenci"

Di gran pupazzi e bambole
Gli artefici noi siam,
E l'arte nostra amiam:
Cantando lavoriam.

Della gentile industria
La bella novita
Gia celebre Torino
Ovunque fa.

Sotto ogni ciel
Va con ardore
La novella umanita.
Non ha cervel,
Di stoppa ha il core
Ma rifulg di belta.

Pel mondo inter,
Sempre gioconda
In sua varia ilarita,
Reca il piacer,
La baraonda
Che i bambini
Lieti fa.

Malia di fiabe e fascini
Di sogni e realta,
Di grazie e di belta
Donar la Lenci sa.

Pel bene che diffondesi
Dal genial oprar,
Piu bella e dolce a noi
La vita appar.

Third and fourth stanzas are repeated.

Song Of The "Lenci"

We are the makers of
Wonderful puppets and dolls,
We love our craft:
And sing while we work.

The wonderful novelty
Of this supple work
Makes Turin famous.
The world around.

In stride
Goes the new being
Under every sky.
A brain it lacks,
And its heart is of straw,
But with beauty it glows.

In its cheerful mood
And frolicsome pose
From land to land,
Among happy children,
Merriment and joyful
Commotion it brings.

The bewitchment of fables and charms
Of dreams and reality,
of beauty and graces
The "Lenci" knows.

When handled with care
It radiates love,
And sweeter and kinder
Life comes to us.

Illustration 7. The word "Lenci" stamped on the bottoms of both feet belonging to the 23in (58.4cm) Lenci girl from the 109 series circa 1928/1929.

Illustration 6. The Lenci advertisement as printed in Italian and its general translation.

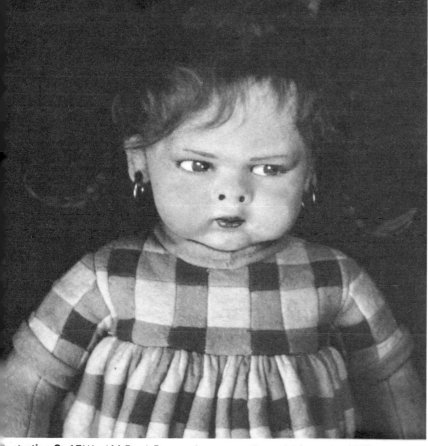

Illustration 8. 17½in (44.5cm) Pouty, almost scowling, girl from the 1500 series; tiny umps of mohair sewn separately into her scalp, the brown hair almost matches her brown de-glancing eyes; all-felt construction with a hollow felt-covered torso. She has several usual features note the *pierced ears* with hoop earrings. This doll also has *separately itched big toes*, which few Lenci dolls possess. The thumb and forefinger of each hand are nnected with thin cording, possibly to enable her to hold a jump rope. Her patchwork-style t dress is of varying shades of pink and cream; she has pink shoes with quilted soles; her derclothing has three pieces, half-slip and panties, with picot-edged ruffles, both attach the short waist with the three-hole buttons of milk glass. This close-up view shows her ce area which is very short with very plump cheeks. Her eyes have two highlights, as does r lower lip. She is circa 1930.

Illustration 9. 14in (35.6cm) Scottish boy in colorful costume; pale blue eyes and blonde hair; red plaid felt kilt trimmed with strips of navy, light blue, white and yellow felt to form its design; green socks are made the same way and the green matches his plain green felt jacket; white cotton shirt with black wool tie. Under his kilt are felt pants that match his maroon vest. On the back of the kilt a cloth ribbon strip reads: "Lenci//Made in Italy." *Annette Palm Collection. Photograph by Lynn Palm.*

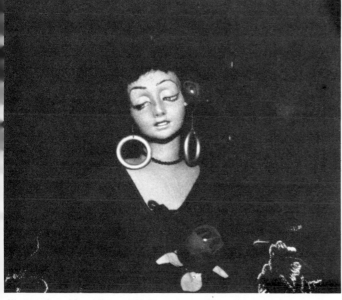

Illustration 10. 27½in (69.9cm) long-limbed Spanish lady; half-closed brown eyes, a row of tiny painted teeth in her smiling mouth; head, arms and upper torso of felt, lower torso and legs are muslin; black mohair under black felt sombrero with tasseled trim; large gold hoop earrings and a red beaded necklace; red felt dress has many tiers of ruffles; white organdy ruffled petticoats and pantaloons edged with red scalloped trim; long silk stockings and black high-heeled slippers, garters with roses; a rose in her hair and at her waist, plus a black shawl with embroidered roses complete her outfit. *Annette Palm Collection. Photograph by Lynn Palm.*

Illustration 11. This view shows the unusual body construction of the Lenci long-limbed lady named *L Gish.*

127

Illustration 13. 17½in (44.5cm) lovely Russian girl of the 300 series circa 1929; she has extremely long mohair in braids; brown eyes; body is all-felt construction with hollow torso; marked "Lenci" on the bottoms of both feet; fantastic outfit is a riot of colors -- orange, purple, deep red, yellow, gold, blue, gray, green, pink and cream; felt hat and skirt have felt appliques and vest has two rows of scalloped trim; sheer cream material forms veil falling from the back of the hat and is edged in pinked felt; blouse, teddy, slip and pantalets are all made of organdy; tall deep red leather boots complete her outfit—they have leather soles and leather-covered heels. The front of each boot is embroidered with wool in an intricate design. This close-up view shows that her eyes have double highlights, as does the pink lower lip. Note also the intricate design of the hat.

Illustration 16. 27in (68.6cm) Lenci long-limbed lady with sultry, half closed eyes; pale blonde mohair sewn into her head in tiny clumps; all-felt construction, unusual hollow torso with molded bust; extremely lovely shapely lady. She has her original square cardboard tag reading "Bambola-Italia//Lenci//Torino//Made in Italy//L Gish 26." The "L Gish" might indicate that this is a portrait doll of the famous actress Lillian Gish. Her gown is cream organdy with turquoise dots and scalloped edging on the ruffles; her bonnet, slip and pantalets match the dress and she wears silk stockings with turquoise high-heeled slippers; she wears her original pearl necklace. A Lenci lady almost identical to this one is shown on page 17, upper left corner in the **Doll Reader**, December 1980/January 1981 issue, with Shirley Temple.

Illustration 15. 30in (81.3cm) *Valentino*. A rare and dramatic portrait doll, circa 1927/1928, of the actor, Rudolph Valentino, in his famous role as *The Sheik*. He has brown eyes and hair; an all-felt body; an arrogant expression and stance -- with head high, elbows bent and hands at waist, which was a typical Valentino pose; his lavish felt costume has cream as the basic color; felt appliques, stripes and other accessories are a combination of colors set off by rich embroidery and gold braid; stripes of the robe are cream, dusky orange, rose and gold; cream jodhpurs have maroon, rose, magenta and white trim; the turquoise vest is ornately embroidered with gold braid; high maroon leather boots complete the outfit. *Billie Nelson Tyrell Collection. Photograph by Paul Port.*

Dolls Made in America Prior to 1925 *Part I*

by MADELINE O. MERRILL
Photographs by RICHARD MERRILL
copyrighted in 1976 and 1977 by Madeline O. & Richard Merrill

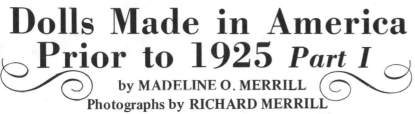

The Doll World has lost an ardent collector and researcher with the passing of Mrs. Madeline O. Merrill. This article and subsequent parts are presented as a tribute to her talents.

All photographs are copyrighted by *The Handbooks of Collectible Dolls.*

Many of the dolls illustrated are from the author's collection. Others are credited to present owners where known. Several dolls are from collections since liquidated and present owners are unknown to the author.

Illustration 3. 15in (38.1cm) primitive rag doll; head and arms have an overall coat of paint; features are embroidered in red and black thread; hair of tow; wears original woolen clothes and hand knit stockings; 19th century; from the State of Maine.

Illustration 1. 8in (20.3cm) primitive cloth doll; gauze covered cloth face has tinted cheeks, embroidered features; human hair wig; circa 1820; from New Hampshire.

Illustration 2. 16in (40.6cm) primitive boy doll of hand sewn linen; well worn, ankle length feet of wood; wears braid-trimmed black trousers, black velvet vest, white shirt, red coat, brown velvet cap; 19th century.

The history of the American doll industry of today is relatively short-lived when compared to the European. It took less than a century for America to dominate the commercially made doll field following its entry in the 1850s. This rapid advance may be dramatically illustrated by an assemblage of American-made dolls. Let us see what dolls might be included by listing those that were made in America and omitting those that, although American designed, were produced elsewhere - - generally in Germany.

From the early days of the colonies, dolls were made at home from the most easily available materials - - usually cloth or wood. Surviving examples have become much sought

after, especially in the last few years, and, because of this, have been accorded their rightful place of importance in the field of doll collecting. They are not only desired by doll collectors but are also being acquired by those who fancy American folk art. The result has been that they have, in recent years, increased enormously in price and demand.

These beguiling old dolls are often surprisingly well made and meticulously costumed in fashions of their day. Such is the case with an unforgettable, elegantly dressed top-hatted gentleman in the collection of the Rhode Island Historical Society at Providence. His creator must surely have been an unsung artist.

Other materials such as dried apples, corn cobs and corn husks were also used in primitive dolls. It is said that Indian children were playing with corn husk dolls when the first colonists reached our shores and that this type of doll was soon adopted by the white children of the settlements. If so, they rank among the earliest of American dolls for corn was unknown in the Old World.

Dolls were not commercially made in the United States until shortly after the middle of the 19th century. A report of the Bureau of Statistics of Labor in Massachusetts mentions that "the oldest existing manufacturing plant of toys and games for children was established in 1835," but there is no specific reference made to dolls. In the *History of Manufactures in the United States* by Victor S. Clark, which covers the period from 1860 to 1893, it states, "Dolls were a large article of manufacture in New York, Boston and Philadelphia, although their porcelain and china heads were generally imported."

Early rubber dolls were made under the patent of Charles Goodyear of New Haven, Connecticut, who was born in 1800 and died in 1860. After ten years of labor amidst abject poverty, he discovered and patented,

Illustration 4. 21in (53.3cm) artistically made 19th C. gentleman; oil painted features are extremely well done; wears finely tailored wool suit, brocade vest and white shirt; carries top hat; 19th century. *Rhode Island Historical Society, Providence, Rhode Island.*

Illustration 5. 27in (68.6cm) doll having a well modeled head of rubber mounted on a cloth-stuffed body; molded hair is painted black; painted features include large dark eyes with lower lashes only; mid 19th century. *Essex Institute, Salem, Massachusetts.*

in 1844, vulcanized rubber. Involvement in almost 60 infringements to his patent kept him impoverished while enriching many others. He stated in his 1855 book, *Gum Elastic,* that the New York merchant, Benjamin E. Lee, was licensed in the United States to manufacture dolls of rubber. Charles Goodyear is thought to have manufactured toys of rubber as early as 1839.

Illustration 6. 15in (38.1cm) doll; manufactured under the 1851 patent of Nelson Goodyear; made by the Indian Rubber Comb Company of New York; head of hard rubber; blonde molded hairdo; blue painted eyes; marked on back shoulders: "I. R. Comb Co."

In 1851, Nelson Goodyear, brother of Charles, received a patent for hard rubber which was extended in 1865. Doll heads may be found made under this patent which bear the mark of the India Rubber Comb Co. of New York (I. R. Comb), plus the patent date of May 6, 1851 - - - Ext. 1865.

These early rubber dolls came in various molds and sizes. Most have molded painted hair but occasionally one may be found with the remains of a tacked on lambs wool wig. A bonneted rubber head, now in the Margaret Woodbury Strong Museum a Rochester, New York, is illustrated in delicate water colors in the 1869 catalog of the New York Rubber Company. This firm manufactured dolls under the 1851 patent of Nelson Goodyear and they exhibited at the

Illustration 8. 19in (48.3cm) doll; made by Ludwig Greiner of Philadelphia under his extended patent of 1872; papier-mâché head on cloth-stuffed body; black molded hair; blue painted eyes; back shoulders labeled: "Greiner's//Patent Doll Heads// No. //Pat.March30'58.Ext.'72."

1876 Centennial in Philadelphia. By 1897 they were making all-rubber dolls.

As is well known by all doll collectors, the first American patented doll head was made by Ludwig Greiner of Philadelphia in 1858 with a patent extension granted in 1872. Probably a doll maker in his native Germany, Greiner carried on his craft after arriving in Philadelphia about the year 1840. His patented papier-mâché heads, with cloth reinforcement, have painted features and molded hair. Only on rare occasions will a *labeled* Greiner head be found with *glass eyes.*

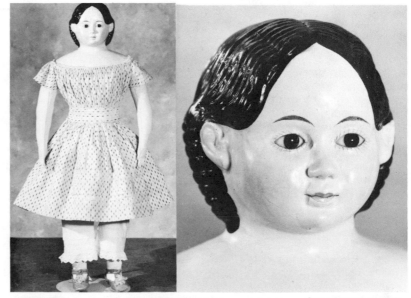

Illustration 7. A 30in (76.2cm) labeled, glass-eyed papier-mâché doll by **Ludwig Greiner** of Philadelphia; extremely rare as, almost without exception, labeled Greiner dolls have painted eyes; labeled on back shoulders: "Greiner's//Improved//Patent Heads//Pat. Mar. 30th. '58."

Heads came in various sizes and molds, both blonde and brunette, with the latter being more plentiful. The Greiner label is applied to the back shoulder and is generally found intact. The firm closed in 1873.

The J. B. Sheppard & Company of Philadelphia operated between the years 1860 and 1935. They are particularly well known for their cloth dolls with molded, painted features - - called *Philadelphia Babies* or *Sheppard Dolls*. It is not known with certainty how long this doll was manufactured, but it was carried over from the last quarter of the 19th into the early 20th century.

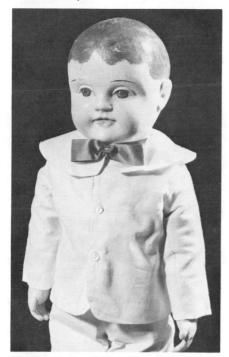

Illustration 9. 22in (55.9cm) cloth *Sheppard* or *Philadelphia Baby;* made by J. B. Sheppard and Company of Philadelphia, Pennsylvania; molded and painted features include brown eyes and hair; early 20th century. *Pearl D. Morley Collection.*

Enoch Rice Morrison of New York patented, in 1862, the walking doll with a pressed cloth head called *Autoperipatetikos.* It is key wound and lumbers along on rather clumsy, metal feet. It is not uncommon to find it in it's original, labeled box. Rarely seen is the colorfully costumed *Walking Zouave* Autoperipatetikos with his bearded, pressed cloth head. Autoperipatetikos dolls were also made using imported heads of china or untinted bisque - - the china having a gold lustre touched, ruffled snood with a bunch of molded grapes at the center front. The patent date of July 15, 1862, is printed on the base of the doll. D. S. Cohen and the Joseph Lyon & Co. of New York, Martin & Runyon of London and possibly others made and/or distrib-

Illustration 10. 9½in (24.2cm) *Autoperipatetikos* or walking doll with original box; patented July 15, 1862, by Enoch Rice Morrison of New York; key-wound clockworks, hidden beneath skirt, operates metal feet which causes doll to walk.

uted these dolls under the Morrison patent.

Lucretia E. Salle of Decatur, Illinois, patented, in 1865, a doll head of leather with a plaster reinforcement added to maintain its shape.

In 1866, Franklin Darrow of Bristol, Connecticut, patented a doll's head of pressed leather or rawhide. The paper label on the chest of these heads is often missing. When retained, it reads "F. E. Darrow's//patent// May 1st 1866." Although Franklin Darrow seems to have been the most prominent, there were others who patented or made leather dolls in the United States, such as in 1903, Gussie Decker; 1912, Emma Gleason; 1917, Clark Downey.

It is worth mentioning at this point the fine, handcrafted dolls of leather that were made by the American Indians. Costumed in their fringed and beaded tribal dress, they are a far cry from the cheaply made ones offered to today's tourists. The early ones appeal not only to doll collectors but to those interested in Indian lore as well.

A seldom seen doll today is one with the head of papier-mâché patented by Philip Lerch of Philadelphia in 1866. Conrad Lang became part of the firm in 1867 when it became known as Lerch & Company, and they were joined about three years later by Klag. Doll heads by this firm bear a paper label on the back shoulder printed either "Lerch & Co." or "Lerch and Klag//Manufacturers//Philadelphia, Pa."

Edward S. Judge of Baltimore, Maryland, and Philadelphia, Pennsylvania, patented a papier-mâché doll head which bears a paper label on the back shoulder reading "Judge's

Patent Indestructible Doll Head" along with the date, "March 24th, 1868" or "Judge & Early" plus the patent date of July 27, 1875. These dolls are infrequently found.

A patent was granted on a pressed cloth head to George H. Hawkins of New York on September 8, 1868. These hollow molded heads are usually found on the familiar Goodwin mechanical toys of the doll riding a tricycle and the walking doll pushing

Illustration 11. Three dolls with pressed leather or rawhide heads ranging in size from 15in (38.1cm) to 24in (61.0cm); made by F. E. Darrow of Bristol, Connecticut; the painted finish is usually in poor condition on these seldom found dolls; 1866 to 1877.

131

Illustration 12. 25in (63.5cm) handcrafted Seminole Indian doll; leather head, on cloth body, has shaped nose and mouth, painted features, horsehair wig; circa 1915.

a carriage. Although scarce, Hawkins also made heads for larger play dolls. It is interesting to see that, feature for feature, even to the molded necklace and earrings, the head was copied from a fine, imported, untinted bisque head of the day.

Robert J. Clay, in 1868, invented a mechanical creeping baby with wax-over-composition head. This was later taken over by the well-known firm of Ives, Blakeslee - Williams Company of Bridgeport, Connecticut, in the early 1870s. It was advertised in their 1893 catalog at $48.00 a dozen, and is referred to as the *Ives Creeping Baby.*

One of the most coveted cloth dolls among today's collectors is the winsome, oil painted doll patented by Izannah Walker of Central Falls, Rhode Island, on November 11, 1873.

Illustration 15. Girl pushing carriage; a mechanical toy by William F. Goodwin of Washington, D.C. It is spring operated - - set in motion by winding rear wheel. Doll's head, of stiffened cloth, was made by George H. Hawkins of New York and is labeled with his patent date of September 8, 1868.

Illustration 13. 24in (61.0cm) rarely seen doll; by Philip Lerch of Philadelphia, Pennsylvania; papier-mâché head, black molded hair; blue painted eyes; cloth body; labeled on back shoulders: "Lerch & Co.,// Manufacturers.//No. 6." *Miss Jessie F. Parsons Collection.*

Illustration 16. A girl riding tricycle. A key-would mechanical toy by William F. Goodwin of Washington, D.C.; doll's head, of stiffened cloth, was made by George H. Hawkins of New York and is labeled with his patent date of September 8, 1868.

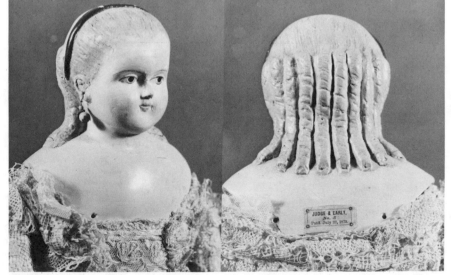

Illustration 14. 22in (55.9cm) seldom seen doll; by Edward S. Judge of Baltimore, Maryland, and Philadelphia, Pennsylvania; black banded hair has curls falling low on shoulders; pale blue painted eyes; pierced ears; labeled on back shoulders: "JUDGE & EARLY,//No. 5//Patd. July 27, 1875." *Louise H. Lund Collection.*

Illustration 17. The die-pressed cloth head of this 18in (45.7cm) doll was patented by George H. Hawkins of New York on September 8, 1868. It has black painted hair with a red band, blue painted eyes and gilded, molded-on earrings and necklace.

Illustration 18. 16in (40.6cm) all-cloth doll; patented by Izannah Walker of Central Falls, Rhode Island in 1873; brown painted hair is brush marked at sides and in back; molded features are painted including overly large, dark brown eyes.

They are said to have been made as early as 1855. Resembling quaint children who appear in early portraits of the 19th century, they have molded painted features and painted hair with brush marks and/or corkscrew curls.

Wooden dolls made in Springfield, Vermont, during the 1870 to 1880 period are uniquely American and need no introduction to doll collectors. Joel Ellis of the Co-operative

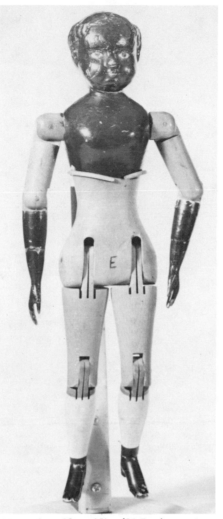

Illustration 20. 12in (30.5cm) wooden jointed black doll; patented by Joel Ellis of the Co-operative Manufacturing Company of Springfield, Vermont; features are painted and the slightly parted lips show a row of tiny white teeth; mold is identical to that of white dolls by this firm.

Illustration 19. 12in (30.5cm) fully-jointed wooden doll, dressed and undressed; patented in 1873 by Joel Ellis of the Co-operative Manufacturing Company, Springfield, Vermont; painted features include black hair, blue eyes and closed lips; hands and feet only are of metal.

Manufacturing Company was the first to patent, in 1873, these all-wooden, jointed dolls with hands and feet of metal. Some were painted to represent blacks. After 1874, when Mr. Ellis gave up the manufacture of his dolls, similar ones were made by the Jointed Doll Company using the patents granted to Frank D. Martin for an improved head (April 29, 1879), the patent granted to George W. Sanders (December 7, 1880) for improvements in joints and the November 7, 1882, patent to C. C. Johnson for improvement in the construction of dolls' heads. In 1881, Henry Hubbard Mason and Luke Taylor were granted a United States patent for an improved doll's head and neck joint. An interesting type of doll made by these partners, Mason-Taylor, is the so-called *Witch* or *Wizard,* a cheaply made doll representing an Oriental. A toggle arrangement at the neck of this doll allowed for its simulated decapitation by a knife provided for the purpose.

Illustration 21.   133

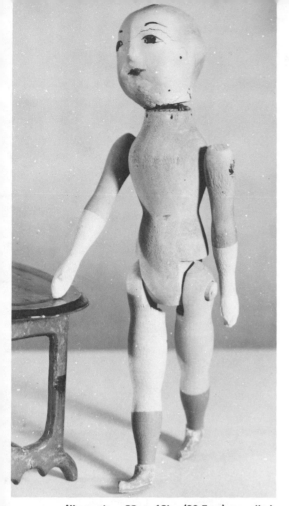

Illustration 22. 12in (30.5cm) so-called *Witch* or *Wizard* wooden doll; made by the Jointed Doll Company of Springfield, Vermont; attributed to Mason and Taylor; Oriental characteristics; jointed wooden body has up-turned metal feet. When a knife is passed through the neck, a toggle arrangement allows the head to remain on the body while giving the illusion of decapitation.

According to testimony of the sons of the Springfield doll makers, it would seem that all of the wooden dolls made at Springfield, Vermont, during this 1870 to 1880 period were either by Joel Ellis of the Cooperative Manufacturing Company under his own patent, or by the partners, Mason - Taylor, using their own and the assigned patents of Sanders, Martin and Johnson. Presumably the jointed wooden dolls by Mason - Taylor were made at the Jointed Doll Company. Manufacture of these dolls ceased by the mid 1880s.

Lucinda Wishard of Indianapolis, Indiana, assigned her 1883 patent for a stuffed flexible doll's body with wire skeleton, to Robert E. Springsteen and Harry E. Drew of the same

PREVIOUS PAGE: Illustration 21. Top: 12in (30.5cm) jointed wooden doll; molded hairdo, painted features; metal hands and feet. Bottom: 12in (30.5cm) jointed wooden black doll; metal hands and feet. Both made by the Jointed Doll Company, Springfield, Vermont and attributed to the partners, Mason and Taylor.

city. She also showed her dolls at the New Orleans Exposition in 1884.

Thomas A. Edison manufactured, under his 1878 to 1889 patents, his talking doll with the mechanism housed in the metal torso. The bisque head, marked "S. & H.," was made in Germany. Other firms making phonograph dolls in following years were the Jenny Lind Doll Company of Chicago, Giebeler-Falk Company of New York, Samuel Haskell of New York and the Averill Manufacturing Company of New York. The *Edison Talking Doll* was by far the best known and was successfully manufactured in large numbers.

Lazarus Reichman of New York patented a doll's head in 1877 that had a shell of beeswax, paraffin and turpentine with inner reinforcement of sawdust, glue and paste. The wig was of real hair. In the same year, Kimball D. Atwood of New York City also obtained a patent for a doll of metal.

In 1881, Ernst Martin and Henry C. Rippel of New York produced wax dolls. They were joined, in 1883, by Carl Wiegand of the same city, to form the National Doll and Novelty Company. This firm, also known as Wiegand, Martin - Rippel, made both wax and papier-mâché dolls.

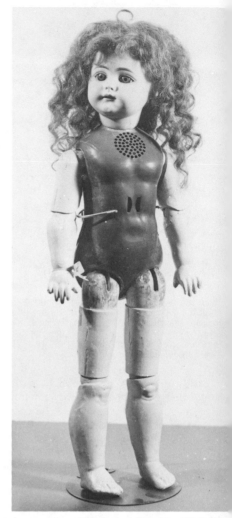

Illustration 23. 22in (55.9cm) *Edison Talking Doll* with 1878 to 1889 patent dates on mechanism within metal torso; invented and made by American inventor, Thomas Alva Edison; has an imported German head by Simon and Halbig. When a cylindrical record is inserted in mechanism and set in motion, doll recites nursery rhymes in a childish voice. *Louise H. Lund Collection.*

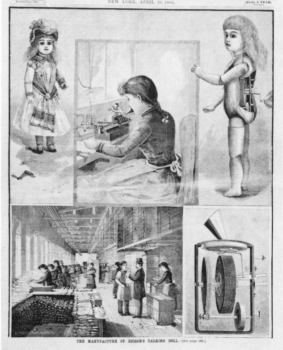

Illustration 24. Cover from the *Scientific American*, New York, April 26, 1890, which contains an article on the *Edison Talking Doll*.

Illustration 25. Wax-over-composition Webber "singing" dolls. *Left:* 26in (66.0cm) plays "Sleep My Child." *Middle:* 22in (55.9cm) plays "I Sing Greenville." *Right:* Shown undressed to illustrate body construction. Pressure on bellows in cloth-stuffed bodies causes organ within to play one of a variety of tunes. Patented in the United States and foreign countries by William Webber of Medford, Massachusetts in 1882; distributed by the Massachusetts Organ Company of Boston, Massachusetts.

Dolls Made in America Prior to 1925 *Part II*

by MADELINE O. MERRILL
Photographs by RICHARD MERRILL

All photographs are copyrighted by *The Handbooks of Collectible Dolls.*

Many of the dolls illustrated are from the author's collection. Others are credited to present owners where known. Several dolls are from collections since liquidated and present owners are unknown to the author.

Probably the most famous American-made doll with a wax head is the *Webber Singing Doll* by William A. Webber of Medford, Massachusetts, who, in 1882, patented it in both the United States and Europe. The cloth body is stamped in back with the maker's name and patents, and in front with the tune it plays. The fine wax-over-composition heads were

From the April/May 1982 Doll Reader.®

imported from both France and Germany and the music boxes, inserted in the torsos, played either an English or German air. The heads on these marked Webber dolls are always of *wax.* By pressing a wooden button on the chest, the doll "sang" one of the more than 20 tunes available. The dolls were distributed by the Massachusetts Organ Company of Boston, Massachusetts, who also manufactured the dolls' music boxes.

In 1890, Philip Goldsmith made, under a patent granted to Julius J. Wolf of Cincinnati, wax-over-composition dolls' heads.

Beginning in 1886, and for a number of years thereafter, Emma L. Bristol of Providence, Rhode Island, made a composition-headed doll with

Illustration 26.   15in (38.1cm) cutout Santa Claus doll; design for doll was patented by E. S. Peck of Brooklyn, New York, December 28, 1886, and was assigned to the New York Stationery and Envelope Company; printed on cloth to be cut out, stitched and stuffed at home.

painted eyes and hair wig. A paper sticker applied to the doll's chest reads: "Bristol's Unbreakable Doll// 273 High Street//Providence, R.I." One of these rare dolls was sold recently at a New Hampshire auction to the Margaret Woodbury Strong Museum. A happy circumstance, since, at the same auction, a rare doll by Lerch - Klag of Philadelphia was lost to American collectors by way of the high bid of a London buyer.

In 1887, Rebecca Johnson was granted a patent for dipping a cloth doll's head in wax.

In the same year, 1887, William White Jacques of Newton, Massachusetts, assigned his patent for a record playing doll to the Edison Phonograph Toy Manufacturing Company of Maine. This doll varied greatly from the phonograph doll that was actually manufactured by Edison in his New Jersey plant.

The first design patent for a doll was awarded on December 28, 1886, to Edward Peck of Brooklyn, New York, for his well-known rag Santa Claus which was printed on cloth to be cut out and stuffed at home. The New York Stationery & Envelope Company was the assignee of patented dolls by Peck.

The late 19th and early 20th century saw the introduction and manufacture of countless cutout cloth dolls. It was the Peck patented dolls that influenced the 1893 dolls designed by the sisters, Charity and Celia M. Smith and others who followed. Commerically printed cloth dolls are typically American.

In 1876, the Arnold Print Works of North Adams, Massachusetts, was established and they are particularly well known for their printed cloth dolls and animals that were sold by the yard to be cut out and stuffed at home. They printed the 1892 copyrighted *Brownies* by Palmer Cox, and, in 1893, *Little Red Riding Hood* by Celia M. Smith. They also made the calico cat which was designed by Celia and her sister, Charity Smith, both of Ithaca, New York. One of their most colorful cutouts was the commemorative *Columbian Sailor Doll* of 1893. The Arnold Print Works continued in business beyond 1925. Their output was great and their designs many.

Cloth dolls, designed by Celia and Charity Smith as well as those by Ida Gutsell, were handled in 1889 by Lawrence - Company of Boston, Philadelphia and New York City, who were printers and distributors.

Not only were cloth dolls popular at this time, but hand knitted and crocheted dolls came in vogue with

Illustration 27. Cutout cloth *Brownie* dolls; designed by artist, Palmer Cox, and printed by the Arnold Print Works of North Adams, Massachusetts, to be sold by the yard in stores. Twelve different *Brownies* were included in each yard. *Top:* An uncut *Brownie* called the *Irishman*. *Bottom:* Two made up *Brownies*. Copyrighted in 1892.

black dolls seemingly favored. *Harper's Bazaar* of 1892 carried full directions for making both doll and costume. Both boy and girl types were made. One particularly fine example may be seen in the Essex Institute of Salem, Massachusetts, a black girl jauntily wearing her red, white and blue costume. She was knitted by 78 year old Mrs. Sarah Kimball in 1892.

The *Columbian Doll,* made by Miss Emma E. Admas of Oswego, New York, was introduced in 1891 and marketed for quite a few years. She was assisted in making her hand-painted, cloth-stuffed dolls by her sister, Marietta. Well made and artistically painted, they are desirable collectors' items. The *Columbian Dolls* received a diploma of merit at the 1893 Chicago World's Fair. Made as both boys and girls, they came with blue or brown eyes, and a few blacks were also included. They were not patented but are identified by a stamping on the back of the bodies. Emma Adams died in 1900 but her sister, Marietta, carried on the business for about ten years longer.

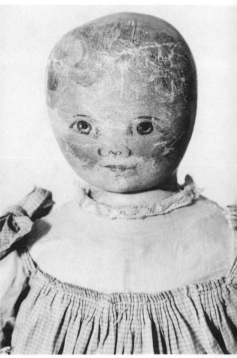

Illustration 28. All-cloth doll produced by Miss Emma E. Adams of Oswego, New York. Named "The Columbian Doll," it was accepted in 1893 by the Commission of the Chicago World's Fair where it received a diploma of merit. Both boy and girl dolls were made as well as some black dolls. They were painted by the artist and maker, Miss Adams, and came in sizes from 15in (38.1cm) to 29in (73.7cm). Dolls were not patented but carry rubber stamp identification on back of bodies. *Fidelia Lence Collection.*

Illustration 29. Stuffed rag doll; originated by Mrs. Julia Jones Beecher, wife of the pastor of the Congregational church in Elmira, New York; came in several sizes, both black and white; constructed of silk jersey underwear with looped wool for hair; face, hands and feet were shaped by carefully placed stitches. Dolls were made by the sewing circle of the church from 1893 to 1910. All proceeds from their sale was used in missionary work.

In 1893, Julia Jones Beecher of Elmira, New York, wife of the pastor of the Congregational church, originated a stuffed rag doll. Constructed of pink silk jersey, it was made in several sizes up to life - - in both white and black. Faces are hand painted, hands and feet are shaped by stitches and looped wool was used for hair. Proceeds from the sale of these dolls were used to promote missionary work. They are considered very collectible.

Samuel M. Schwab, Jr., of New York City, patented, in 1893, a rag doll made of two pieces of printed cloth - - seamed and stuffed.

From 1893 to 1917, Steinfeld Bros., New York City, manufactured and imported dolls. They made Maurice F. Oppenheimer's *Racketty Packetty Kiddy.*

The first decade of the 20th century saw an expanding American doll industry. Many new and interesting stuffed cloth dolls were introduced, among them *Mother's Congress Doll* patented by Madge L. Mead of Philadelphia on November 6, 1900. Manufactured by the Mothers' Congress Doll Company of Philadelphia, the well-printed features included blonde hair with a blue ribbon bow. These very collectible dolls carry their name, maker and patent date on the front of their torsos.

Illustration 31. 12½in (31.8cm) upside down doll with one head black, the other white; made by Albert Bruckner of New Jersey; black has black mohair wig, laughing mouth showing two rows of white teeth; white has printed blonde hair, closed lips; neck band labeled: "Bruckner Doll//Made in U.S.A;" also stamped with patent date of July 9, 1901. When properly positioned, skirt covers unused doll's head.

On July 9, 1901, Albert Bruckner of New Jersey was granted a patent for a cloth doll with a lithographed, molded facial mask. It was made in both black and white dolls as well as a topsy-turvy or upside-down doll with one face black, the other white. When the latter is held in an upright position, the skirt completely covers the unused doll. A cloth label was sewn to the neck bands of both type dolls stating: "Bruckner Doll - - Made in U.S.A." The patent date is also stamped on the right front edge of the neck.

Ella Smith of Roanoke, Alabama, in 1904, designed and made the much sought after cloth doll called the *Alabama Indestructible Doll.* Heads, limbs and features of these dolls are painted, and, although most models came with painted hair, occasionally one may be found with a hair wig. They were made to represent both black and white children and the bodies are well stamped with the maker's name and patent date of September 26, 1905.

Illustration 30. 24in (61.0cm) stuffed cloth doll; patented Nov. 6, 1900, by Madge L. Mead; made by the Mothers' Congress Doll Company of Philadelphia, Pennsylvania; blonde hair with a blue bow; blue eyes; black slippers; marked on body: "BABY STUART//Mothers' Congress Doll//CHILDRENS' FAVORITE/PHILADELPHIA//PA.//Pat. Nov. 6, 1900." *Jean Dyer Collection.*

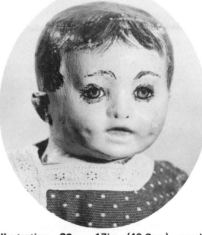

Illustration 32. 17in (43.2cm) much sought after all-cloth *Alabama Indestructible Doll;* designed and made by Ella Smith of Roanoke, Alabama, from 1904 to 1924; brown painted hair; blue painted eyes; dimpled face; body marked: "Mrs. S. S. Smith//Manufacturer//Roanoke,--Ala.;" lower torso marked: "No. 1//Patented Dec. (?) 1907." *Pearl D. Morley Collection.*

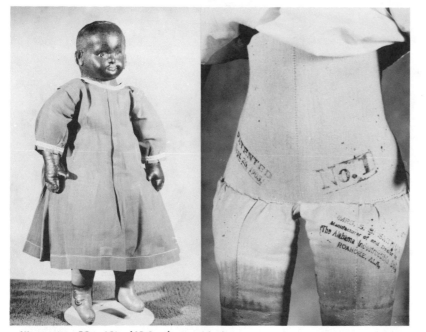

Illustration 33. 19in (48.3cm) rare, black all-cloth *Alabama Indestructible Doll. Left:* doll dressed showing its painted head, arms, and legs with typical painted on shoes. *Right:* doll undressed showing its well marked body; on torso: "PATENTED// Sept. 26, 1905/No. 1;" on leg: "MRS. S. S. SMITH/Manufacturer of and Dealer in The Alabama Indestructible Doll// ROANOKE, ALA." *Pearl D. Morley Collection.*

Cloth dolls made to be cut out and stuffed at home were still numerous and varied in the early 20th century. There were some designed in the likeness of storybook characters while others were made to commemorate special events. Many were obtained by sending coins and box tops to manufacturers who, through this method, advertised and promoted the sales of their products. This was particularly the case with the makers of breakfast foods which led to the creation of such characters as the Davis Milling Company's *Aunt Jemima and family,* Cream of Wheat's *Rastus* and Kellogg's *Goldilocks and the Three Bears.* Many of the cloth cutout dolls were printed by the Arnold Print Works of North Adams, Massachusetts, and the Art Fabric Mills of New York.

Artist Carl E. Schultz of New York obtained, in 1903, a United States patent for a *Foxy Grandpa* cloth cutout doll based on a popular character in his comic strip drawings. Designs vary of this bespectacled, bald-headed little man. An early version printed by the Art Fabric Mills of New York shows him carrying a rabbit under one arm while a watch fob with a Masonic emblem dangles from his hip pocket. Another and perhaps later version shows *Foxy Grandpa* with the rabbit and watch fob missing while his bald head is covered by a derby hat.

Illustration 34. 18in (45.7cm) *Rastus,* the Cream of Wheat advertising doll; printed in color on cloth, it came ready to cut out, sew and stuff; first appeared in 1922; obtained by sending a box top and ten cents to the cereal manufacturer.

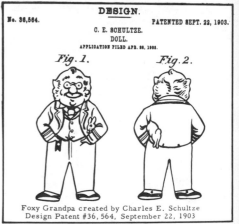

Illustration 35. 20in (50.8cm) stuffed cloth doll in likeness of *Foxy Grandpa,* a comic strip character created by artist, Carl E. Schultz. He appears exactly as drawn on the design patent (# 36,564) granted to Mr. Schultz on September 22, 1903. This commercially made cloth doll was manufactured, under this patent, by the Art Fabric Mills of New York.

A variant among cloth-stuffed dolls may be found in those with children's faces printed in color from photographs. The Dreamland Doll Company of Detroit claimed to be the originator when these innovative dolls first appeared in 1906. E. I. Horsman of New York also made this type doll in 1907.

The still famous and much loved *Raggedy Ann* cloth doll was registered in 1915 by John B. Gruelle of New York, a newspaper writer and cartoonist. Its success led to his writing, in 1918, the Raggedy Ann stories. The Georgene Novelty Company produced, in 1918, the first manufactured *Raggedy Ann* dolls. Today's *Raggedy*

Ann and companion, *Raggedy Andy,* are both constructed in the same manner with widely smiling faces, button eyes and looped red yarn hair. *Raggedy Ann* is said to have been inspired in the beginning by an old rag doll which once belonged to Mr. Gruelle's mother.

Illustration 36. 24in (61.0cm) cloth doll, circa 1910, whose colorfully printed face is from a photograph of a child. This type doll was made by several manufacturers including the Saalfield Publishing Company of Akron, Ohio.

The Vargas family of New Orleans created miniature wax figures in likenesses of the black street vendors of that city. These realistically sculptured little street criers were made by the descendants of Sr. Francisco Vargas who emigrated to the United States from Mexico in the early 19th century and gained fame from his beautifully modeled waxen saints. He was commissioned to make all the flowers, fruits and vegetables for the Louisiana Exposition in 1894. His wax works were carried on by his family following his death in the late

Illustration 37. 6½in (16.5cm) chicken vendor. One of the many street criers realistically modeled in wax by the Vargas family of New Orleans, Louisiana. Created in the late 19th and early 20th centuries, they are no longer being made.

Illustration 38. 14in (35.6cm) roly-poly *Rolly Dolly* by Schoenhut; patented in 1908 by A. Schoenhut & Company of Philadelphia; painted costume is orange with yellow trim, ruffle at neck is of pleated cotton; *Rolly Dollies* were made in various sizes and designs; labeled: "Schoenhut Rolly Dolly."

1890s. The quaint, realistic little street criers, hawking their miniature wares, were made by five generations of Vargases but are now no longer available.

The A. Schoenhut - Company of Philadelphia, makers of dolls and toys, was founded in 1872 by Albert Schoenhut who had earlier emigrated from his native Germany. His colorfully painted papier-mâché *Rolly Dolly* was patented in 1908 and, in 1909, he filed for a patent for a spring-jointed wooden doll. A patent was granted in 1911. Called the *All Wood Perfection Art Doll,* it was extremely well made, painted in oil colors, and, with the exception of the curved-limbed baby and the walking doll, came with pierced feet which enabled it to assume many postures when mounted on a provided metal stand. Both boy and girl dolls were available, and they came with either painted hair or mohair wigs. Movable eyes were used in 1921 and, in 1924, a cheaper line of elastic-strung, cloth bodied dolls were brought out. Production continued for a short time but

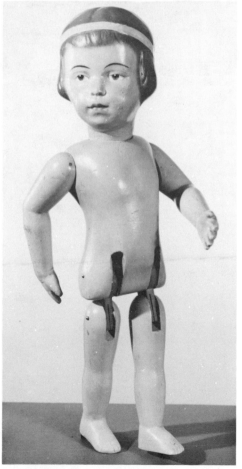

Illustration 39. 14in (35.6cm) wooden walking doll; made by A. Schoenhut & Company of Philadelphia, Pennsylvania; painted head, molded hair with pink painted band; intaglio eyes; stiff wooden legs, swinging freely from hips, allow doll to walk when hand propelled; copyrighted in 1913.

the 1930s witnessed the end of the line for what is considered by many to be the finest of American-made dolls.

Equally famous are the earlier Schoenhut circuses which consisted of a great variety of wooden performers and animals along with their paraphernalia and big top. Another imaginative wooden toy was a 53 piece set called "Teddy's Adventures in Africa" which was dominated by an excellent little figure representing Teddy Roosevelt complete in hunting gear.

Illustration 41. 9in (22.9cm) jointed wooden circus performers. *Left:* Ring master. *Right:* Clown riding lion. Part of an elaborate circus made by A. Schoenhut & Company of Philadelphia, Pennsylvania. Circus performers also came with heads of bisque.

Illustration 40. 21in (53.3cm) all-wooden spring-jointed boy doll; patented by A. Schoenhut & Company of Philadelphia in 1911; painted head has intaglio eyes and mohair wig. He is able to assume many postures upon insertion of stand's peg into either one of the two holes on bottom of his feet. These dolls were made as both boys and girls and came with choice of molded hair or mohair wigs.

Illustration 42. 9in (22.9cm) all-wooden jointed doll; an excellent likeness of Theodore Roosevelt in African Safari garb; made by A. Schoenhut & Company of Philadelphia, Pennsylvania; wears khaki uniform and carries hunting gear; main character in an elaborate set called "Teddy's Adventures in Africa."

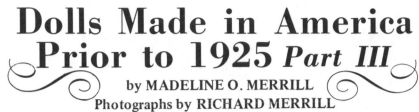

Dolls Made in America Prior to 1925 *Part III*

by MADELINE O. MERRILL
Photographs by RICHARD MERRILL
copyrighted in 1976 and 1977 by Madeline O. & Richard Merrill

Part I of this article was presented in the February/March 1982 issue of the DOLL READER pages 3 to 8 while Part II appeared on pages 10 to 15 of the April/May 1982 issue.

All photographs are copyrighted by *The Handbooks of Collectible Dolls.*

Many of the dolls illustrated are from the author's collection. Others are credited to present owners where known. Several dolls are from collections since liquidated and present owners are unknown to the author.

Illustration 43. 15½in (39.4cm) composition doll in likeness of the sou'wester-clad boy pictured on the Uneeda Biscuit package; wears original yellow raincoat but is missing his rain hat and miniature box of Uneeda Biscuits which he carried in the crook of his arm; patented December 8, 1914, by Morris Michtom of the Ideal Toy and Novelty Company of New York.

The beginning of the great American composition doll industry is seen with the granting to Solomon G. Hoffman of his 1892 patent for the Can't Break 'Em dolls. Hoffman, a Russian immigrant, founded, in 1892, the First American Doll Factory of Brooklyn, New York which was renamed, in 1895, the American Doll - Toy Manufacturing Company. In 1909, the Aetna Doll & Toy Company

From the June/July 1982 Doll Reader.®

Illustration 44. 16in (40.6cm) *Soozie Smiles,* the *Surprise Baby;* made by the Ideal Toy and Novelty Company of New York; two-faced composition head mounted on cloth body with composition arms; a crying or smiling face is exposed by rotating the flange-necked head; "Mama" and "Papa" voice box is embedded in torso.

bought the rights to the Can't Break 'Em patent following the death of Mr. Hoffman. Aetna's output was distributed, in 1909, by Borgfeldt and in later years by the E. I. Horsman firm.

Morris Michtom of the Ideal Toy and Novelty Company of New York patented, on December 8, 1914, a 15in (38.1cm) composition-headed doll in the likeness of the sou'wester-clad little boy pictured on the outer wrapper of the well-known Uneeda Biscuit crackers. The body is of cloth with arms and high black boots of composition. Often missing are the hat and miniature box of Uneeda crackers he carried in the crook of his arm. The

doll itself is unmarked but the sleeve carries a label reading: "Uneeda Kid//Patented Dec. 8, 1914//Ideal Novelty and Toy Co.//Brooklyn, N. Y." This was but one of the many dolls made by the Ideal Toy and Novelty Company which was founded in 1907 by Morris Michtom who became famous for his Teddy Bears and composition character dolls. They included such as the coquette *Naughty Marietta, Dolly Varden,* World War I's *Liberty Boy,* two-faced *Soozie Smiles* and an extremely good likeness of *Baby Snooks* as portrayed by the comedienne Fanny Brice.

Another prominent American doll manufacturer is the E. I. Horsman Company of New York. In the late 19th century they made mostly toys but turned primarily to doll making around the turn of the 20th century. Among their many composition character dolls sought after by today's collectors are the *Campbell Kids, Baby Bumps* in both black and white models and *Tynie Baby. Tynie Baby* also came with an imported German bisque head.

The well-known firm of Fleischaker - Baum was established in New York in 1910. Their American-made composition dolls, trademarked "EFFanBEE," included such characters as *Miss Coquette,* with side-glancing eyes and a molded ribbon in her hair, *Baby Grumpy* with many variations, and, in 1924, the baby *Bubbles* followed by a line of *Patsy* dolls.

The background and career of Martha J. Chase of Pawtucket, Rhode Island, is well documented. Her factory in Pawtucket established in the early 20th century, produced hand-painted, cloth-stuffed dolls representing babies and children, life-sized hospital mannequins and, on occasion, fashion mannequins. Her portrait and character dolls are of particular interest and include *George Washington, Mammy and Pickaninnies,* and various characters from Dickens' tales and Carroll's *Alice-in-Wonderland.* The Chase factory remained under ownership of the Chase family until the late 1970s. Production in later years consisted mainly of their widely used hospital mannequins. The famous Chase stockinette dolls were supplanted, in 1935, by the introduction of molded vinyl plastic versions which were made in both white and black models.

In 1917, ventriloquist Harry H. Coleman patented in both Britain and the United States his rather large, clumsy, hand-propelled walking doll which was called *Dolly Walker.* The composition head and wooden limbs are attached to a wooden torso which

Illustration 45. 11in (27.9cm) boy, 12in (30.5cm) girl, *Campbell Kids,* made in the likeness of the Grace E. Drayton drawings for the Campbell Soup Company; made by the E. I. Horsman Company of New York; smiling heads of composition have painted features with eyes cast to the side and molded hair; bodies of flesh-colored cotton with composition hands; copyrighted in 1910.

mask faces of composition with painted features and black mohair wigs. Lifelike in appearance, the dolls were made as braves, squaws with papooses, little boys and girls. They are marked on the foot with a paper label reading: "Skookum Indian//Trademark registered//U.S.A.//Patented."

Madame Georgene Averill, wife of J. Paul Averill of the Averill Manufacturing Company of New York, designed and patented, from 1913 on, numerous character and baby dolls. Dolls by this firm also used the name "Madame Hendren" and "Madame Georgene." Their composition-headed dolls included one of the first American Mama dolls, the phonograph doll called *Dolly Record,* whistling dolls dressed as sailors, cowboys and "cops," plus a number of baby dolls. At the close of the first World War, Georgene Averill designed and copyrighted the all-bisque laughing baby called *Bonnie Babe* which was made in Germany

is covered with wire mesh. The wooden legs were so jointed as to allow the doll to dance as well as walk. Made in three sizes, 18in (45.7cm), 21in (53.3cm) and 28in (71.1cm), it came with painted features, painted or sleep eyes and painted hair or glued on wig. It was distributed by Harry Coleman and made by the Wood Toy Company of New York.

Artist and designer, Rose O'Neill, copyrighted her famous *Kewpies* in 1913, followed by *Scootles* in 1925. Most of these winsome little dolls were produced in Germany and made of bisque. However, a few bisque *Kewpies* were made, circa 1920, by the Fulper Pottery Company of Flemington, New Jersey, but these are relatively scarce. Also considered collectible are the American-made composition *Kewpies* and *Scootles* which were manufactured by Joseph L. Kallus' Cameo Doll Company.

In 1913, Mary McAboy of Missoula, Montana, designed and made the first *Skookum* Indian dolls. They continued to be made for many years. These inexpensive, blanket-wrapped American Indian dolls were dressed in various tribal costumes and had

Illustration 46. 12in (30.5cm) black *Baby Bumps;* made by the E. I. Horsman Company of New York; composition head; open/closed smiling mouth; painted features; brown cloth body; also came as a white baby; circa 1912. *Pearl D. Morley Collection.*

Illustration 47. 15in (38.1cm) all original *Tynie Baby;* made by the E. I. Horsman Company of New York; smoothly finished composition head, light brown molded hair; sleep eyes; cloth body with composition limbs; marked on head: " © 1924//E. I. Horsman Co., Inc.;" was also available with the entire doll or head only of imported German bisque.

Illustration 48. 24in (61.0cm) *Bubbles;* made by Fleischaker & Baum of New York whose trademark was Effanbee; composition head and upper body molded in one piece, molded hair; sleep eyes; open mouth with two upper teeth; cloth body with voice box, composition limbs; arms are so modeled as to allow doll to put finger in mouth; marked: "Effanbee//Bubbles//Copr. 1924//Made in U.S.A."

for George Borgfelt & Company of New York.

From 1916 to 1920, hand-painted, lightweight composition Art Dolls were made by Jessie McCutcheon Raleigh of Chicago, Illinois. Many were made in the likenesses of storybook characters. The heads that were on jointed composition bodies had painted eyes and molded hair, while those on cork-stuffed bodies had sleep eyes and human hair wigs. Complete outfits for the dolls were also available.

In 1916, Gertrude F. Rollinson designed a painted stockinette doll which closely resembled the earlier, well-known doll by Martha J. Chase. Manufactured by the Utley Company of Holyoke, Massachusetts, it came with painted eyes, a wig or painted hair, pierced nostrils and a mouth either closed or showing painted-in teeth between parted lips. The cloth torsos are stamped, often times indistinctly, with a circular trademark lettered: "Rollinson Doll//Holyoke, Mass."

In 1911, Louis Amberg & Sons, notable importer, distributor and manufacturer of dolls and toys, moved from Cincinnati to New York. His *New Born Babe* with an imported German bisque head, introduced in 1914, was apparently the first doll modeled after a newborn infant.

In 1918 he introduced an all-composition doll on a jointed, elastic strung body. It strongly resembled, in mold and construction, the earlier bisque-headed German-made dolls. The socket head, with a mohair wig over unpainted, molded hair, had an open mouth with teeth and metal sleep eyes. The head was marked: "L.A.&S.//40" and the shoulders were marked: "Amberg's Victory Doll//50." It was probably made as a substitute for the then unattainable, imported German bisque dolls. Amberg, in 1918, also used bisque heads by the Fulper Pottery Company of New Jersey.

Illustration 49. 20in (50.8cm) stockinet baby doll with raised, oil painted features, painted limbs, sateen covered body. First made by Martha J. Chase of Pawtucket, Rhode Island, in the 1890s. Mrs. Chase founded her doll making firm (M. J. Chase Co., Inc.) at Pawtucket and her stockinet dolls were made until 1935. In addition to her regular line of dolls, she produced a variety of portrait and character dolls which are considered rare.

Among the most appealing of Louis Amberg's American-made composition dolls was *Mibs* which appeared on the market in 1921. This little character was a Phyllis May doll designed by Hazel Drukker and came with painted features, molded hair, a cork-stuffed body and a lace trimmed white lawn frock. Attached to the latter was a tag which read: " 'Please love me', I'm Mibs."

In 1919, a well made and, for that time, expensive cloth doll was brought

out by the L. R. Kampes Studio of Atlantic City, New Jersey. Its molded mask face had hand-painted features and, instead of the usual wig, real hair was sewn directly to the head in circular rows. Dolls were made to order to resemble their new little owners as to coloring and hair style and they could also be returned to the studio should they need to be repaired or refinished. New outfits for the dolls were designed each spring and fall.

During this period, when German-made bisque dolls were unavailable, several United States firms made dolls, doll heads and/or parts of metal. In 1915, an interesting metal-headed baby, in squeeze toy form, was manufactured by the Art Metal Works of Newark, New Jersey, under the patent of Louis V. Aronson of the same city.

From 1918 to 1921, the Giebeler-Falk Corporation of New York made

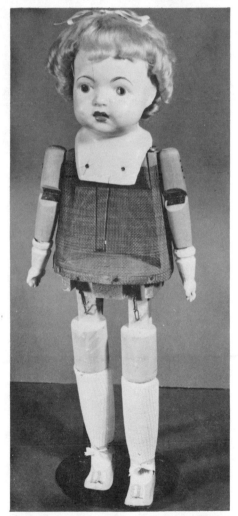

Illustration 50. 28in (71.1cm) hand-propelled walking doll *Dolly Walker;* patented in 1917 by ventriloquist Harry H. Coleman in both Great Britain and the United States; made in three sizes by the Wood Toy Company of New York; composition head, mohair wig; painted features; wooden frame torso is covered with wire mesh. *Eloise M. Thomas Collection.* (On exhibition at Yesteryear's Museum, Sandwich, Massachusetts.)

143

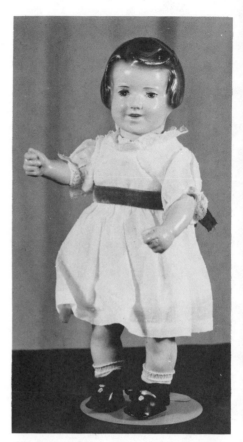

Illustration 52. 13½in (34.3cm) light-weight all-composition spring-jointed doll; one of a variety of artistic dolls by Jessie McCutcheon Raleigh of Chicago, Illinois, which came in three sizes; distributed, from 1916 to 1920, by Butler Brothers of New York; brown hair with blue barrette; painted features including eyes; smiling open/closed mouth showing four upper teeth. *Pearl D. Morley Collection.*

a doll with head, hands and feet of aluminum on a ball-jointed, elastic-strung body of wood. The well-painted head had metal sleep eyes, an open/closed mouth with painted-in teeth and a human hair wig. It resembled, in mold and construction, the familiar bisque-headed dolls that had earlier been imported from Germany.

Attempts to fill the bisque doll hiatus were made by a few American firms. Lenox, Inc., of Trenton, New Jersey, made a few experimental bisque-headed dolls for EFFanBEE (Fleischaker & Baum) which bear the names of both companies. The Paul Revere Pottery of Boston, Massachusetts, produced all-bisque dolls as well as dolls whose bisque socket heads, with porcelain sleep eyes, were mounted on elastic-strung bodies. Marked "P.R.P.," these dolls were rather inferior and the venture in the end was not successful.

However, the output of bisque dolls by the Fulper Pottery Company of Flemington, New Jersey, was well received and quite substantial. They made the familiar all-bisque *Kewpie* by Rose O'Neill as well as bisque-headed babies and children. All bear the Fulper name.

In 1921, David Weiner of New York obtained a patent for a doll's

head with a threaded neck plug which allowed the head to be screwed into the shoulders of the doll's body. Under this patent, Change-O-Doll Company of New York made unbreakable dolls' heads that came boxed with a single body. The heads were interchangeable, represented various characters and nationalities and numbered from three to 12. In 1924, the *Famlee Doll,* with detachable heads, was introduced to the market and was handled by the New York firms of Berg Brothers, Inc., and the Berwick Doll Company.

Although some celluloid dolls were produced in the United States, by far the greater number were manufactured in Germany. In 1880, the Celluloid Novelty Co. of Newark, New Jersey, was making celluloid dolls under patents 235,033 and 237,599 granted to William B. Carpenter and M. C. Lefferts. The first named patent, (235,933) granted on December 28, 1880, was for a method of coloring hairlines of doll faces as well

Illustration 53. 20in (50.8cm) American-made *Victory Doll;* made by Louis Amberg & Son of New York; composition head, mohair wig applied over unpainted molded hair; metal sleep eyes; open mouth with teeth; jointed body; head marked: "L.A.&S'//50;" shoulders marked: "Amberg's Victory Doll//50;" circa 1918.

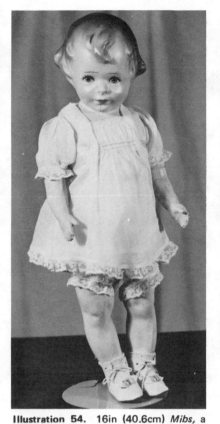

Illustration 54. 16in (40.6cm) *Mibs,* a character doll considered to be one of the most appealing of American composition dolls; designed by Hazel Drukker; composition head, molded hair; painted features; cork-stuffed cloth body; composition limbs; wears lace trimmed white lawn frock. A ribbon which came with doll is printed: " 'Please love me', I'm Mibs." *Pearl D. Morley Collection.*

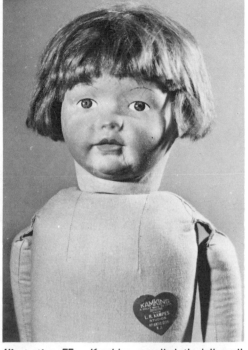

Illustration 55. *Kamkins,* an all-cloth doll, well made and expensive, brought out by the L. R. Kampes Studio of Atlantic City, New Jersey, in 1919. Made on order to resemble their new little owners, they could be returned to the studio for repair, and, in the spring and fall, newly designed outfits could also be purchased. *Ruth E. Whittier Collection.*

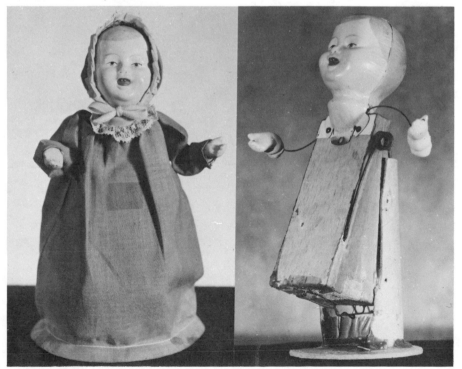

Illustration 56. 9¼in (23.6cm) painted metal head baby attached to wooden bellows which, when pressed, cry: "Mama/Papa;" made by the Art Metal Works of Newark, New Jersey; wears original blue cotton dress and bonnet; label attached to dress reads: "Fully patented//Mama Doll//I talk!!//Squeeze me Easy//Made in America//Cop.1915 by Louis V. Aronson."

as giving the material a flesh-like appearance. Fine lines were cut into the celluloid with a sharp knife and coloring matter worked into the incisions to form eyebrows, lashes and other features. The natural appearance was achieved by rubbing the glossy surface of the entire face with an abrasive (pumice). Celluloid-headed dolls produced under this patent *may* be the rare, swivel-necked, French-type ladies with their glass eyes, incised and colored eyebrows and lashes and mohair wigs. They are unmarked.

In the early 1920s, Louis Sametz of New York City, toy importer, also made celluloid dolls using an Indian head as a trademark in addition to his Rose O'Neill *Kewpies* which were marked: "O'Neill."

The Parson-Jackson Company of Cleveland, Ohio, in 1910, produced a baby of a celluloid-like material advertised as Biskolene. The company's name and trademark, a stork, are carried on the head and shoulders of the doll. Features, including the hair, are painted. The typical baby body is steel-spring jointed and, being watertight, will float.

During this period, Marks Brothers Company of Boston manufactured as well as imported celluloid-headed dolls. His American-made dolls have heads marked, within a shield: "Made in U.S.A.//Marks Brothers Co. Boston."

The Seamless Toy Corporation of New York was in business from 1918 to 1920. Among their production was *Pretty Polly,* a celluloid baby doll with "bisque finish."

By 1922, German-made dolls returned to the American market. One of the first to be introduced in this postwar period was the popular all-bisque and/or bisque-headed *Bye-Lo* baby designed by American artist, Grace Storey Putnam. Manufactured by several German firms, it was distributed by George Borgfelt & Company of New York who advertised, in 1925, that it was for sale in all leading department stores in seven sizes from 9in (22.9cm) to 20in (50.8cm). Despite its imitators, the Putnam baby still remains uppermost in the minds of doll collectors.

The 1930s saw the demise of the German bisque dolls. They were supplanted by the unbreakable composition and plastic dolls which were manufactured in great quantities by the burgeoning doll industry in the United States. The day of the artistically made dolls of finer materials was over. Plastic, mass-produced dolls have completely taken over today's

Illustration 57. 25in (63.5cm) doll; made by Giebeler-Falk Doll Corporation of New York from 1918 to 1921; head, hands and feet of painted aluminum on ball-jointed elastic-strung wooden body; human hair wig; metal sleep eyes; open/closed mouth with painted-in teeth; marked on head: "G (within star)//22//U.S. PAT."

Illustration 58. 14in (35.6cm) doll; made by the Paul Revere Pottery of Boston, Massachusetts, during the World War I period; bisque head, mohair wig; blue sleep eyes, rather poorly painted eyebrows; open mouth with teeth; jointed composition body; marked: "P.R.P.//No.2."

Illustration 59. A swivel-necked, celluloid doll head with *incised* and colored eyebrows and lashes; unmarked. Although not proven, it may have been made by the Celluloid Novelty Company of Newark, New Jersey, under the December 28, 1880, patent granted to William B. Carpenter for this method of coloring hairlines on dolls.

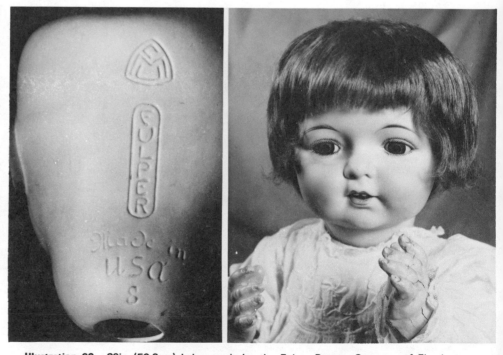

market. Time will tell whether these dolls will become the cherished heirlooms of tomorrow as have their predecessors of earlier years.

Illustration 60. 20in (50.8cm) baby; made by the Fulper Pottery Company of Flemington, New Jersey; bisque head, mohair wig; sleep eyes which were patented in 1918 by Samuel Marcus; open mouth with teeth; marked: "Fulper//Made in U.S.A.//8."

Illustration 61. *The Famlee Doll* in original box; made by the Berwick Doll Company of New York; patented April 12, 1921. Consists of one doll body and five interchangeable heads, each with its own costume. Heads differ as to race and nationality. Extra heads and costumes could be purchased separately from a list of 18.

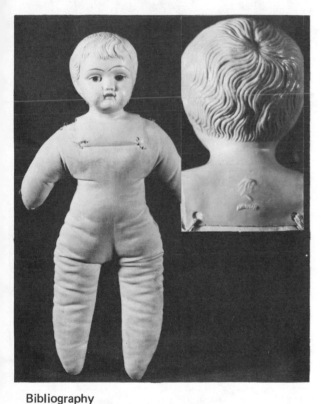

Illustration 62. 10in (25.4cm) doll; made by Louis Sametz of New York in the 1920s; celluloid head, molded hair; blue painted eyes; back of shoulders bears trademark of an Indian head over the word "America."

Illustration 63. Baby doll, with molded hair and painted features, made entirely of a lightweight celluloid-like material advertised as biskoline. It is jointed with steel springs, is watertight and will float. Manufactured by the Parsons-Jackson Company of Cleveland, Ohio, whose name and stork trademark are carried on head and shoulders.

Bibliography

The Doll Collectors of America, Inc. American Made Dolls & Figurines, 1940. Published by The Doll Collectors of America.

The Collector's Encyclopedia of Dolls 1968. By Dorothy S., Elizabeth A. and Evelyn J. Coleman. Published by Crown Publishers, New York.

The Handbooks of Collectible Dolls, Vol. 1, 2, 3. 1969-1974. By Madeline O. Merrill and Nellie W. Perkins. Published by Woodward & Miller, Melrose, Mass.

The Dolls of Yesterday. 1948. By Eleanor St. George. Published by Charles Scribner's Sons, New York.

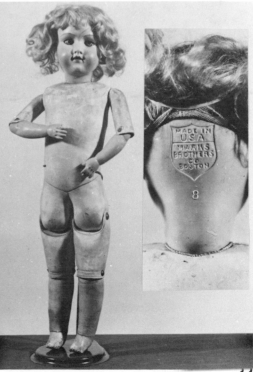

Illustration 64. 23in (58.4cm) doll; celluloid head is spring mounted on leather-covered body; mohair wig; sleep eyes; open mouth with teeth; arms, of leather and celluloid, are elastic-strung through wooden tube in shoulders; head marked within shield: "MADE IN//U.S.A.//MARKS //BROTHERS//CO//BOSTON."

American Clockwork Dolls and *Lady Figures*

by BLAIR WHITTON

LEFT: Illustration 1. The English *Autoperipatetikos* with a molded black hair parian head and molded blouse top. This photograph illustrates the narrow shaped cardboard body from the waist down. While it appears more natural than the wide flaring American version, this type is more susceptible to falling because of the rather heavy head and shoulders.

RIGHT: Illustration 2. The *Walking Doll With Hoops* is an attractive and rare clockwork toy. The double hoop unit with the power unit was patented by George Brown of Forrestville, Connecticut. As the doll, patented by Goodwin, walks forward, the painted tinplate boy holding the flag rocks and the bell rings.

Many of the more than 125 early clockwork toys patented before 1900 featured doll or lady figures that would be of interest to doll collectors. Some, such as Enoch Rice Morrison's *Autoperipatetikoes* and William Goodwin's *Automatic Walking Doll* pushing a carriage, have appeared in feature articles in various doll publications. Yet many collectors are not aware that the *Autoperipatetikoes* was made in two other forms or variations. The English form consists of a slender body, doing away with the wide hoop-like skirt found on the American version. Both the American and the English versions used an assortment of both china and parian heads. Unfortunately this tended to make the figure a bit top heavy (Illustration 1.) The American version was also found with a head formed of buckram or muslin that had been saturated with hot size and pressed

between two molds. When the pressed features were dry they were painted their natural colors. The second variation is the *Walking Zouave* which was patterned after the original French regiments originating in Algeria in 1831. Volunteer militias of Zouaves became popular during our Civil War. Goodwin's *Walking Doll* pushing a three wheel carriage was made with either a wooden or a tinplate body and came with or without a clockwork mechanism. A very rare variation of Goodwin's walking figure was that of a walking doll pulled by a pair of clockwork driven hoops. The mechanism hangs from a short axle connecting the two hoops, one being slightly larger than the other, causing the toy to run in a wide circle when activated. (Illustration 2.)

The child's riding velocipede was a popular toy back in the 1860s and 1870s and it was understandable that toy versions of them were manufactured. Arthur M. Allen, H. C. Alexander and Nathan S. Warner were early patentees of these toys which were made with dressed girl or boy figures. Later they were provided with monkey riders and still later in the 1890s with a figure of Uncle Sam.

Another popular toy was the *Girl Skipping Rope* patented by Joseph Hoffman of Waterbury, Connecticut. The young girl holds short horizontal jump rope handles which turn in her hands, while the skipping rope, made of fine wire, turns. The figure, in an upright position, moves up and down as the rope passes under her feet. The entire motion gives a natural illusion of a young girl skipping rope. (Illustration 3.)

Edward Ives of Bridgeport, Connecticut was probably the largest producer of clockwork toys in the United States. He used doll figures in many of his toys. The following is a list of some of these toys: *The Hand Velocipede* (Illustration 4.), the Warner swing with a girl figure, the *Doll Cradle,* the *Single Galloper With Lady Driver,* the *Hippodrome Chariot With Female Driver,* the *Churning Toy,* the *Drum Dancer, Daughter Of The Regiment* (Illustration 5.), the *Empress Eugenie,* the *Pendulum Dancer,* the *Old Nursemaid & Child* (Illustration 6.), *Old Aunt Chloe,* the *Washerwoman* and the *Old Woman Who Lived In A Shoe.*

During the same time period, Robert J. Clay of New York City patented a number of toys activated

148

Illustration 3. The *Automatic Rope Skipper* was patented by a Joseph Hoffman of Waterbury, Connecticut. Notice the German china head and lower legs and feet used on the figure.

Illustration 4. The *Girl On The Hand Velocipede* was patented by Ives in 1873. The figure has a molded composition head, a wood body, stamped tinplate hands and is colorfully dressed. The horse's head and the three wheels are cast iron.

by clockwork. He established the Automatic Toy Works in the early 1870s. It was Clay who patented the *Creeping Doll*. This was a dressed baby doll with a clockwork mechanism within its body, that, when wound, would move along the floor in a lifelike crawling or creeping action. A crying sound was also built into the mechanism.

Clay also developed the *Child In A Cradle* in 1874. A partial quote from the patent description follows: "This invention relates to the applica-

tion of a clock mechanism to a figure representing a child in a reclining position in a cradle. The invention consists in the combination of the clock mechanism with the body, head and limbs of the figure, in such a manner as to give a rising and lowering motion to the body and arms and a reciprocating rotary motion to the head."

Clay's *Mechanical Sewing Machine Girl* consisted of a dressed china head doll seated at a cabinet sewing machine. When the clockwork is

Illustration 5. *Daughter Of The Regiment* is a variation of the Ives' *Drum Dancer*. A jointed wooden doll activated by a clockwork mechanism concealed in the tinplate drum base. The other variations, all with the same drum base but with different figures, were titled *Colored Recruit*, *Veteran of 76* and *Drummer Boy*.

activated, her foot pumps the treadle and the machine starts to sew. The figure bends forward from the waist, puts the material in position, then straightens up. These movements are repeated again and again. (Illustration 7.)

The *Woman's Rights Advocate* depicts a black woman standing behind a podium, delivering a speech. When wound she turns her head from side to side, bends forward at the waist, straightens up and brings her right hand down, striking the podium, emphasizing a strong point in her speech. It is possible that this toy figure represents Sojourner Truth who lectured against slavery and for equality for women during the period the toy was made.

Clay obtained the patent rights for the *Grandmother Rocking The Cradle* in 1878. Very few examples of this great toy exists today. The toy is made up of an elderly lady rocking and fanning a baby in a cradle. Her head moves up and down, her right arm moves with the fan while her left arm extends to the cradle to give it a rocking motion.

149

Illustration 7. Robert Clay's mechanical *Sewing Machine Girl* gives a very realistic performance of a dressmaker working at a sewing machine.

Illustration 6. The *Old Nursemaid & Child*. This early rare version was manufactured by the Excelsior Toy Company of New York City.

Illustration 9. Jerome Secor's *Mechanical Piano Player* has a sectional cast iron body shell that contains the clockwork. The placement of the arms extending from the hips rather than the shoulders and the lack of legs and feet are two of its unusual features that are covered up when the figure is dressed.

Illustration 8. Clay's Automatic Toy Works obtained the patent rights for the *Grandmother Rocking The Cradle*. The grandmother figure has three distinct movements.

All are mounted on a varnished wood box base that contains the clockwork mechanism. (Illustration 8.)

Jerome B. Secor of Bridgeport was another active toy producer in the period between 1875 and 1885. His *Mechanical Piano Player* was an outstanding clockwork toy. The early models had a lady figure, seated at a piano, that had a French bisque head with a flanged neck and a real hair wig. Later models had a similar looking head cast in white metal with painted features and a hair wig. When activated, the head moved from side to side while the hands glided over the keyboard in time with the music from the music box inside the piano. (Illustration 9.)

Elie Martin of Paris invented a swimming doll that he patented both in France and in the United States.

Illustration 10. This *Swimming Doll* was patented in the United States by Elie Martin of Paris, France. It floats on water and when activated moves forward with a breast stroke.

This doll was manufactured in three sizes by Charles Bertran in Paris from 1878 on. A very rare variation of this swimming doll is one that is mounted on wheels and moves along the floor in a swimming motion. (Illustration 10.)

These toys with doll figures, along with others and numerous clockwork toys, are pictured and described in detail in a new book called *American Clockwork Toys 1862-1900.* The book has 224 pages of clockwork toy information, 153 black and white photographs, patent drawings and pages from manufacturers catalogs and 12 color plates of the rare and unusual. It presents factual information in chronological order, of the toys, the people who invented them and the companies that manufactured them.

Modern "Mama Doll" Patents Validated

Reprinted from the November 1924 issue of *Novelty News.*

Through a decision recently rendered in Philadelphia by the Circuit Court for the Third District of the United States, Louis V. Aronson, President of the Art Metal Works of Newark, N.J., has had validated his patents for the modern "mama doll."

The decision, which was unanimous, was rendered by Judges Davis, Woolley and Buffington. It was in an infringement suit brought against Michael Rabb and Toy Devices, Inc.

"To obtain simplicity is the highest trait of genius," says the court in its decision, thus paying a real tribute to the inventor. In its findings the court refers to the making of the "mama doll" as an art and says this art "remained practically in the old complicated condition from 1890 until Mr. Aronson's invention of 1915."

The decision goes somewhat minutely into mechanical technicalities, referring to the "crank arms, pinions, roller shafts, bearing, rods, handles, links, levers, pivots and springs" which went into the anatomy of this type of dolls under the old system of manufacture, and says that Mr. Aronson's invention changed these "complicated devices into a simple one less likely to get out of order and less expensive, but which accomplished the same results in a new and more practical manner."

As an evidence of the commercial importance of the decision, and also of the alertness of the average American child to the superior qualifications of the doll that cries out "Mama!" "Mama!" just as baby does, it is stated that about 5,000,000 of these dolls are sold in this country every year. This is saying nothing of the big foreign demand.

(This reprint appeared in the March 1975 *Doll Reader.*®)

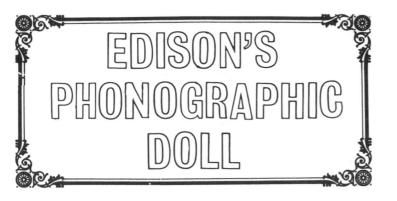

EDISON'S PHONOGRAPHIC DOLL

Reprinted from the April 26, 1890 issue of *Scientific American*.

Ed. Note: This is a most interesting reprint from the April 26, 1890 issue of *Scientific American*. The cover picture of this issue is reproduced along with the article. Top left shows a dressed doll, top middle shows a worker recording what the doll says, top right shows an undressed doll with mechanism, bottom right shows the actual talking mechanism of the doll, bottom left shows the boxing of the finished dolls. Below is the text that accompanied the cover picture about the manufacture of the fabulous ''talking doll.''

The new ''talking doll industry,'' established upon the basis of the Edison phonograph, has reached such proportions as to entitle it to more than a passing notice. At Orange, N.J., within a short walk of the world-renowned laboratory of Edison, are located a number of buildings occupying a ground space of many acres, in which over 500 people are engaged in the manufacture of the phonograph in its two principal forms, one of which is the commercial instrument repeatedly described in our columns, the other the phonographic doll, which we now present to our readers for the first time. This interesting toy forms an attractive object at the Exhibition of the Wonders of Electricity now in progress at the Lenox Lyceum, in this city.

As near as we can judge from a tour of the works, about one-half of the plant is devoted to the doll industry. Necessarily much of the mechanism of the doll is made in the regular phonograph works; but the adjustments, the manufacture of the record cylinders which determine the story which the doll shall tell, as well as the packing and shipping, are all conducted in an extensive building exclusively devoted to the manufacture of talking dolls.

The finished doll, shown in the upper left hand figure of our engraving, has the same appearance as other dolls; but its body is made of tin, and the interior thereof is filled with mechanism very much like that of the commercial phonograph, but of course much more simple and inexpensive. The cylinder of the phonograph of the talking doll is mounted on a sleeve which slides upon the shaft, the sleeve being screw-threaded so as to cause the cylinder to move lengthwise of the shaft. A key is provided by which the cylinder may be thrown out of engagement with the segmental nut, and a spiral spring is provided for returning the cylinder to the point of starting. The cylinder carries a ring of wax-like material, upon which is recorded the speech or song to be repeated by the doll. Upon the same shaft with the record cylinder there is a large pulley which carries a belt for driving the flywheel shaft at the lower part of the phonographic apparatus. The key is fitted to the main shaft, by which the photographic cylinder is rotated, and the flywheel tends to maintain a uniform speed.

Above the record cylinder is arranged a diaphragm, such as is used in the regular phonograph, carrying a reproducing stylus, which is mounted on a lever in the same manner as the regular phonograph. The funnel at the top of the phonographic apparatus opens underneath the breast of the doll, which is perforated to permit the sound to escape. By the simple operation of turning the crank any child can make the doll say ''Mary had a little lamb,'' ''Jack and Jill,'' or whatever it was, so to speak, taught to say in the phonograph factory.

In passing through the works it is noticeable that order and system reign in every department. Everything is done upon the American, or ''piece,'' system. The tools and machinery here used are the finest procurable. Every piece without regard to its size or importance is carefully inspected by aid of standard gauges, so that when the parts are brought together, no additional work required to cause them to act properly.

The works of the doll are to some extent adjustable, and any adjustment necessary is effected in an extensive department in which the little phonographs are received from the assembling rooms. Here they receive the finishing touches, and are passed on to another room where they are placed in the bodies of the dolls. From this department the finished dolls pass on to the packing room, where they are carefully stored away in boxes having on their labels the name of the story the doll is able to repeat. This department is illustrated by the lower left hand figure of our engraving. The central figure shows the manner of preparing the wax-like records for the phonographic dolls. They are placed upon an instrument very much like an ordinary phonograph, and in the mouth of which a girl speaks the words to be repeated by the doll. A large number of these girls are continually doing this work. Each one has a stall to herself, and the jangle produced by a number of girls simultaneously repeating ''Mary had a little lamb,'' ''Jack and Jill,'' ''Little Bo-peep,'' and other interesting stories is beyond description. These sounds united with the sounds of the phonographs themselves when reproducing the stories make a veritable pandemonium.

The manufacture of this interesting toy calls into requisition the skill of mechanics in almost every branch, and it has necessitated the construction of new tools which are interesting of themselves. Mr. Batchelor, engineer of the Edison laboratory and works, and Mr. English, manager of the phonograph works, are continually devising means for facilitating the manufacture of these interesting toys. The factory has at present a capacity for making about 500 talking dolls a day.

From the June 1975 Doll Reader.®

THE MANUFACTURE OF EDISON'S TALKING DOLL.—[See page 263.]

The Chase Doll:
An American Classic

by VYRLIN BRUCE

Illustration 1. On most play dolls the brim said "STOCKINET DOLL" instead of "HOSPITAL DOLL."

Illustration 2. *Back row, left to right:* 12in (30.5cm) Chase girl, purchased from the family of the original owner and dressed in original clothes. Construction is the same as dolls made in the 1890s. This one was probably made between 1904 and 1910. She has white lace-edged drawers with drawstring waist. Petticoat is white cotton, lace-edged with waistband fastened with button and buttonhole. Socks are white cotton with pink stripe at top and shaped heel and toe. She came with one original shoe and dark brown leather with ribbon tie and metal buckle with leather "bow." Her dress is of pink and white checked cotton, hand-finished with tucks, lace trim and buttons and buttonholes at back closing. Chase trademark on left upper leg.
17in (43.2cm) Chase girl purchased from the daughter of the original owner. There is much wear to both head and body of this doll. She is dressed in the same manner as the 12in (30.5cm) girl except for dropped waist with belt loops and sash. Chase trademark on upper left leg.
12in (30.5cm) Chase boy, purchased along with the 12in (30.5cm) girl and same construction. He is dressed in a cotton knit union suit with ribbon edging around neck. According to one source, union suits did not appear on dolls until 1904. He has long cotton knit stockings and a rose-colored cotton two-piece suit with white trim and belt in the so-called Russian style. His shoes are beautifully-made leather two-strap sandals with two tiny buckle fasteners and cut-out design on toes. No trademark.
18in (45.7cm) Chase boy, dressed in a contemporary romper which actually belongs to another Chase doll. No trademark.
Front row, left to right: 13in (33.0cm) Chase baby in old but not original clothes. She was found in poor condition and has had restoration to both head and body but still retains her Chase trademark stamp. Her eyes are brown.
13in (33.0cm) Chase baby, well dressed in what appears to be original clothes, but homemade. She has no panties but a cotton slip, a hand-tucked white lawn dress with lace trim and a lovely pink wool coat and bonnet. This is trimmed with satin stitch and ribbon. Shoes and socks are not old. Chase trademark is on upper left leg.

Martha Chase of Pawtuckett, Rhode Island, who designed and made the Chase dolls, was born in 1851. She was the daughter of a physician, Dr. James L. Wheaton; when she married, it was to another physician, Dr. Julian A. Chase. She eventually made a very important contribution to the medical field due to this double association.

As a child, she owned and played with an Izannah Walker doll; when her own daughters were young, Mrs. Chase made dolls for them suggested by her own Walker doll. However, her dolls were more natural-looking and easier for a child to carry about. The dolls were correctly jointed at hips, knees, elbows and shoulders; the feet were shaped with a flat sole and natural-looking toes; the hands were cupped with each finger individually fashioned and a separately applied thumb. The ears were well defined and were also applied separately.

After much experimenting, Mrs. Chase perfected a head that satisfied her, with a childish, lifelike face covered with the same kind of stockinet cloth that was stretched over the underbody. The construction was quite intricate and painstaking. The head, which consisted of two pieces - the face and the back - was joined by a stitch similar to that used on baseballs. Like the body, it was stuffed tightly with cotton. The head, shoulder plate, arms and legs were finished with flesh tone waterproof oil paint. The face, which was very solid, with meticulously contoured features, was painted, by hand, in natural tones. The hair was also painted with a textured short bob, and as far as I know, never in the history of the Chase doll was a wig ever used. The early dolls always had a short bob and only the clothing denoted the sex. Later, dolls had either boy or girl style painted hair.

The earliest dolls had pink or tan sateen bodies; later bodies were heavy white cotton cloth, and in 1910, dolls were advertised that could be washed in warm water - which suggests that by this time they were covered with stockinet and painted all over with waterproof paint. Still later, the dolls were made without elbow and knee joints (probably in the 1920s). Many of these later dolls had a molded "Dutch-cut" hair style and are much sought after by collectors because of their rarity.

Changes in the dolls were made after Mrs. Chase was persuaded to open a factory and manufacture them commercially. Late in the 1880s, Mrs. Chase took one of her larger dolls to a department store in Boston (Jordan Marsh) to have it fitted for shoes and the buyer convinced her to start manufacturing them. In 1891 the Chase family opened a factory and until Mrs. Chase's death in 1925, toy dolls were made and sold around the world. They have become museum pieces and collectors' finds. They were made in sizes from 9in (22.9cm) to life-size, portraying mostly babies and children. Baby dolls had fatter faces and bodies and slightly different eyes from those of the child dolls. There were also a few made in 7in

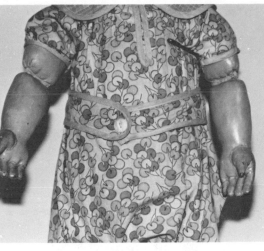

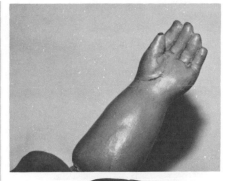

Illustration 3. 12in (30.5cm) Chase boy showing body construction with stitched joints at elbows and knees and early sateen body covering. Thumbs and ears are well formed and separately applied. All parts except sateen covered area were painted with waterproof enamel paint. By 1910 all parts, including torso were covered with stockinet and painted with oil paints so that doll was totally waterproofed.

Illustration 5. Detail of separately applied ears on early Chase dolls.

dolls was designed by Mrs. Gretchen Murray. Suits and dresses as well as underclothing were beautifully made in the same manner as children's clothing of the day. Socks and stockings had fitted heels and toes instead of the usual tubular kind found on most dolls. Shoes were made of leather and constructed like children's shoes with inner and outer soles and tiny buckles and buttons for fastenings. Buttonholes on dresses and suits were handmade and closed with tiny pearl buttons in most cases. The clothes were contemporary in style, usually of cotton or wool, and represented

play or school clothes. Most were simple - not trimmed with ruffles and flounces as were so many imported dolls that were sold at the time. However, a child-size boy doll is

(17.8cm) and 8in (20.3cm) sizes, but these are very difficult to find today.

In 1921, the Chase factory advertised characters from *Alice in Wonderland*, including Alice, Tweedledee and Tweedledum, the Mad-Hatter, the Duchess and the Frog-Footman; characters from books of Joel Chandler Harris, including Mammy Nurse and two Pickaninnies (color plate C9 in *The Collector's Encyclopedia of Dolls* by the Colemans); also George Washington. The characters from Dickens, Mrs. Gamp, Little Nell and others were probably made about this same time, and it is believed that Mrs. Chase was the first doll maker to create dolls that portrayed characters in books. A descendant of Mrs. Chase states she may have developed all these character dolls at an earlier date - perhaps as early as 1905.

The excellent condition in which most of these toy dolls are found today speaks well of the careful workmanship and sound construction used in their manufacture. The clothing and shoes were all made by local people, probably on a piece-work basis. Special clothing for the Chase

Illustration 6. *Back row, left to right:* 17in (43.2cm) early Chase doll with jointed elbows and knees; tan sateen covered body; Chase trademark on upper left leg; not in original clothes. 20in (50.8cm) early Chase doll with jointed elbows and knees; tan sateen covered body; Chase trademark stamped on upper left leg; old but not original romper. 16in (40.6cm) early 1930s Chase girl; all surfaces, including torso, painted with oil paint; no joints at elbows or knees; molded side-parted hair and hand-painted features; hand construction still the same as older dolls; old but not original clothes. *Front row, left to right:* 16in (40.6cm) early Chase doll similar to the above early dolls; romper is contemporary to doll but homemade of pink checked cotton with narrow white braid trim; doll may be meant to be a baby as the face is rounder and broader. 13in (33.0cm) Chase baby made for UFDC Region 14 Conference, May 1977; hard vinyl head; five-piece vinyl-covered stuffed body; handmade white cotton baby clothes by The New London (Connecticut) Doll Club.

Illustration 7. 12in (30.5cm) Chase boy in his knit union suit which is believed to be original.

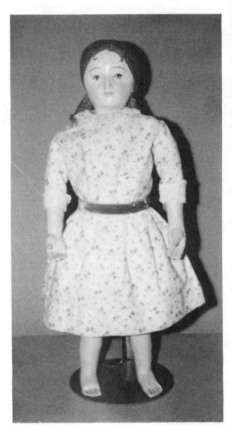

Illustration 8. 15in (38.1cm) *Little Nell* Chase character doll; body design is the same as the early babies and children with painted head, shoulder plate, arms and legs; torso, including upper arms and tops of thigh, is sateen covered; brown hair; blue eyes; has extra joints at elbows and knees; trademark stamp is on sateen of upper left leg; dress is a cream challis print with small flowers and green sash and came with the doll, is contemporary, but may not be original: 1910 to 1920, but may have been designed as early as 1905. *Regina A. Steele Collection.*

pictured in *Spinning Wheel's Complete Book of Dolls* (p. 176) in his "Sunday best:" high button shoes, a white shirt with Peter Pan collar, and a black velvet suit!

In 1909, R. H. Macy and Company advertised Chase Stockinet Dolls in sizes 16in (40.6cm), 17in (43.2cm), 21in (53.3cm) and 24in (61.0cm); prices ranged from $2.49 to $4.96. These dolls were priced higher than many of the imported bisque-head dolls sold at the time.

Apparently, a patent to cover the construction of the toy dolls was never applied for, although all dolls carried the Chase trademark (often worn off), either on the thigh or under the arm. An additional sewn-on label read: "The Chase Stockinet Doll.// Made of stockinet and cloth.// Stuffed with cotton.// Made by hand.// Painted by hand.// Made by especially trained workers.//"

Eventually, Mrs. Chase's rag doll grew up to take part in the adult world of education. In 1911, she made up a life-size adult doll, the result of an inquiry by Miss Lauder Sutherland, an instructor of nursing in the Hartford (Connecticut) Hospital, for use in nurses' training. *The Chase Hospital Baby,* developed from the original play doll, was first marketed in 1913. These hospital dolls were completely waterproof, had internal containers for practicing nursing procedures, and could be bathed and handled like human patients. They are still being used in nurses' training schools today

and as basic equipment by the American Red Cross, various state health departments, and home economics classes in schools.

Several years ago, when I took nurses' training for my L.P.N. license and was introduced to a dummy called "Mrs. Chase," no one seemed to know why this was her name. It was not until a few years ago, when I became interested in doll collecting and, in particular, Chase doll collecting, that I realized the significance of the name.

According to one source, when Martha Chase died in 1925, the family discontinued making Chase play dolls, but the hospital training dolls were manufactured for many years. However, I have recently found evidence that play dolls were made almost continuously up until today. After the molded "Dutch-cut" hair style in the 1920s, a molded side-parted hair style was made in the early 1930s. These were still all hand-made and hand-painted but minus the elbow and knee joints and separately applied ears. The hand construction remained the same and is one of the easiest characteristics to recognize.

Since the late 1930s or early 1940s, up until today, the Chase factory makes a small play doll that is similar in appearance and construction to the original Chase doll, but made with a hard vinyl head and covered with vinyl fabric. For me, much of the charm has been lost. There is nothing more exciting than finding an old Chase child or baby with its sweet expression and lovely hand-painted face. Best of all is when one is found with its original handmade clothing and tiny leather shoes. Once you learn to recognize the Chase doll, you will find it is not necessary to have the name stamped on it - the characteristics are unmistakable.

In Time For Christmas 1900

BY ALMA WOLFE

"Christmas is Coming." This ad caption from *The Cosmopolitan*, November, 1900, heralded the news that COOK'S Flaked Rice Company of New York City had stocked thousands of "Miss Flaked Rice" dolls for "the children's pleasure" on that joyous day, the first Christmas of the twentieth century.

The rice company maintained that "there is nothing like a rag doll for making a child happy. The finest wax or china baby Paris ever produced will not be treasured like a clumsy, roly-poly doll that can be thrown around and abused, and loved all day long,

and will only cease to smile when her face is so dirty that the smile is blotted out." Ah, yes, remember the beloved rag doll of your childhood.

And the price was also right—ten cents in stamps and the coupon found in a package of COOK'S Flaked Rice. The 24in. (60.96cm) tall "Miss Flaked Rice" was "printed in natural colors on strong muslin." She was to be cut out and sewn at home and then "stuffed with three cents' worth of

cotton." Her total cost was less than one dollar. In 1978, the stuffing alone would cost more than did the package of rice, doll and cotton in 1900.

The ad not only told the readers how to procure a delightful doll, but also enticed them to enjoy a "delicious and tempting...perfect food...simply the best rice, sterilized and steam cooked." A recipe book was included with every package "telling" the homemaker how to serve the rice "in countless different ways, for Breakfast, Luncheon and Dinner."

Christmas was coming. Happy were the little people of that era whose mothers took advantage of this offer. Fortunate are today's collectors who can count "Miss Flaked Rice" among their treasured dolls.

*The photo of "Miss Flaked Rice" was "lifted" from the ad via the expertise of photographer, James W. Giokas.

THE COSMOPOLITAN.

Christmas is Coming.

THE children's pleasure must be planned for. There is nothing like a rag doll for making a child happy. The finest wax or china baby Paris ever produced will not be treasured like a clumsy, roly-poly doll that can be thrown around and abused, and loved all day long, and will only cease to smile when her face is so dirty that the smile is blotted out.

COOK'S Flaked Rice Co. has thousands of these dolls all ready to make Xmas happy for thousands of little people. They are the size of a small child (24 inches high), are printed in natural colors on strong muslin, and only need to be sewed up and stuffed with three cents' worth of cotton to look like this picture. One will be mailed to any address on receipt of the coupon contained in each package of COOK'S Flaked Rice, and ten cents in stamps.

Address COOK'S Flaked Rice Co., 1 Union Square, N. Y. City.

The rice is never sent by mail.

COOK'S Flaked Rice is a perfect food for every member of the family. Delicious and tempting, it may be prepared on the table in less than a minute. ABSOLUTELY NO COOKING.

Can be served in countless different ways, for Breakfast, Luncheon and Dinner. Is equally satisfactory as Breakfast cereal, entree and dessert. Is not a new food. Simply the best rice, sterilized and steam cooked. Book of tested receipts with every package.

You must buy a package of COOK'S Flaked Rice of your Grocer, and get the coupon. We will **not** supply the rice to consumer.

COOK'S FLAKED RICE CO., 1 Union Square, N. Y. City.

24 inches high.

Ad from *The Cosmopolitan*, November, 1900.

Right:
"Miss Flaked Rice" advertising doll.

Trademark of Art Fabric Mills

BY ALMA WOLFE

"Rag Doll FREE." A most enticing ad caption! And the photographic likeness of the doll was an eye-catching 8-1/2in. (21.6cm) tall in the ad on page 47 of the October 1905 issue of *The Ladies' Home Journal* (*Illustration 1*).

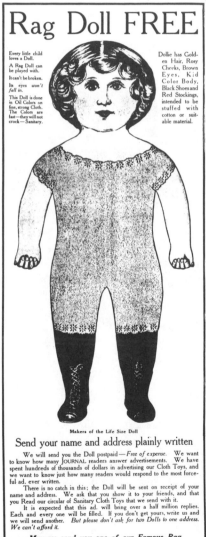

Illustration 1.

Surprisingly, this promotional doll offered by Art Fabric Mills of New

York could be obtained without peddling any type of merchandise or without purchasing a product. The ad specifically stated, "There is no catch in this; the Doll will be sent on receipt of your name and address."

Why was the firm offering the doll gratis? Art Fabric Mills stated that they wanted "to know how many *Journal* readers answer advertisements. We have spent hundreds of thousands of dollars in advertising our Cloth Toys, and we want to know just how many readers would respond to the most forceful ad ever written."

The manufacturers expected "over a half million replies," and promised to fill "each and every one." A circular describing their line of "Sanitary Cloth Toys" would be enclosed with each doll.

Also featured was a bonus offer—for 10 cents in stamps, the reader could obtain "a pair of Good Luck Kittens printed on durable cloth." The "most forceful ad" might also be termed a "bonanza ad."

Under the picture of the doll was the phrase "Makers of the Life Size Doll." Art Fabric Mills had used as their trademark, since March 1899, a doll figure, incorporating the words "Life Size." The doll they were offering "free of expense"......"with our Compliments" was a replica of their logo. The trademark was registered with the U.S. Patent Office as Patent No. 34,728, and was issued to Edgar Newell, president of the company. All dolls and toys produced by the Mills were marked with the patent date, "February 13, 1900" and "Art Fabric Mills."

The "Life Size Doll" was produced in two sizes. The larger doll was 36in. (91.4cm) tall; the smaller version was 20in. (50.8cm) tall. The height of the promotional doll was not mentioned—most likely, she was the 20in. (50.8cm) size.

"The Doll" or "Dollie" (as referred to in the ad) was "done in Oil Colors on fine, strong Cloth. The colors are fast—they will not crack—Sanitary." Her virtues were further subtly compared with the fragile elite of dolldom. Little girls could enjoy playing with her, for she could withstand many childhood adventures. She was unbreakable, and her eyes definitely would not "fall in."

Blonde hair encircled her round face. Her cheeks were rosy. Her eyes were brown. A pretty child. Her chemise was enhanced with cutwork. She wore black ankle-high laced boots and red stockings and a red bow in her hair. "Dollie's" wistful expression appeared to be pleading for a home and a dress, PLEASE (*Illustration 2*).

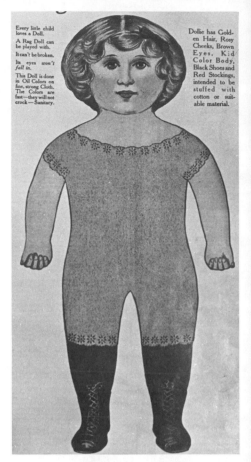

Illustration 2. Photograph by James Giokas.

This promotional doll represented a prolific and diversified line of dolls, animals and toys which were produced by Art Fabric Mills from 1899 to 1910. All of the "Sanitary Cloth Toys" were printed on fabric and were to be cut, sewn and stuffed at home. Easy-to-follow instructions were printed on each sheet.

Art Fabric dolls, animals and toys were offered as premiums by the Malted Cereal Company, 1904-1905. The dolls offered included the Famous Life Size Doll, Foxy Grandpa, Buster Brown and Tige, Punch and Judy, a Topsy doll and the Family of Dolls—mother, father, brother and sister in Continental costumes. The National Medicine Company also employed the Family of Dolls and the Life Size Doll as sales helpers.

In 1911, Selchow and Richter became the successor to Art Fabric Mills. According to the Coleman's *The Collector's Encyclopedia of Dolls*, this company had been the sole distributors of the dolls and toys manufactured by Art Fabric Mills.

Bibliography

Coleman, Dorothy, Elizabeth and Evelyn, *The Collector's Encyclopedia of Dolls.*

Hart, Luella, *Directory of United States Doll Trademarks 1888-1968.*

------"The Rag Doll Made in the United States," *Spinning Wheel Magazine,* July/August 1962.

Walker, Frances and Margaret Whitton, *Playthings By The Yard.*

From the June/July 1979 Doll Reader.®

COLLECTIBLE/MODERN

COMIC STRIP "PILLOW" DOLLS FROM THE 20'S PERIOD

BY MARGARET GRONINGER
Photographs by Jane Giberson

Pillow dolls — flat items with figures stamped or printed on them — are popular today in many forms, from familiar advertising characters like the Eskimo Pie boy or the Burger King to television personalities like Fonzie of "Happy Days." Such dolls were equally popular in the 1920's period, where they were generally of an oilcloth-like material (sometimes called "imitation leather") rather than of soft cloth, and often represented comic strip characters.

The largest set of such dolls appears to be that portraying members of "Gasoline Alley." To refresh the memory a bit, "Gasoline Alley" was a comic strip drawn for many years by Chicago Tribune cartoonist, Frank O. King. When the strip began in 1919, it centered around a group of small town men who met in an alley on Sunday mornings to talk about cars. Its main appeal then was to males, especially males who liked cars. The accent changed drastically on February 14, 1921, when pudgy Uncle Walt Wallet found an abandoned newborn infant boy on his doorstep. Being a decent chap, Uncle Walt adopted the baby, named him Skeezix, and, with the aid of his black cook Rachel, raised the child. Later Walt was assisted by Mrs. Phyllis Blossom, whom Walt married in June, 1924. All of which was calculated to win hundreds of female followers, and indeed did catapult the strip into the family interest ring. Thereafter, the action in "Gasoline Alley" was slow paced, down-to-earth and unashamedly sentimental (witness the Valentine's Day arrival of Skeezix, and Uncle Walt's traditional June wedding).

King, made wealthy by his comic art, died in 1969. "Gasoline Alley" continued in the hands of his assistants, who had assumed control when King more or less retired in 1959.

A whole series of "Gasoline Alley" dolls evolved from Frank O. King's comic strip. Some were trademarked as follows:

Nov. 27, 1922 — Skeezix
Mar. 10, 1923 — Uncle Walt
June 23, 1924 — Rachel
June 23, 1924 — Mrs. Blossom
June 23, 1924 — Puff

Of course, the dates mentioned above might not have to do with the *oilcloth* King dolls, as other types of "Gasoline Alley" figures existed, such as nodders. More conclusive are the U.S. Patent design drawings, which appeared as follows (dates given are those of filing):

Oct. 16, 1922 — Skeezix as a toddler
June 23, 1924 — Mrs. Blossom
June 15, 1925 — Jean
Jan. 30, 1926 — Skeezix as a young boy

All of the above can be verified as flat pillow dolls, since the drawings show them as such.

Illustration 3. Patent design: Skeezix as a young boy (1926).

Illustration 4. Patent design: Mrs. Blossom (1924).

Illustration 1. Skeezix, Walt, Jean and Skeezix.

Illustration 2. Toddler Skeezix in two sizes.

From the February/March 1980 Doll Reader.®

Toddler Skeezix, a blond topknotted lad in bright red baggy romper outfit, was available in at least two sizes, 10 in. (25.4 cm) and 11½ in. (29.2 cm). The larger one's bottom is stamped "Skeezix // Reg. U.S. Pat. Off. // Pat. Feb. 27, 1923;" the date on the smaller one examined is no longer clear, but is probably the same. From the patent drawings it is evident an older Skeezix child, no longer a toddler, must have been sold in doll form around 1926. He has long pants of a better fit, but the same distinguishing topknot. The Mrs. Blossom doll from 1924 is a svelte lady in outdoor attire, including a floor length coat, while Jean is a pert little girl about 13 in. (33 cm) tall, wearing a hat, a red coat and high button leggings. Uncle Walt is the last known member of the flat form clan (though a Rachel may well have existed, too); the plump patriarch of the group ranges a full 26 in. (66 cm) in height. Like the others examined, his clothes are printed on in a simple color scheme of red, black and yellow. All dolls are two-sided and of oilcloth.

Illustration 6. Orphan Annie, showing body construction.

Illustration 7. Freckles (left) and Orphan Annie.

Illustration 5. Small toddler Skeezix and Jean.

That the dolls covered a space of some years and that the series included Skeezix at several different stages of his life is not surprising, for investigation reveals "Gasoline Alley" was reputed to be the first comic strip in which its characters actually grew up. In fact, Frank King once admitted he hoped to see the family he created go on for many generations. They just about did! Skeezix eventually became a man, went off to war, got married and became a father himself. But by that time, interest in depicting "Gasoline Alley" characters in doll form had faded.

Other flat pillow dolls from the same period do exist, some depicting comic strip characters by artists other than King. Harold Gray's Little Orphan Annie, 15½ in. (39.4 cm) tall, is unusual in that extra arms and legs were attached to the basic flat form (and at an angle), giving the doll a little more dimension. Also, unlike the others surveyed, which have

their clothes printed on them, her blue cloth dress is removable.

(For the record, Little Orphan Annie was first conceived as a boy, Little Orphan Otto, but by the time Gray's strip appeared in print in 1924, Annie — the name taken from the James Whitcomb Riley poem — had triumphed. When Gray died in 1968, other hands took over the Annie strip, none successfully. Finally the Chicago Tribune / New York News Syndicate resorted to rerunning the earlier Annies. Earlier the subject of two movies and a radio show, Annie is still with us in the form of a popular theatrical production, called simply "Annie." And countless other Orphan Annie items, from Ovaltine mugs to many dolls in a variety of materials, have been offered over the years; cloth Annie dolls are on the market even today. But the latter are not the oilcloth type like the 1920's version.)

A more traditional kind of pillow doll is a 10½ in. (26.7 cm) lad of oilcloth whose flowery neck sash may remind many of Percy Crosby's Skippy. However, the jaunty lad with big orange shoes, short brown pants, striped socks, "blind" eyes and freckles is instead the hero of a strip called "Freckles and His Friends," a Merrill Blosser creation. Freckles first saw the light around 1915, stayed the same eight years of age for a long time (at least until 1927, which should help date this doll somewhat), though he eventually — and almost overnight — became a more adventurous 16 years old. Blosser's strip continued to be turned out by another artist after the originator semi-retired in the mid 1960's.

United States Patent drawings turn up one more flat pillow doll, this time of Herby, kid brother of the office boy

urchin, Smitty (oddly enough, no patent design for Smitty has surfaced). Cartoonist Walter Berndt of Brooklyn, New York, took out the patent for the Herby doll in 1926, four years after starting the segments starring Smitty (with Herby in tow), but four years before Herby got his own separate-but-equal strip. Smitty and Herby, parented by the Chicago Tribune/ New York News (after a brief fling at the New York World under the heading of

Illustration 8. Patent design: Herby (1926).

"Bill the Office Boy"), continued to lope along until Berndt's retirement in 1973.

Though Herby's material is not known, the rest of the dolls described in this article are of an oilcloth type fabric. Now, oilcloth dolls do not age well. If overheated, they become sticky; if bent, segments flake off. Consequently, most that have survived from the 1920's are no longer in mint condition; yet comic strip doll devotees cherish them anyway.

⇒ Boudoir Dolls ⇐

by MARGARET GRONINGER

Illustration 2. Early Victorian Lady, English doll, 1928.

We call them bed dolls today, but in their own era, the 1920s to 1930s period, they were known as boudoir dolls. These dolls differed greatly from other dolls of the period in that they were never intended for play by children, but were meant solely to decorate the *adult boudoir!*

In fact, boudoir dolls were almost art objects. Thus, they could be exaggerated in form (and many were). Legs might be overlong, hands tinier than normal or eyes over-painted. Bodies were not important. Faces were! Even more important was the costuming, which had to be exotic and fanciful. Emphasis was on the surface, the more surface the better.

Materials used for the dolls varied. Generally, the best dolls had pressed cloth faces, many with cloth bodies also (although the French imports often had composition limbs with cloth heads). The composition, shoulder headed versions were mostly cheaper dolls. Even there exceptions can be found, such as a composition headed lady with jewel-like stones imbedded around the neck.

Fashion and women's magazines loved boudoir dolls. Indeed, many of those publications heavily promoted the flashy figures. A 1926 *Good Housekeeping* displayed one vamp under the heading, "dolls with long dangling legs and arms in costumes reminiscent of the Louis periods in France are quite the vogue. This proud lady with powdered wig is dressed in lavendar silk and printed velvet; satin shoes with amusingly high heels; $11.50." Shown was a blonde lady with (in spite of the write up) contemporary flapper dress and eye makeup.

Earlier, in 1923, the *Ladies' Home Journal* devoted a full page to four elaborate dolls from Paris, 30in (76.2cm) to 34in (86.4cm) high, all with cotton-stuffed muslin bodies attached to heads of composition with a linen finish and painted features. One was a (male) Moor, in yellow taffeta attire (including turban); another was called *Butterfly,* and a third was supposed to represent actress Sarah Bernhardt. *Butterfly* had hair of white silk embroidery floss "sewed on crinoline, loops forming puffs." As might be expected, her gown was in a period style, complete

Illustration 1. Patent design by Charles E. Gibson, New York, 1922. *Drawing by author from patent design.*

with butterfly bows of lavender fringed taffeta on her long, full gown. The darker haired Sarah Bernhardt was in white satin adorned with white camellias. Now, none of these was called a boudoir doll, for the term was just evolving at that point; but they definitely were not playthings, and did fit the general description (decorative, exotic, elongated, adult).

If you did not want to buy a finished boudoir doll, many magazines were delighted to help you make one - - from kits. The December 1934 *Woman's Home Companion* pictured "demure Mademoiselle Jeanette," designed by Madame Lisa des Renaudes of Vienna. You could buy the doll in undressed form from the magazine for a mere $1.75; for an additional sum, stamped panne silk for the dress could be acquired, too. Jeanette had several other typical characteristics; her hairdo of braids looped over the ears was a popular one on such dolls, and her skirt could be used to hide pajamas during the day.

Other countries also had boudoir dolls. A 1928 *Illustrated London News* included a sketch of a "fancy doll," a Marie Antoinette shepherdess lady "daintily dressed in Sateen and Cretonne." Her height was about 30in (76.2cm). From the same year and the same magazine was an "Early Victori-

an Lady dressed with exquisite care, ready to adorn a luxurious sofa or cushion."

A 1929 American magazine offered not boudoir dolls but clothes for them. One was a kind of Civil War costume with "tight bodice, bouffant skirt, long pantalettes and wide-brimmed bonnet to match." The other outfit was a contemporary pajama (lounging) suit. Concluded the magazine, "The dolls should be dressed to match their owner's bedroom color scheme."

Not all magazine depictions of boudoir dolls were outright pitches to sell. Some were descriptions in passing,

Illustration 3. Patent design by Leonore Bubenheim, 1924. *Drawing by author from patent design.*

From the February/March 1981 Doll Reader.®

FRENCH CHOCOLATES, BONBONS AND FAVORS

NEW YORK *Louis Sherry* PARIS

Illustration 4. "Harper's Bazar, May 1925."

Illustration 5. Boudoir dolls in ethnic costume, 1923.

as in a 1923 *Harper's Bazar* ad for a woman's peasant-type blouse. The model just happened to be holding two large, overlong dolls in ethnic dress, kind of a new approach to boudoir dolls. Said the article, "The dolls sketched are actual models of peasants in native costume, quite the smartest dolls we have seen and much newer than the mournful Pierrot and decadent bad ladies who generally accompany him." Actually, Pierrot — the sad, always elegant, generally asexual clown in droopy white with

Illustration 6. *Mademoiselle Jeanette* from 1934.

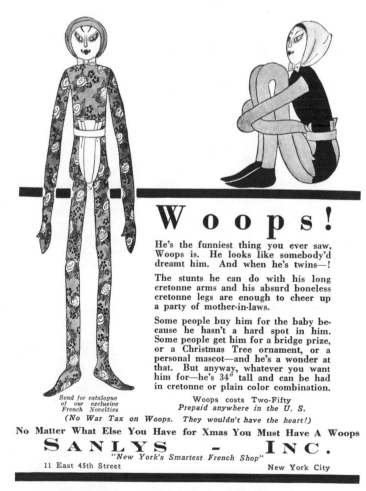

Woops!

He's the funniest thing you ever saw, Woops is. He looks like somebody'd dreamt him. And when he's twins—!

The stunts he can do with his long cretonne arms and his absurd boneless cretonne legs are enough to cheer up a party of mother-in-laws.

Some people buy him for the baby because he hasn't a hard spot in him. Some people get him for a bridge prize, or a Christmas Tree ornament, or a personal mascot—and he's a wonder at that. But anyway, whatever you want him for—he's 34" tall and can be had in cretonne or plain color combination.

Send for catalogue of our exclusive French Novelties

Woops costs Two-Fifty
Prepaid anywhere in the U. S.

(No War Tax on Woops. They wouldn't have the heart!)

No Matter What Else You Have for Xmas You Must Have A Woops

SANLYS - INC.

"New York's Smartest French Shop"

11 East 45th Street   New York City

Illustration 7. *Drawing by author from patent design.*

Illustration 8. Patterns for clothes for boudoir dolls, 1929.

Illustration 10. Patent design by Eugene Goldberger, 1926.

black accents — turned up himself in a 1923 *Ladies' Home Journal,* lolling beneath a lampshade of Pompadour printed taffeta. Perhaps this was the 24in (61.0cm) Pierrot by Lenci, perhaps not.

Some advertisements used boudoir dolls, too. The Louis Sherry candy concern ran a number of ads in the 1925 *Harper's Bazars* in which Lenci-like boudoir dolls draped themselves around boxes of candy. The ads are notable for another reason; famed artist Howard Chandler Christy painted them! Along the same line, a 1925 *Vogue* included a corset ad in which three modern women held or admired several boudoir dolls dressed as flappers.

Designers were busily patenting boudoir dolls during this period. Eugene Goldberger (Eegee) filed designs for two such dolls in 1926. Both were flappers, one in a short skirt and the other in natty lounging pajamas. Also in contemporary dress was a lady in a Scotch plaid golfer outfit, this doll patented by Leonore Bubenheim for Madame Lenore Art Doll. Her design, along with two others by the same woman (a winking clown and a lady sprite), was filed in 1924. Yet another boudoir doll was patented by Charles E. Gibson in

1922. His was a simpler type, probably intended to be dressed by its buyer. In fact, it was much like the Woops dolls, 34in (86.4cm) cretonne bodied creatures sold during the same period by Sanlys, "New York's Smartest French Shop."

Because boudoir dolls were not played with, finding one in good condition today is not an impossible task. Happy hunting!

Illustration 11. Boudoir dolls in corset ad, 1925.

Illustration 12. French doll shown by English magazine, 1928.

Mozart by Lenci

BY JOHN AXE

The Mozart is not a common doll from Lenci. Although the Lenci factory in Turin, Italy, was a commercial doll making firm, Lenci dolls were never manufactured in the ample quantities of many other doll makers. A Lenci doll is an "art doll." Lencis have always transcended being just playthings for children and today are considered among the most desirable of dolls that enter collections.

Wolfgang Amadeus Mozart was born in Vienna, Austria, in 1756. His father, Leopold Mozart, was a composer who encouraged Wolfgang's musical accomplishments. At the age of five the child was composing minuets and other pieces and was proficient on both the harpsichord and the violin. Mozart toured Europe in concert from 1762, at age six, until 1781, playing the pianoforte. During the winter of 1763-1764 he published his first compositions. In 1767 he composed his first German operetta and his first Italian opera. A list of the compositions and types of music that Mozart composed would comprise several pages. He wrote in all forms— Masses and other church music, vocal music, instrumental pieces, chamber music, sonatas, concertos, operas and symphonies. The most famous operas are "The Marriage of Figaro," "Don Giovanni" and "The Magic Flute;" the best symphonies are considered the last three—No. 39 in E flat, No. 40 in G minor and No. 41 in C. In spite of this wealth of production, Mozart died in poverty in Vienna on December 5, 1791 at 35 years of age. He was buried the next day in a ceremony attended only by the gravedigger.

The 14 in. (35.6cm) Lenci doll portrays Mozart as the child prodigy. The doll is fully-jointed of stiffened felt. The painted eyes are brown, with pale green shading underneath which gives him a rather alert expression. The blond mohair wig is intricately stitched to the scalp. The clothing, with the exception of the cotton neck ruffle, is all of felt. The flared waist coat is a pale green, lined in lavender. The breeches are lavender and so is the three-cornered hat under his left arm. Beneath the coat he wears a tan vest trimmed with flowers and six buttons. The shoes are the same shade of green as the jacket. The stockings are ribbed cotton.

Stitched to the back of the coat are two cardboard tags. The first reads: PRODVZIONE // ORIGINALE // LENCI (in script). The second reads: LENCI (in script) DI E. SCAVINI // TURIN (ITALY) // MADE IN ITALY // N MOZART is hand-written. The last two lines carry patent and date information.

Fortunately for lovers of Lencis, Dorothy S. Coleman has written *Lenci Dolls* (Hobby House Press, 1977). The name Coleman when associated with dolls means accuracy of research and thoroughness of presentation. Unfortunately, in the case of the doll shown here, it is not cited in the study, which makes dating difficult, although a 20 in. (50.8cm) version was in the 1925/6 Lenci Catalog. The former owner of Mozart purchased him "sometime around 1930." (This system of dating a doll is never reliable.) Mrs. Coleman reported on all Lenci dolls up to 1930. After that time company records are sketchy and catalogs are not available. According to Mrs. Coleman's research, the first cardboard tag is from 1923;

the other tag was used from 1922 to 1928. The clothing is stitched in place and the author will not remove it to search for button tags or stamped marks, which would be a further aid in dating.

It would be a shame to disturb the all-original condition of the doll to determine if he is from before 1930 or after that time. Wolfgang Amadeus Mozart was not an ordinary person. The Lenci Mozart is not a common doll.

Detail from the painting "Mozart Singing His Requiem" by Thomas W. Shields, 1882. The invalid composer is seated. Of the "Requiem," a Mass for the dead, Mozart said, "I well know I am writing this 'Requiem' for myself." It was uncompleted when he died.

The Rudolph Valentino Doll

by JOHN AXE

Illustration 1.

Rudolph Valentino has been dead for longer than the majority of people in the world today have been alive. Yet his name is still well-known in spite of the fact that his film career only lasted about seven years. Rudolph Valentino was the first great male sex symbol of American films. He was handsome and muscular and he usually essayed exotic roles in his films. He was elevated to major stardom in 1920 after having played bit parts in minor films for about two years. His screen roles always included a mandatory dressing or undressing scene during which women screamed, swooned or fainted. All of this seems rather corny and naive today but during the 1920s his was the first passionate lovemaking that most women had seen on the screen. There has only been one other sex symbol of the magnitude of Valentino. That was Elvis Presley. Neither was a very good actor, but it never mattered to their devoted fans.

For doll collectors there was never a commercially popular Rudolph Valentino doll. Lenci of Italy made a doll that resembled Valentino in his most famous role, *The Sheik,* released in 1921. This is a felt doll made in the traditional Lenci manner and it has an adult face and a body with slim proportions. The doll wears an Arab costume as Valentino did in the picture. This film also created a demand for Arab motifs in fashion and in interior design that lasted for years.

From the August/September 1980 Doll Reader.®

Another of Valentino's most popular pictures was *Blood and Sand* in 1922. The doll shown here wears a costume very similar to the one that he wore in this film in which he played a gypsy who became a bull fighter. This doll is also probably from the 1920s, and like the Lenci doll, did not carry tags that credited it to Valentino. Buyers knew who the dolls represented and the companies who produced the dolls were spared royalties. The doll in the accompanying illustrations is 22½ in. (57.2cm) tall and has a papier-mâché head with painted features and a black mohair wig under the gypsy bandana. The body is cloth with elongated limbs in the manner of the boudoir dolls of the 1920s. The clothing is very well made and includes a soft cotton shirt with tiny buttons, a black velvet vest trimmed with gold beads and black velvet trousers that have gold stenciling on them. The leather shoes have high heels. The doll is not marked. An identical doll has a wind-up music box that plays "Sonny Boy" inside the stomach area. This doll has an attached paper tag that reads GESTELZICH, which may be a company name, and tells that the doll was made in Germany. Rather than being an actual portrait of Valentino, these dolls capture the essence of his rather dreamy screen presence.

Illustration 2.

Rudolph Valentino was 25 years old in 1921 when he was chosen to play his first major role in *The Four Horsemen of the Apoclaypse,* the part that catapulted him to fame. He had arrived in New York from Italy in 1912, where as a teenager he worked as a taxi dancer and an exhibition dancer until the famous Russian actress Nazimova, whom he had met through mutual friends, helped him to get a part in a touring company of players that folded in Ogden, Utah. He then went to San Francisco where he resumed his dancing career until 1917 when he went to Hollywood. Valentino was married to two protégés of the rather scandalous Nazimova. The first brief marriage to actress Jean Acker led to divorce and to a jail sentence because he married his second wife, actress and designer Natasha Rambova (born Winifred Shaunessy), before the divorce decree had become final. Valentino went on salary suspension from Famous Players-Lasky Studios when it would not meet Rambova's demands to manage his career. She was barred from the sets of his pictures as a condition of his resuming his film work and shortly thereafter she left him. (Most of Valentino's biographers report that neither of these marriages was ever consummated.)

While he was promoting *The Son of The Sheik,* his last film, Valentino was stricken with a perforated ulcer in New York City. He died on August 23, 1926 at the age of 31. His funeral caused riots because of the thousands of mourning women who wanted a last glimpse of "the great lover." There were even reports of suicides by those who "could not live without Rudy." Polish screen actress Pola Negri, claiming to be his fiancée, even offered to restage her fainting spells for the benefit of the cameramen at the funeral. Valentino fan clubs grew after his death, aided by the publicity of the "mysterious lady in black" who laid a rose on his tomb every year on the anniversary of his death. Rudolph Valentino is buried in Hollywood in the family crypt of June Mathis, the influential screen writer who insisted that he be cast in his first important role, that of Julio in *The Four Horsemen of the Apocalypse.*

Illustration 3. Rudolph Valentino in *Blood and Sand,* **1922.**

Interview with
Madame Alexander

BY JOHN AXE
with the participation of
Patricia Gardner

Richard Birnbaum, President, Alexander
Doll Company and Madame Alexander.

Madame Alexander. Those two words alone are very exciting to collectors who love the collectible and modern dolls. And we were privileged to meet Madame Alexander herself at the National U.F.D.C. Convention in New York City held August 7th-12th, 1979. To us the whole tone of the Convention carried an aura of Madame Alexander. The dolls from the Alexander Doll Company were very prominent in the Exhibition Room; they were everywhere in the Sales Room. They looked better than ever.

On Thursday, August 9th, Madame Alexander spoke to her fans at F.A.O. Schwarz on Fifth Avenue. The store was so packed with people that we could not see the merchandise for sale. The lines for the refreshments were so long that we forgot about being hot and thirsty. But no one missed the extensive exhibition of Madame Alexander dolls that were on loan for the occasion. These were special dolls from past years that were displayed by

doll designer and collector Ted Menten. There were all-original and unusual Little Women, Maggies, Cissettes and Cissys galore; there were many prime examples of the dolls from the hard plastic era; Tommy and Katie, the dolls that were created exclusively for the 100th Anniversary of F.A.O. Schwarz in 1962 were among our favorites. Seeing Madame Alexander in person was an exciting event for everyone. We were also privileged to meet Miss Frances, Madame Alexander's gracious secretary, who had made many of the arrangements for this special function.

One of our most rewarding experiences was on Saturday evening, August 11th, before the Covention Banquet, which was addressed by Madame Alexander. Miss Frances had arranged for us to interview Madame Alexander and to be presented to Richard Birnbaum, Madame Alexander's son-in-law, who has responsibility for operations at the Alexander Doll Company.

Madame Beatrice Alexander will be 85 years old in March. But that is just a chronological fact. Madame Alexander told us that she has her work prepared and planned for the next ten years. Her vigor was apparent in the enthusiasm with which she told us this and many other things. She was vivacious and lovely in a flowing gown reminiscent of some of the fashions in which her lady dolls are costumed. We could have spent hours with Madame Alexander but time would only permit us to ask her a part of what we would like to know about her dolls.

QUESTION: Madame Alexander, how did you become interested in making dolls?
MADAME ALEXANDER: My father had a doll hospital in New York City. Many times I watched him reglue a shattered bisque or china doll head. The repair process could take three hours and he only got 25 cents for his

Miss Frances, Madame Alexander's secretary (left) and Madame Alexander.

From the October/November 1979 Doll Reader.®

work. So in 1923 I began making unbreakable cloth dolls.

QUESTION: What was your goal when you began the Alexander Doll Company?

MADAME ALEXANDER: I had to satisfy my artistic temperment and my financial temperment, even though we did not make money in the early years. Now other people are making more than a living on Madame Alexander dolls!

QUESTION: Why do you think that your dolls are the favorites of collectors?
MADAME ALEXANDER: I have always tried to maintain the highest standards of quality in my dolls. I have been very fortunate in picking my friends and my employees. My employees are my friends and they have had the same high standards as I have. I have always appreciated talent and I was always fortunate to have talented people around me.

QUESTION: Did you personally sculpt the models for any of the dolls that your company made?

MADAME ALEXANDER: Yes I did. But I work in fantasy. I did not try to imitate a real child or a real person in my dolls. My sculpture was always done to make the finished product look like a doll.

QUESTION: Of all the dolls that you have created which is your favorite?
MADAME ALEXANDER: Does a mother have any favorites among her children?

QUESTION: Do you have a personal collection of Madame Alexander dolls?
MADAME ALEXANDER: In my apartment I have a Scarlett O'Hara and a Renoir Mother and Child [set from 1967].

QUESTION: What is the significance of some of the names, like Wendy, Elise and Janie in naming your dolls? Were they the names of people in your family?
MADAME ALEXANDER: Wendy was named for my granddaughter, who died when she was 20. I have never named another doll after a living person. [She was not referring to the many Madame Alexander personality dolls.] In my religion [Jewish] we never name anyone after a living person. I am not a superstitious person but I did not want to do this with dolls either.

QUESTION: What are some of the Madame Alexander dolls that we can look forward to in the future?
MADAME ALEXANDER: I am ten years ahead in my work. I plan to bring the First Ladies Series up to Rosalynn Carter. My work is just beginning!

We were impressed with the sincerity and the warmth of Madame Alexander. She does not need publicity to sell her dolls. We know that she appreciates the respect and the love that collectors have for her work. She is amused to see the high prices that some of her more desirable collectible dolls bring now as she began her doll company to express her own talents and to make a living. Before Madame Alexander took her place of honor on the dais at the Convention Banquet, she consented to pose for pictures with her old friends who had accompanied her to the Waldorf-Astoria and with some of her new friends whom she had met there.

The Kewpies' Mother

The following is reprinted from "All Doors Open to Jell-O," an advertising brochure copyrighted in 1917 by the Genesee Pure Food Co.

The beautiful and brilliant young woman whose genius produced the captivating Kewpies is Rose O'Neill, the most famous of living women artists.

For the last eight years, while she has been busy studying and painting in Europe, illustrating stories in American books and magazines, drawings and modeling Kewpies and writing Kewpie verses in her New York studio, Rose O'Neill has found time to draw most of the pictures that have appeared in Jell-O advertisements.

One day, on being asked her opinion of Jell-O, she said: "Well, when I tell you I haven't time to be a

housewife and have never in my life made up anything eatable except Jell-O, you will know that I must appreciate the advantages offered by the "easy Jell-O way."

Good cooks are constantly praising Jell-O. It has devolved upon Rose O'Neill to furnish the strongest endorsement from the other side -- the women who can't cook.

Every woman who has ever made up Jell-O desserts or salads wants to make more of them. She has discovered that without special training and even without practice she can prepare dishes as fine as any made by chef or cook, and every one as "pretty as a picture!" In the case of Rose O'Neill it may have been the beauty of the Jell-O dishes as much as the easy way of making them that fascinated her.

From the June/July 1979 Doll Reader.®

CHILD STAR DOLLS OF THE 1930S & 1940S

by John Axe

Anne Shirley (born 1918) from ca. 1923 when she was child star Dawn O'Day.

All-original *Anne Shirley* by EFFANBEE in the late 1930s wearing a pale pink sheer cotton dress. (It is possible she is from the early 1940s, which would make her a "Little Lady" rather than Anne Shirley.) She is 14in. (35.6cm) and has a brown human hair wig, blue sleep eyes and the large hands of the Anne Shirley doll. The head is not marked, the torso is embossed: EFFANBEE//ANNE SHIRLEY.

UNESCO (United Nations Educational, Scientific, and Cultural Organization) has proclaimed 1979 the International Year of the Child. The United States, like the other participating nations, will observe this project. International Year of the Child is stimulating attention and concern regarding the needs of children all over the world, especially in the developing countries.

For doll collectors, every year is the Year of the Child. Most doll collections feature dolls of children and babies that are loved more than many real children are. No true doll collector ever lives a day during which he or she does not think of their collection or do some work in connection with it. Without a doubt, doll collectors will take an active part in the awarness program to aid children, whether it be by support of the UNESCO project or in their own personal way.

The all-composition dolls included in this photographic essay are dolls of some of the most famous and popular children of all time. The dolls are portraits of child movie actresses from the 1930s and the 1940s who earned tremendous adult attention, interest and admiration because of their celebrity status. There are no contemporary children who have achieved the fame and popularity of the children who were the inspiration for these dolls. We will probably never again see so many famous children capture public adulation in a single generation as these did.

Who would not envy having a collection such as the one shown here? And these acclaimed children of a past era help to make us more aware of those unfortunate children all over the world in our own time.

Shirley Temple (born 1927) from the 1934 film *Eyes*. The doll Shirley is holding is probably a Pats by EFFANBEE. The doll in Jane Withers' arms loo a LENCI.

Above:
All-original 16in. (40.6cm) *Shirley Temple* by IDEAL. This is the "knife-pleated" organdy dancing costume from the film *Curly Top* in 1935. The dress is pink and is labeled; the underclothing has a paper label with "16" on it. Head mark:

16
SHIRLEY TEMPLE
IDEAL
N. & T. Co.

Back mark:

SHIRLEY TEMPLE
16

Above right:
An imitator of the Shirley Temple doll is this 14in. (35.6cm) HORSMAN *Bright Star*. She has a blond mohair wig, blue tin sleep eyes and an open mouth with four teeth. She is almost mint. The organdy dress is white with red flowers and is trimmed in red. The doll is unmarked. The tag in front that shows a doll that looks like the Shirley Temple doll reads: HORSMAN'S//BRIGHT STAR//"With eyes that shine//and hair so fine." The second tag, showing that is was probably a salesman's sample carries the information: REGAL DOLL CORPORATION//HORSMAN DOLLS, INC.//TRENTON, N.J.// Style No. 526.

Right:
18in. (45.7cm) *Margaret O'Brien* in a labeled dress of heavy cotton from MADAME ALEXANDER in 1946. She has a brown mohair wig and blue sleep eyes. The hat is original; the shoes and socks are replacements. The doll is marked both on the head and back: ALEXANDER

Left:
17in. (43.2cm) *Jane Withers* doll by MADAME ALEXANDER with an open mouth that has teeth and a metal tongue. She, like most Jane Withers dolls, has an auburn mohair wig and green sleep eyes. The outfit is most likely a replacement. The head is marked: JANE WITHERS
                    ALEXANDER DOLL
The back is marked: 17
(*Lois Barrett Collection.*)

Right:
Jane Withers dolls were issued by MADAME ALEXANDER in various sizes in 1937. This 13in. (33cm) version is all-original in a tagged Jane Withers dress of pink organdy. She has an auburn mohair wig and green sleep eyes. The doll is not marked. (*Connie Chase Collection.*)

Margaret O'Brien (born 1937) in 1942. Margaret O'Brien was the last really popular child star; the doll was the last all-composition movie star doll.

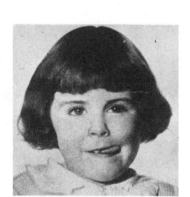

Juanita Quigley (born 1931) who performed in the movies under the name Baby Jane.

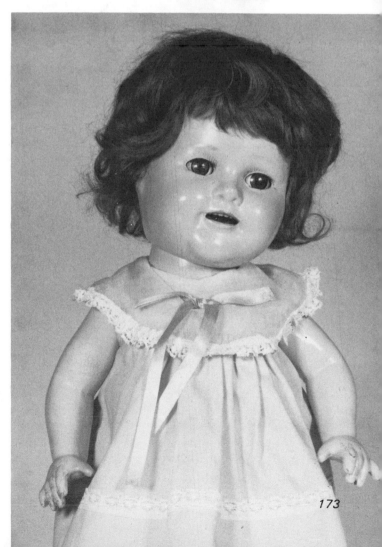

One of the most rare child movie star dolls and one of the most rare ALEXANDER dolls is *Baby Jane* from 1935. She is 17in. (43.2cm). She has an auburn mohair wig, brown glass-like sleep eyes, teeth and a metal tongue. The costume is not original. The head of the doll is marked: BABY-JANE//REG// Mme ALEXANDER
(*Betty Shriver Collection.*)

173

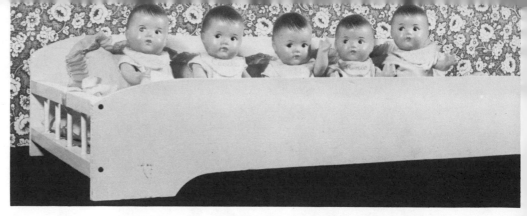

All-original *Dionne Quintuplets* in their original, fully-equipped bed by MADAME ALEXANDER in the 7in. (17.8cm) size from 1935. The fully-jointed babies are wearing diapers, undershirts and bibs. This is the "straight hair" 7in. (17.8cm) set with painted eyes which is marked ALEXANDER on the back and marked on the head: DIONNE//ALEXANDER

23in. (58.4cm) *Marie* with a cloth torso. The pink flannel coat and hat is an original Dionne outfit, but pink was the color for Yvonne in the ALEXANDER dolls. The white dress carries one of the more rare labels: DIONNE QUINTUPLETS//Marie// EXCLUSIVE LICENSEE//ALEXANDER DOLL CO. N.Y. The straight, painted hair, open mouth with teeth and the clothing dates the baby from 1935. The head is marked: "DIONNE"//ALEXANDER

Left:
From ca. 1937 is the all-composition Alexander toddler Dionne Quintuplet. This is an all-original *Yvonne* in a pink labeled dress of dotted swiss to which her name pin is attached. She has an open mouth with four teeth, brown sleep eyes and a human hair wig. Only the body is marked: ALEXANDER (*Lois Barrett Collection.*)

Right:
11-1/8in. (28cm) *Baby Sandy* by RALPH A. FREUNDLICH, INC., ca. 1940. She has yellow-painted hair and blue tin sleep eyes and an open mouth with two teeth and a felt tongue. The head is marked: BABY SANDY

Grande Dame of Doll Makers and her American Children

by CHIP BARKEL   Photographs by the Author

Illustration 1. 21in (53.3cm) *Barbara Lou* by Effanbee; all-composition; blonde human hair; green sleep eyes; open mouth with teeth; larger proportioned child's body; wears original long taffeta dress of light aqua and maroon, an aqua hair ribbon with maroon rosettes, a full taffeta slip with attached underwear, white socks and imitation white leather tie oxfords; head unmarked; body marked: "Effanbee// ANNESHIRLEY;" late 1930s.

Dewees Cochran surely has earned her unofficial title of "Grande Dame of American Doll Makers." No other person has so totally dedicated himself to all phases of doll making, consistently maintaining rigidly self-imposed standards of the highest caliber, as has Mrs. Cochran.

She began her career while living in the village of New Hope, Pennsylvania, in October 1933 after making three black cloth character dolls and dressing three china head dolls as early Philadelphia ladies. These dolls sold rather quickly through a gift and antique shop in Wayne, Pennsylvania, on a consignment basis. With this successful endeavor as encouragement, Dewees decided to make other samples and travel to New York. Saks' Fifth Avenue were equally enthusiastic and ordered a dozen sets; however, at F.A.O. Schwarz Dewees was admonished for poking fun at black people.

After Christmas Saks' asked Dewees to design something more lifelike than they currently sold. Before she had arrived at her next **appointment,** she conceived the idea

Illustration 2. 14in (35.6cm) *Barbara Joan* by Effanbee; all-composition; light brown human hair; green sleep eyes; open mouth with teeth; wears original red and yellow plaid wool short jacket with six yellow covered buttons, a yellow wool beret with attached ribbon that ties under the chin, a yellow wool skirt with attached sleeveless white blouse and brown imitation leather shoes; marked: "EFFANBEE" on head, "EFFANBEE// ANNE-SHIRLEY" on body; late 1930s.

of making dolls to represent specific children. As a result of sharing her idea with the buyer of Young Books on Madison Avenue, Dewees Cochran received her first commission the following day. Using the two daughters of Mr. and Mrs. Irving Berlin, her portrait dolls would become a reality.

On the train back to Pennsylvania while attempting to carve those first experimental heads from balsa wood, Dewees knew that she must move to New York immediately. In a matter of days, she and her husband, Paul, were on their way to their new home on Madison Avenue in New York City. Additional orders were already waiting for her to bring them to "life." With these dolls finished, she was forced to find an

alternative to the time-consuming balsa wood carving. The answer was a plastic wood composition, which could be used with molds and slight differences sculpted by hand. It was not only expediency which prompted Dewees to look for a method to produce her special dolls in quantity. She feared that a toy manufacturer might steal her idea and mass-produce them. She decided that she must beat them to it.

Since Dewees had studied art in Munich and at the Philadelphia Academy of Fine Arts, she had some background with which to begin her study of American children. After

Illustration 3. 20in (50.8cm) *Gloria Ann* by Effanbee standing next to her original box; all-composition; blonde human hair; sleep eyes; closed mouth; wears original maroon taffeta dress with ruffles, under black and white checked coat trimmed in maroon piping, maroon felt hat and real leather maroon gloves that fit on specially designed hands with individual fingers (note: all bodies marked "ANNE SHIRLEY" had this innovative feature); marked: "EFFANBEE//AMERICAN// CHILDREN" on head, "EFFANBEE//ANNE-SHIRLEY" on body; late 1930s. *Glenn Mandeville Collection.*

From the February/March 1982 Doll Reader.®

husband walked the streets of New York finding living examples of her face type theory. She quickly made models of six children from her collection of borrowed photographs.

Publicity from her specially commissioned portrait dolls poured forth from all over the city including the *New Yorker,* the *New York Sun,* the *New York American* and *Vogue* magazine. This led to an introduction to Bernard Baum and Hugo Fleishaker of the Effanbee Doll Company in December 1935. Contingent on the success of six samples to be shown at the Toy Fair the following March, Effanbee offered Dewees a three year contract to produce the designs of her *American Children* portrait dolls. Three months for six samples meant working night and day, but she finished in time for Toy Fair. Everything for the dolls, wigs, clothes and shoes as well as the dolls themselves, was handmade by Dewees.

The next three years brought many more exhibitions of Dewees Cochran's work and even more orders, careful research and tediously examining sheaves of childrens' photographs, she identified six common face types. Dewees felt victorious as she and her both for the commercially-made dolls from Effanbee and for her specially commissioned portrait dolls. On April 3, 1939, Dewees Cochran's *American Children* were featured on *Life* magazine's cover. This triumph was the classic "light before the storm" because Dewees' Effanbee contract expired and was not renewed. Since World War II had begun, many of her imported materials were no longer available. Furthermore her attempts to find suitable replacements with which to work failed repeatedly. When, in 1941, the United States entered the war, Dewees' hopes of using yarn hair and stuffed cloth bodies were also dashed, because the kapok stuffing was no longer available to her. During the war her doll making came to a standstill.

The year 1946 brought new hope and enthusiasm for her doll making. Dewees found a chemist who suggested she use a latex compound which could be used in molds. She formed a partnership with two small companies to produce a *Cindy* doll in latex. This was to be a commercially-produced American girl doll made with the same attention to quality that her custom orders had received. *Cindy* was well received in the retail outlets, but soon a disagreement between partners occurred and Dewees withdrew from the project. Only *Cindy* dolls embossed "Dewees Cochran Dolls" on their torso can be

considered authentic, according to Mrs. Cochran, because the partners continued marketing unmarked dolls of lesser quality after her departure. With this business experience behind her, Dewees vowed only to produce dolls which she personally made to insure that her superior standards would be guaranteed.

With the help of a local seamstress, Dewees resumed making latex dolls in 1948. These portrait dolls were 15in (38.1cm) and 17in (43.2cm) tall and were made from her six basic face types. Marshall Field's department store in Chicago ran a Doll Look-Alike promotion with Dewees available to answer questions and to match face types to children. This promotion meant adapting dolls already completed by Dewees and in their stock to match little girls by changing wigs, clothes and other small details. This really put Dewees' face type theory to the test because the dolls were not custom orders like her other portrait dolls.

In the fall of 1951 Dewees decided to create a dream child for herself. The first doll would be a child of about three, but older editions would follow as the doll "grew up." After showing *Stormie* at an exhibition, Dewees was asked to make others like her with different hair colors. This would be the birth of her *Grow Up Series. Susan Stormalong (Stormie)* had red hair; *Angela Appleseed (Angel),* blonde; and *Belinda Bunyan (Bunnie),* brunette. All three girls had different personalities, but shared fictional ancestors from American folklore. Two boys completed the set, *Jeff Jones,* a brunette introvert and *Peter Ponsett,* a blonde extrovert. The *Grow Up Series* was an instant success at various lectures and exhibitions Dewees attended in New England and in New York City. The *Grow Ups* did indeed grow, hastened somewhat ahead of reality by their anxious creator. Each year for five years a new age became a reality. This time frame was designed so that a child of five could watch her *Grow Up* doll age from five to seven to 11 to 16 to 20 by her tenth birthday. Children were not the only proud owners of *Grow Up* dolls, since collectors who appreciated Dewees' artistic talents also found her dolls irresistable.

Dewees left Norwich, Vermont, permanently in March 1960 for her new home near Saratoga, California. She was the recipient of a resident scholarship to Montalvo, a non-profit organization for artists. Montalvo gave artists a place to live and to further their artistic interests. Dewees' intentions were to retire from doll making

Illustration 4. 17in (43.2cm) (Custom order) *Portrait Doll* by Dewees Cochran; made entirely of latex; jointed at neck, shoulders and hips; painted eyes with real lashes; blonde human hair in pulled-up pony tail; open/closed mouth with teeth; wears original handmade fishing sweater, gray slacks and red leather sandals; marked: "Dewees Cochran Dolls ©1954" in script on small of back, tag: "Dewees Cochran// Dolls" (obverse) "Girl in// Portuguese// Fishing// Sweater" (all hand written). *Glenn Mandeville Collection.*

except for her *Grow Ups.* Orders for portrait dolls kept pouring in, Dewees kept working and her retirement never materialized.

In 1976 the Effanbee Doll Company again sought a business agreement with Dewees. They hoped she would design a self-portrait doll for their Limited Edition Club. Dewees was very enthusiastic about the venture because she knew that Effanbee would not compromise her standards. She granted them permission and chose a self-portrait doll she had made for a Gibson Girl display at the 1970 UFDC convention. This doll represented Dewees Cochran at age eight, and was the third annual offering of the club for 1977.

Following the agreement with Effanbee, Dewees returned to her latest project. This project would highlight almost half a century of doll design and manufacture. In 1979 her autobiography *As If They Might Speak* was published. This milestone does not imply that Dewees Cochran's

Illustration 5. Left to right: 20in (50.8cm) *Peggy Lou* by Effanbee; all-composition; brown human hair; blue painted eyes; closed mouth; wears original white voile dress with red hearts, red leather shoes and belt, red straw hat and organdy slip/underwear combination; marked: "EFFANBEE//AMERICAN//CHILDREN" on head, "EFFANBEE//ANNE-SHIRLEY" on body; late 1930s. 17in (43.2cm) *American Child Boy* by Effanbee; all-composition; blue painted eyes; blonde human hair; wears original navy wool suit, white cotton shirt, paisley print tie and black imitation leather tie shoes; marked: "EFFANBEE//ANNE SHIRLEY" on body; late 1930s. *Glenn Mandeville Collection.* 20in (50.8cm) *American Child* by Effanbee; all-composition; light brown human hair; brown sleep eyes; open mouth with teeth; wears original aqua cotton dress and pink cotton pinafore and white imitation leather shoes; marked: "EFFANBEE//ANNE-SHIRLEY" on body, "EFFANBEE//DURABLE//DOLLS (in heart)//Made in U.S.A." on dress label; late 1930s. *Glenn Mandeville Collection.*

active association with or interest in dolls has diminished. At age 89 she is still diligently designing and making her special portrait children.

At this time Mrs. Cochran is currently working on unfilled back orders. Anyone wishing information and/or to be placed on her waiting list should contact her directly. Please send a business-size self-addressed stamped envelope to: Mrs. Dewees Cochran, 155 Quail Hollow Road, Felton, California, 95018.

Illustration 6. Left to right: 18in (45.7cm) *Susan Stormalong (Stormie)* at age 20 by Dewees Cochran; all latex; painted eyes with real lashes; red human hair; wears original light blue, pink and white cotton outfit of one piece blouse/shorts and matching skirt and white leather sandals; marked: "D.C.//S.S.- 58//1" behind right ear; 1958. 15½in (39.4cm) *Belinda Bunyan (Bunnie)* at age 16 by Dewees Cochran; all latex; painted eyes with real lashes; shoulder length dark brown hair; wears original navy and green cotton plaid dress under navy wool coat with matching wool hat, white socks and red leather shoes; marked: "D.C.//B.B.-'54// # 9;" 1954. 18½in (47cm) *Jeff Jones* at age 20 by Dwees Cochran; all latex; painted eyes with real lashes; brown human hair; wears original navy and green plaid shirt, navy wool slacks, black leather belt, white socks and shoes; marked: "D.C.//J.J.-'60//2" 1960. 12½in (31.8cm) *Angela Appleseed (Angel)* at age five by Dewees Cochran; all latex; blue painted eyes with real lashes; very long platinum blonde human hair; wears original light blue flower print dress with sash that ties in back, white socks and white leather shoes; marked: ⋈ embossed into the latex and signed Dewees Cochran in semi-circle around intials on back of torso; 1953(?). (The last number refers to the order they were made for *Susan Stormalong* and *Jeff Jones*.)

177

Illustration 1 *12in (30.5cm) (to peak of cap)* Auguste Clown, *original creation by Elizabeth Watkins; porcelain shoulder head and hands; white face with red nose; blonde caracul hair; red calico suit with white pompons; 1967.* Elizabeth Watkins Collection.

Illustration 2. *10½in (26.7cm) (15in [38.1cm] to peak of cap) white-face bisque clown with black dots and green, red and blue lines on face; pupil-less black glass eyes; open mouth with five teeth; fully-jointed five-piece body; original costume of red satin, white silk faille and coarse lace ruff. Marked:*

Elizabeth Watkins Collection.

Collecting Clowns

See article and additional illustrations on pages 191-193.

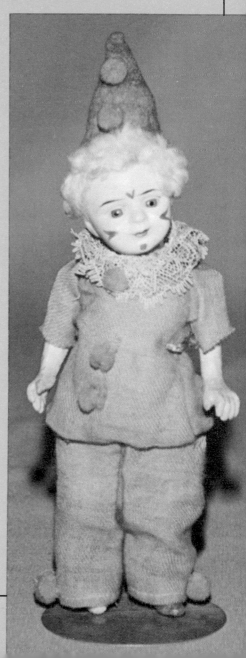

BELOW: Illustration 4. *9in (22.9cm) (to peak of cap) clown; white bisque face, blue face paintings; blue glass eyes, red eye lines, brown brows; closed mouth with two dimples; white lambs wool wig; five-piece body; tan shoes; black socks with red line at top; once-red felt cap; original beige suit with two yellow pompons. Marked: "19/0." Thelma Bouchey Collection.*

Illustration 3. *14in (35.6cm) (to peak of cap) clown; papier-mâché head shellacked to resemble old celluloid; blue dots of color on face with red brush strokes; red brush strokes also on chin and outer corners of eyes; violet glass eyes of high quality; open mouth with teeth; carefully done brows and upper and lower lashes; five-piece body; once-white felt cap with black pompon has bits of Christmas glass icicles sewn to it. Celluloid dog has glass eyes and jointed head and legs. Thelma Bouchey Collection.*

"It's Howdy Doody Time" —
A Photographic Essay
by John Axe

BELOW: 25in (63.5cm) *Howdy Doody* by Ideal, circa 1953. *(Photograph by John Axe.)*

The September 1981 issue of Good Housekeeping had a cartoon story from the "It's All in the Family" series showing the mother and father and the two children at a flea market. The final picture showed the family returning to their car with the father clutching a large bag of puppets. To justify his purchase he said to his wife, "You heard what the man said — 'Howdy-Doodiana is an investment!" I still love Howdy Doody and the gang from "Doodyville" and I will always admit it.

Howdy Doody was one of the first "stars" on television. His show debuted on December 27, 1947, on NBC-TV. "Howdy Doody" was seen until September 24, 1960 totaling 2,543 performances. As a show for children, "Howdy Doody" did not pretend to have any educational value. It was to entertain and children loved it. Howdy Doody himself is now an American folk hero. He and his twin brother, Double, were born in Texas on December 27, 1941, and they lived on a ranch for six years. Then their rich Uncle Doody died and left the twins some property in New York City. Double wanted to remain in Texas but Howdy saw his chance to fulfill his dream of operating a circus. When NBC wanted to purchase Howdy's land for a television studio a deal was made for NBC to construct a circus for Howdy on the grounds. Bob Smith, called Buffalo Bob because he was from Buffalo, was appointed as Howdy's guardian and he helped Howdy operate the circus. Then NBC gave Howdy his own television show and brought in a "Peanut Gallery" of children to enjoy it. The show was about a circus troupe that tried to perform against the wishes of Phineas T. Bluster, a mean old man whose main interest in life was to prevent people from having fun.

Some of the characters on the show were puppets and others were human performers. Clarabell Hornblow, the mute clown, was played by Bob Keeshan (later Captain Kangaroo) and then by Bob Nicholson, followed by Lou Anderson. Among the live performers were also Arlene Dalton as the Story Princess and Judy Tyler as Princess Summerfall-Winterspring. The most important puppets were Howdy, whose voice was supplied by Bob Smith; Phineas T. Bluster, who was 70 years old and "as spry as a pup;" Heidi Doody, Howdy's cousin; the Flubadub, the main circus attraction; and Dilly Dally, who could wiggle his ears.

Illustration 1. Buffalo Bob with his creation, *Howdy Doody,* from the cover of *TV Guide,* June 23, 1953. Buffalo Bob's *Howdy Doody* had red hair, a big grin and 72 freckles on his face. He is dressed in blue jeans, a plaid work shirt, wore a bandana around his neck and cowboy boots on his feet.

Illustration 2. 25in (63.5cm) and 20in (50.8cm) *Howdy Doody* dolls by Ideal, circa 1953. Both dolls have hard plastic heads, vinyl spatula-shaped hands and stuffed cloth bodies. They have dark red hair, blue sleep eyes with lashes, mouths with painted teeth that operate with a pull string at the back of the neck and, of course, freckles. The larger doll is on the cover of this magazine; the smaller one is missing some of his accessories. Both are embossed on the neck: "IDEAL DOLL."

Illustrations 3 and 4. Marionettes by Peter Puppet Playthings, Inc., circa 1950. Above, from left to right: 14½in (36.9cm) *Princess Summerfall-Winterspring,* 17½in (44.5cm) *Howdy Doody* and 15½in (39.4cm) *Clarabell.* Each has a composition head with painted features, moving mouths, composition hands and feet and a flat wooden section for the torso. The Princess also has black yarn braids. No markings. The marionettes were designed by Raye Copelan and copyrighted by Bob Smith. Another version of the *Howdy Doody* marionette is pictured below with his original box.

OPPOSITE PAGE:
Illustration 6. 12in (30.5cm) and 19in (48.3cm) *Howdy Doody* dolls by Eegee. Both dolls have vinyl heads with painted features, vinyl hands and stuffed cloth bodies. The smaller one has a movable mouth and his clothing, except for the neckerchief, is part of the body. He is Style # HD 12, made in Hong Kong in the 1970s and the markings on the head are obliterated. The larger doll has a painted molded open mouth with painted teeth and removable clothing and was also made in Hong Kong in the early 1970s. He is marked on the head: "EEGEE CO.// ©NATIONAL 72 // BROADCASTING // COMPANY INC."

ABOVE: Illustration 5. 7¾in (19.8cm) *Howdy Doody* in all hard plastic, maker unknown, circa early 1950s. Fully jointed; dark blue sleep eyes. A lever in the back of the head operates the mouth with its painted teeth.

From the February/March 1982 Doll Reader.®

Illustration 7. Howdy Doody china cup and silver plate spoon with a blue plastic Clarabell pipe for blowing soap bubbles. Only the spoon is marked: "CROWN SILVER PLATE // ©KAGRAN."

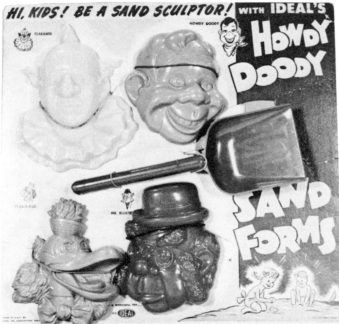

Illustration 8. Howdy Doody "Sand Forms" by Ideal. Clarabell, Howdy Doody, Flub-a-Dub (sic) and Mr. Bluster are each bright plastic. Copyright 1952 by Kagran Corp.

Illustration 9. Howdy Doody Picture Puzzle in a frame by Whitman Publishing Company, No. 2603, 1953. Copyright by Kagran Corporation. At the bottom left is Flubadub, the main circus attraction from the TV program. Flubadub had a dog's ears, a duck's head, a cat's whiskers, a giraffe's neck, a racoon's tail, an elephant's memory and a feather-covered body. He craved meatballs and spaghetti.

Illustration 10. Plastic puppets in different colors by Tee-Vee Toy, Item No. 549, early 1950s. From left to right they are Mr. Bluster, Clarabell, Howdy Doody, Princess Summerfall-Winterspring and Dilly Dally. Each is about 4in (10.2cm) high. A lever in the back of the heads makes the mouths operate, except for Clarabell, who is a whistle.

184

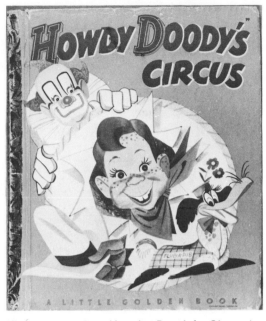

Illustration 11. *Howdy Doody's Circus* by Edward Kean, illustrated by Liz Dauber and Dan Gormley, published by Simon and Schuster, copyright 1950 by Kagran Corporation. This tale tells how Howdy and Clarabell began their circus and encountered the world's only talking Flubadub, who became their ringmaster.

Illustration 13. 26in (66cm) ventriloquist version of *Howdy Doody* by Eegee, 1972. Plastic head with bright red painted hair; painted blue eyes; moving mouth. The hands are vinyl; the body is stuffed cloth. Head marked: "EEGEE // NATIONAL BROADCASTING CO. INC. // 19©72."

Illustration 12. 20in (50.8cm) *Howdy Doody,* circa late 1940s. Composition head and hands; stuffed cloth body. The painted hair is dark red; the mouth does not move and it has painted teeth. The eyes, unlike *Howdy's* own, are brown and have no lashes. The doll is not marked and he is not dressed in original clothing. Compare this doll with that on the cover of this magazine to note that the head proportions are not accurately delineated.

Illustration 14. *Howdy Doody* and *Clarabell* from J. C. Penney, Christmas 1977 catalog. Howdy is seen in Illustration 6. The catalog says that both are 19in (48.3cm) tall. Vinyl heads and hands; stuffed cloth bodies.

Shirley Temple Dolls
The Scarce, The Rare and The Copied
by JOHN AXE

Illustration 1. 19in (48.3cm) Shirley Temple look-alike, manufacturer unknown, late 1950s to early 1960s; all-vinyl and fully-jointed; rooted blonde hair; blue sleep eyes with lashes; open mouth with painted teeth; dimples. This doll seems like it was made from the mold of the 19in (48.3cm) 1957 Ideal doll. The body is the same; the head is of a lighter weight vinyl but the hair is identical. Production savings were made with less careful facial detail painting and the lack of inset teeth. Back marked: "19 // S // A E // 195," left arm marked at joint: "19," legs marked at joints: "19 ST." The replaced costume is a Madame Alexander accessory.

Illustration 2. 9in (22.9cm) Shirley Temple by Ideal; late 1930s; all-composition and fully-jointed; painted, molded curly brown hair; blue painted eyes; marked on the back: " *e* // IDEAL DOLL." All the clothing is replaced. This is one of the rarest of all the Ideal composition Shirley Temple dolls, if indeed it was originally intended to be she. *Marge Meisinger Collection.*

The most famous child ever was little Shirley Temple. The most popular celebrity doll ever was the *Shirley Temple* doll by the Ideal Novelty & Toy Company (later called the Ideal Toy Corporation). It was also the most copied and imitated doll.

Ideal was granted the first commercial license to use Shirley Temple's name. The *Shirley Temple* doll first came on the market in full force in time for Chirstmas of 1934. By the fall of 1934 Ideal was announcing in trade publications that "so many orders are already in hand that orders will be filled in the order received." Ideal secured the rights to manufacture a *Shirley Temple* doll from the Fox Film Corporation (later merged as Twentieth Century-Fox), who had the little actress under exclusive

contract, but this was done with "the authorization of the parents of Shirley Temple." The first ads by Ideal told that the dolls were dressed in "authentic Shirley Temple costumes, and to each doll is fastened a beautiful celluloid button bearing Shirley Temple's picture and a facsimile signature." Stores were already planning promotions for the dolls by staging contests for little Shirley Temple lookalikes. The first dolls came in four sizes and retailed at $3, $5, $6 and $7. The company was so confident of success with the new doll that it did not hand out any samples to retailers, as had been the custom among doll manufacturers for many years.

Ideal heavily promoted *Shirley Temple* dolls and their accessories from 1935 through 1937. In 1936

a contest that was part of "one of the largest national promotions ever undertaken by any doll or toy manufacturer" (*Playthings*, November 1936) was launched to advertise *Shirley Temple* dolls. The contest was an announcement that appeared in 14,000,000 Sunday newspaper's comic sections along with an ad for the dolls. More than 11,000 cash and merchandise prizes were supposed to go to the winners of the contest. The first ten prizes were Scotch Terrier puppies that were like Shirley's dog, Corky. The other prizes were Shirley Temple merchandise, such as doll buggies, shoes and coats. To enter the contest little girls had to present themselves to a doll dealer who would provide them with the contest forms. The application blank showed *Shirley Temple* dolls dressed in six different

From the October/November 1981 Doll Reader.®

costumes. The child had to place the costumes in the order in which she found them the most appealing and come up with reasons for wanting to have her own *Shirley Temple* doll. The contest was rather cruel because the entire object was to increase the desire of little girls to own a *Shirley Temple* doll. Stores liked the plan because the contest form could not be mailed in, but had to be returned to the doll counter where an elaborate *Shirley Temple* doll display was set up, further stimulating the little girl's desire.

Illustration 4. Advertisement from *Film Pictorial,* a British magazine, August 1, 1936. Very little is known about the Allwin *Shirley Temple* dolls. They appear to have been made from cloth.

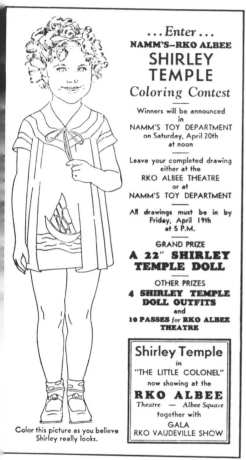

Illustration 3. A Shirley Temple coloring contest that was used for Children's Day promotions. *Playthings,* May 1935. An accompanying article told retailers how to take advantage of the coming holiday, June 15:

"The merchandising of toys is not a simple matter, and in order to build by a large sales volume it is necessary to consider several factors, of which advertising is one of the most important. If Children's Day is to mean anything to the toy dealer, then it is mandatory that advertising be used. It is part of the dealer's job to put the story of Children's Day across to his customers, and advertising offers one way of doing this effectively. The very nature of the day is such that it presents numerous possibilities for writing some very good 'copy.' The ad should strive to tell the purpose of the day in as few words as possible, and the merchandise featured should be of a type highly appealing to all children . . .

"The following are a few suggestions that might be used in preparing 'copy' for the advertisements: 'Every day is Children's Day . . .'; 'Make the youngsters happy and gay - give them toys for Children's Day'; 'Children need toys in June as well as in December - Children's Day is one you should remember'."

Illustration 5. 17in (45.7cm) all-composition Shirley Temple look-alike, circa 1936. This doll is probably Goldberger's *Miss Charming.* Dark blonde mohair wig in a "Shirley Temple" set, although it has been redone; blue tin sleep eyes with lashes; open mouth with teeth; dimples in the cheeks. There are no markings on the doll.

In January of 1937 *Playthings* reported that Ben Michtom, the son of the founder of the Ideal Novelty & Toy Company, had just returned from a promotional trip throughout the country. The purpose of the journey was to "acquaint the public with the Shirley Temple Doll Contest." While Mr. Michtom was in Hollywood he met Shirley Temple and her parents on the set of the Twentieth Century-Fox film *Stowaway.* Mr. Michtom "found Shirley to be an alert, intelligent, unspoiled and thoroughly likable youngster, and a finished actress in spite of the fact that she is not yet seven." (Shirley Temple was actually going on eight; this was during the period when the studio "lied" about her age.) Ben Michtom posed with Shirley and her 11-week-old Pekinese puppy, Chin Chin, and later related in the most laudatory terms his interview with her. He was also impressed with the fact that she collected on a dollar bet from William A. Seiter, the director of *Stowaway,* because she repeated a scene in the film and as she promised, did a better job than during the initial take.

Ben Michtom reported,

"She is a real little girl with determination and acting ability possessed by few adults. *Stowaway* is her best picture, a really fine piece of work that will undoubtedly further increase Shirley's margin as the leading box office attraction of the motion picture screen."

Mr. Michtom's enthusiasm was certainly tempered by the lucrative

187

Illustration 6. Foreign-made *Shirley Temple* dolls, circa late 1930s. The larger doll is 7½in (19.1cm) in a papier-mâché type of composition over plaster; fully-jointed, including the head; painted and molded light brown curls; blue painted eyes; smiling mouth with painted teeth; dimples in the cheeks; stamped on the torso: "JAPAN." The smaller doll is all-bisque and is 4in (10.2cm); only the arms and the legs are jointed; painted and molded light brown curls; black painted eyes; closed mouth; the painted shoes have heels; incised at the neck: "GERMANY // 5649." Neither doll is dressed in an original costume.

contracts that he possessed. Among all child actors Shirley Temple does not rank high in the talent department. Her greatest appeal in the 1930s was that she was so cute and that she took coaching and direction well. But the public loved her. In 1936, 1937 and 1938 she was the leading box office attraction in the motion picture industry. By 1939 she had fallen to fifth place. After that time she was never considered an important performer. As a young adult, Shirley Temple was a very wooden and mannered actress and her characterizations were incredibly amateurish. (This same phenomenon occurred with Margaret O'Brien, who as a child had a greater acting range than Shirley Temple. Other child performers like Natalie Wood and Elizabeth Taylor

achieved tremendous acclaim as adults.)

Ideal's *Shirley Temple* composition child dolls eventually came in 16 sizes. They are 9in (22.9cm), 11in (27.9cm), 13in (33.0cm) and every inch size from 15in (38.1cm) to 27in (68.6cm). The baby doll, based on Shirley Temple at age two, with a cloth body and composition head and limbs was introduced in the summer of 1935. She came in six sizes — 14in (35.6cm), 16in (40.6cm), 18in (45.7cm), 20in (50.8cm), 25in (63.5cm) and 27in (68.6cm) — and had a wig or molded hair. Other *Shirley Temple* dolls appeared that were made from factory parts, such as a cloth body girl in different sizes. This doll is referred to as a *Shirley Temple* toddler doll and is rather scarce now. Special editions of the dolls came packed in a wardrobe trunk with extra costumes. Separate outfits were available for the dolls by early 1936. One of the most interesting of these was a reproduction of the "Cape Cod Slicker," a raincoat like the one Shirley wore in the film *Captain January*. One of the more unusual and desirable versions of the doll was the cowgirl costume in the spring of 1936. This was first called the *Official Doll of the Texas Centennial* and later the *Shirley Temple Texas Ranger Doll*. And no wonder so many of the composition *Shirley Temple* dolls are found with messy hair today. In 1937 Ideal sold all the dolls with "a generous supply of hair curlers and full instructions" for "keeping Shirley curly." Ads proclaimed that "the genuine Shirley Temple Doll is the *only* doll with *enough* hair — and *good enough hair* — to be waved, curled and dressed in all the latest styles."

Special advertising promotions for the dolls were held to coincide with Shirley Temple's birthday — April 23 — and for other events such as Children's Day (the second Sunday in June, originally a holiday begun by the Protestant Churches in the United States) and the traditional present-giving holidays. Each of these occasions became a national merchandising event.

Right from the beginning Ideal had problems with other doll companies who wanted to take part in the market created by the most successful play doll created up to that time. It has been reported in print many times that Madame Alexander was opposed to marketing the *Shirley Temple* doll for this reason:

"I always thought Shirley Temple was extremely talented, but about the time she became a child star I had been quoted in a newspaper interview that I disapproved of commercializing on a child's

efforts. Because I could not go against what I had said, I did not make the doll." (Especially since she had not gained the rights to do so!) Yet in March of 1935 Madame Alexander presented "the only authentic 'Little Colonel' doll." All advertising cited the fact that her permission to produce the doll came from the holders of the copyrights of the children's books based on the character. The dolls look very similar in appearance to the *Shirley Temple* doll by Ideal. Wards 1935 Christmas catalog shows these dolls in various costumes. An interesting feature of the *Little Colonel* dolls is that they have wigs that look just like a *Shirley Temple* doll wig, forehead curl and all. Alexander advertising cited the fact that "the book has been a juvenile classic for innumerable years and is a tremendous seller today" and most importantly of all that "*the film* appeals to adults and juveniles alike." All of this coincided with Shirley Temple's 1934 Fox release *The Little Colonel*.

In March of 1935, the same month in which the *Little Colonel* ad appeared in *Playthings,* Ideal carried an "Important Notice" with their *Shirley Temple* doll ad. It stated:

"We are the only doll manufacturer authorized by the parents of Shirley Temple and by Fox Film Corporation to put out 'Shirley Temple' dolls, dresses and accessories.

"The manufacture or sale of any imitation 'Shirley Temple' dolls will be vigorously prosecuted.

"The sale of imitation 'Shirley Temple' dolls by any store is made a misdemeanor in New York State in addition to civil rights throughout the country. 'Shirley Temple' is our registered trademark."

The Dionne Quintuplets, the most exploited children of the era, were made in doll form by Madame Alexander beginning in 1935. Interestingly enough, by November of 1935 Alexander ads carried the warning that:

"The *only* genuine Quintuplet dolls are Dionne Quintuplet dolls. Warning: The Canadian Guardians of the only Quintuplets will take proceedings against all infringements to the rights of the Dionne Children."

In July of 1936 the E. Goldberger Doll Company (Eegee) introduced *Miss Charming* and *Baby Charming.* The Goldberger *Miss Charming* in all the ads looks just like a *Shirley Temple* doll with a wig and dress style that is much the same. Here is a description of the dolls from *Playthings* in September of 1936:

"LITTLE MISS CHARMING — The doll that everybody loves! This beautifully dressed doll has moving eyes with lashes, a gorgeous head of well set blonde hair, and shiny white teeth showing through her laughing mouth. She stands 17 inches tall and wears a cute celluloid button bearing her name and picture. A pretty ribbon and two golden clips adorn her hair. She is fully dressed, with white shoes and jeweled buckles. A fine assortment of dress styles is available. Placed in a strong, attractive box . . . "Little Miss Charming Dolls are available in all popular sizes from 12 to 27 inches high. 'Baby Charming', a companion line — consists of a complete assortment of baby dolls with and without wigs." The entire description seems like one for *Shirley Temple* dolls! Goldberger and Alexander were not the only infringers of Ideal's *Shirley Temple*. Almost every doll company had a similar doll. Horsman even called its look-alike *Bright Star* to remind buyers whom she looked like.

In the August 1936 *Playthings* along with the advertisement for Shirley Temple Dolls by the Ideal Novelty & Toy Co. this notice appeared:

WARNING!

"We have recently settled a lawsuit in Common Pleas Court of Philadelphia County *by securing a perpetual injunction.* An injunction was issued perpetually restraining the defendant 'from using in connection or in association with any doll not manufactured by plaintiff, Ideal Novelty & Toy Company, its successors or assigns, the trade name 'Shirley Temple' or any deceptive simulation thereof, or the name 'Shirley' or any deceptive simulation thereof, or the picture of the actress 'Shirley Temple;' or from selling or causing to be offered for sale dolls not manufactured and sold by the plaintiff which are deceptively similar in appearance, dress and get-up to the doll of the plaintiff known as the 'Shirley Temple' dolls, etc.'

"*It is the intention of Ideal Novelty & Toy Company to proceed vigouously against any other infringers.*"

Over the years many, many dolls were made who took their inspiration directly from the *Shirley Temple* dolls by Ideal. The largest variety came during the late 1930s in composition. Many of these Shirley Temple look-alikes have fooled the unwary. Enthusiastic sellers have been known to take any old composition doll with a blonde wig and put it in a flea market with a big sign on it proclaiming that it is an "unmarked *Shirley Temple*" with a price on it that is higher than the genuine article would bring. The original *Shirley Temple* doll almost always has the name "Shirley Temple" on it. Authentic *Shirley Temple* dolls have been verified with no markings, but one should be cautious in considering them the "real thing" if they have no original clothing, and particularly if they do not have an original Shirley Temple wig.

After 1939 Shirley Temple declined sharply as a film attraction. Ideal also stopped promoting and producing the dolls, using the molds for other characters like Snow White. (These dolls have "Shirley Temple" markings.) Some molds were sold to companies who tooled out the Shirley Temple name; other molds appear to have been copied.

Several different kinds of dolls that closely resemble little Shirley Temple were imported from Japan until December 7, 1941. None of these were copied from Ideal's dolls, but every other thing about them proclaims who they were supposed to be. Many of them resemble the little actress even more than the Ideal dolls but the Japanese, wishing to avoid trademark violations, were never foolish enough to call the doll "Shirley Temple." Today there is a doll with bisque parts available called "Shirley" that is made in Taiwan. It is a direct lift from a composition Shirley Temple doll, except that it is, to be very generous, *not* a pretty doll. The over-sized curls of the wig are only slightly reminiscent of Shirley's dainty curls and the big painted eyes would be more suitable on a Little Orphan Annie doll.

By the late 1950s Shirley Temple was popular all over again after a period of retirement, during which time she had obtained a divorce and remarried. Shirley Temple films were shown on television and youngsters and the adults who remembered her as a child revived an interest in her that has not ceased yet. From 1958 until the fall of 1961 she appeared on television on a semi-regular basis, presenting an anthology of children's stories in which she sometimes starred. The television shows attracted a following but the critics did Shirley Temple no favors. The revival of Shirley Temple's popularity inspired Ideal to produce a new series of *Shirley Temple* dolls in vinyl.

The vinyl *Shirley Temple* dolls from 1957 to the early 1960s came in sizes of 12in (30.5cm), 15in (38.1cm), 17in (43.2cm), 19in (48.3cm) and 35in (88.9cm). The largest vinyl edition is considered by many collectors as the most desirable of all the *Shirley Temple* dolls. It was relatively expensive - about $26.00 - and was not produced in the huge quantities as the smaller ones were; therefore, it is scarce and the most expensive doll for collectors today. In 1972 Montgomery Wards celebrated its 100th Anniversary and the company issued a special *Shirley Temple* Ideal doll for the event. It was made from the mold of the 15in (38.1cm) 1957 doll, although it is a lighter volume vinyl and measures about 14in (35.6cm). The last *Shirley Temple* doll from Ideal was the one from 1973 that came in two variations. This doll is still around in humongous quantities and many think that it is the most realistic rendition of the little actress that Ideal ever made.

Illustration 7. 14in (35.6cm) all-vinyl *Shirley Temple* made for Montgomery Wards 100th Anniversary in 1972; rooted blonde hair; hazel sleep eyes with lashes; open mouth with teeth; dimples. Everything is original including the bobby pins in the hair and the white vinyl shoes. Head marked: "HONG KONG // IDEAL DOLL // ST-15-N," back marked: "IDEAL ST 15 // HONG KONG." Dress labeled: "MADE IN HONG KONG."

Even the vinyl *Shirley Temple* dolls were copied by other doll manufacturers. One copy was advertised as *Little Miss Movie Star* in the late 1950s. (See Illustration 1).

In 1980 The Ideal Toy Corporation catalog showed a new *Shirley Temple* doll. It was never marketed though. Many reasons have been given for this, to the chagrin of collectors. My best guess is that the doll as shown in the catalog was such an inferior product that it was deemed unwise to put it into production. (See Illustration 8).

During 1981 Ideal will sell the *Patty Play Pal* doll that was first introduced in 1958. This 35in (88.9cm) doll uses the same basic body that the 35in (88.9cm) *Shirley Temple* doll did. All collectors are hoping that for 1982 - or 1984, the 50th Anniversary of the *Shirley Temple* doll - Ideal will again offer a 35in (88.9cm) *Shirley Temple*

Illustration 8. The 11½in (29.2cm) Ideal *Shirley Temple* doll that never was. The 1980 Ideal Toy Corporation catalog showed this doll with Sara Stimson, the child who played the Shirley Temple role in the fourth version of Shirley Temple's hit film *Little Miss Marker.* (The picture was such a bomb that it was not widely distributed.) The small packaged Shirley Temple doll pictured above the larger Shirely Temple doll's head is an even different version in facial modeling and body construction. It is also less pretty. Yet all collectors wish that they could have had this doll anyhow.

doll. No matter what they charge for it, the 35in (88.9cm) *Shirley Temple* will be much less than the $1200.00 that is today usually asked for the version from the late 1950s to the early 1960s.

The very best copy of a *Shirley Temple* doll ever would be one that the Ideal Toy Corporation copied from its own classic design. It would never be considered a copy, just like Shirley Temple herself who will always be an original.

IDENTITY UNCOVERED

by **Jan Foulke**
photograph by **Howard Foulke**

"Dummy Dan". All-original with remains of box.

Everyone called him Charlie McCarthy—dealers who offered him for sale, collectors who owned him, even authors who wrote about him, including us in our *2nd Blue Book of Dolls & Values*, page 190! But now he has come to light in his original box and has revealed to us his true identity: "Dummy Dan, The Ventriloquist Man."

He was made by Ralph A. Freundlich, probably in the late 1930s to early 1940s as a competitive product for EffanBee's Charlie McCarthy. This particular "Dummy Dan" is 21in. (53.3cm) tall, but apparently he came in various sizes. His head and hands are composition, his body is cloth and his hair and eyes are painted. His mouth can be opened and closed with a string at the back of his neck. He is dressed in black and white checked pants and cap, black coat with matching checked trim—a very dapper young man indeed, and its's nice to know who he is!

COLLECTING CLOWNS

A Photographic Essay
by Patricia N. Schoonmaker
Photographs by John Schoonmaker

See color illustrations on pages 178 and 179.

What could be more unique or appealing in a collection than a clown doll? From the court jester of the Middle Ages, there have been clowns through the ages. Pierrot, (or "Little Peter" in French) was the first clown to use white makeup on his face and to wear a "clown suit" as we know it. Enrico Caruso, the noted Italian singer, made famous the role of a heartbroken clown in the opera *Pagliacci.*

The Big Treasure Book of Clowns by Felix Sutton, (Grosset and Dunlap), explains that all real clowns are named "Joey," after Joseph Grimaldi, the first of the outstanding modern clowns. The first of the three most basic types of clowns is "The Auguste," a slapstick clown who will do anything to make you laugh. Second is "The Grotesque" clown, named for his costume which is very exaggerated. The face is usually white with a big red, putty nose. He wears silly hats and possibly carries a little parasol. The third type is a "Character Clown" who is usually dressed as a tramp. Emmett Kelly is the most well-known example, and dolls have been made in his likeness.

Nearly every animal in the circus has performed in a clown costume at one time, and the hardest to train is the bear. However, if you own a clown teddy bear he will train easily and be a star performer.

Illustration 1. *12in (30.5cm)* The Reluctant Court Jester, *original creation by Elizabeth Watkins; porcelain head, arms and legs; separate shoulder; brown hand-painted eyes; gold neck ruff and bells; lavender, yellow and green velour suit; leather boots; Folie dressed in green taffeta.* Elizabeth Watkins Collection.

Illustration 2. *Early print from an antique scrapbook showing a young child playing with a mechanical* Punch *doll.*

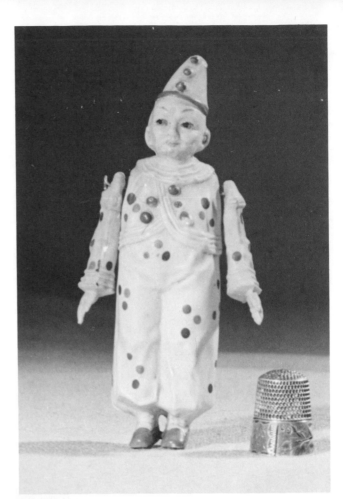

Illustration 3. *3½in (8.9cm) old celluloid clown with creamy look of old ivory by Rheinische Gummi und Celluloid Fabrik Co.; red, green and blue dots of color; green pompons. Marked below waist back:*

"   //GERMANY."

(Sterling thimble for size ratio. Thelma Bouchey Collection.

Illustration 4. *Acrobat Clowns.* **Bottom:** 6½in (16.5cm) (to peak of cap) Humpty *by* Schoenhut Toy Co.; *painted eyes, mouth, red and black face marks; white cotton suit with red and lavender design; red shoes; red trim on wooden cap.* **Top:** 6½in (16.5cm) (to peak of cap) Dumpty *by* Schoenhut Toy Co.; *different face mold with large grinning mouth, red face decorations, black brows; cotton suit is blue with polka dots; cap is of cotton material rather than wood. Both* Elizabeth Watkins Collection.

192

Illustration 6. 8½in (21.6cm) (to top of hat) Chucko the Clown by Hollywood Doll Mfg. Co.; red face paint; red and white suit with blue pompons; white ruff and sleeve and cuff ruffles; hard plastic five-piece body. 1955. Charles M. Runyon is the name of Chucko, a television personality prominent in the 1950s. Willa Koenigsaecker Collection.

Illustration 7. 8in (20.3cm) Jerry Jingle by Kitty Carson Doll Factory, Pioneer, California; yellow yarn hair; plaster face, hands and feet; red and yellow suit. Tag with name and maker and poem which ends: ". . . Talk to me, I won't talk back, but I'll listen and make your heart a little lighter." Florence Mayfield Collection.

Illustration 5. 8½in (21.6cm) (to peak of cap) clown by Herm Steiner; white bisque head with painted eyes, open/closed mouth, blue face markings; five-piece body; yellow suit with blue pompons, red neck ruff; brown shoes, black socks with red line at top. Marked: "GERMANY//HERM STEINER// 16/0." Elizabeth Watkins Collection.

Collectible Sonja Henie

BY JOHN AXE

Illustration 1. The doll is 21in. (53.3cm) tall and is all-original. She has a human hair wig that is essentially in its original set and still has the three original metal barrettes that were in the wigs of Sonja Henie dolls. Her original skating outfit is tagged and is blue taffeta with marabou feather trim. The headpiece also has marabou feathers and the underpants are the same material as the dress. The skates are silver, but the metal blades are missing. The fingernails are painted a light pink, and this is a factory original, not an addition to the doll. This rare size Sonja Henie doll is from the *Pat Slabe Collection* and it was a plaything from her childhood. The doll is not marked.

Illustration 2. (Right) The earlier composition Sonja Henie doll used the Wendy Ann body with the jointed swivel waist. The doll is 13-1/2in. (34.3cm) tall. The blond wig is human hair. The brown sleep eyes have lashes and dark eye shadow, as do the eyes on all the Sonja Henie dolls from Madame Alexander. These graceful dolls were dressed in skating or skiing costumes that carried Madame Alexander clothing tags that also cited that the doll was a "Sonja Henie." This version of the Alexander Sonja Henie doll is not marked on the head. The back of the doll is incised:

WENDY ANN
MME. ALEXANDER
NEW YORK

From the April/May 1979 Doll Reader.®

One of the most popular Hollywood film stars of the late 1930s and the early 1940s was Sonja Henie from Norway. During this same time period she was one of the most popular American all-composition dolls. Sonja Henie films are enjoyed on television now and Sonja Henie dolls are prized collector's items. Sonja Henie is the subject of my monograph, published by Hobby House Press. The book tells of Sonja Henie's fabulous life as an Olympic Gold Medal Skating Champion; her successful "Hollywood Ice Revue" which was enjoyed by millions of people who saw her perform in person, her film career which capitalized on her skating performances;

and of course all the Sonja Henie collectibles that are treasured today. There is a generous sampling of photographs to illustrate these features, as well as rare portraits and stills from Sonja Henie films.

Sonja Henie learned to ice skate at the age of six. She also studied ballet and combined this discipline with her free-skating performances, making her the national champion of Norway by the time she was ten years old. At twelve, in 1924, she competed in her first Olympic Games, placing eighth in figure skating. At the next three Winter Olympics—1928, 1932 and 1936—she placed first in women's singles in figure skating, having already won the world's championship ten consecutive times, an unbeaten record. From 1937 until 1953 she toured the country with her own production company staging ice revues in the major cities, proving that she was an outstanding athlete and an accomplished artist.

In the meantime she was offered a contract to appear in the movies. Being a shrewd businesswoman, Sonja Henie held out for one of the best contracts ever offered to a newcomer at that time. Her initial contract was with Twentieth Century-Fox and her first film, *One in a Million,* indeed proved that she was. The picture set box office records everywhere after it opened for Christmas of 1936 and by 1938 Sonja Henie was Number Three in the popularity polls, right behind Clark Gable, who was topped by Shirley Temple. A Sonja Henie picture was built around the star herself and each film featured skating sequences that were even more spectacular than her touring performances. Many top Hollywood leading men appeared with Sonja in her films, but she was always

Illustration 5. Portrait of Sonja Henie from the 1941 Twentieth Century-Fox picture, *Sun Valley Serenade.*

the headliner. Sonja Henie's last Hollywood movie was in 1948 and it was the remake of *The Countess of Monte Cristo*, which was not as successful as her earlier ventures. Her final picture was lensed in England in 1958 and was an inferior product called *Hello London*, which was never in general release. Sonja Henie films grossed $25 million.

Happily for collectors there were Sonja Henie souvenirs from her Ice Revues, coloring books, paper doll

Illustration 3. One of the Sonja Henie coloring books from Merrill. This is #3491, 1940, drawn by McMein.

Illustration 4. (Right) Back cover from one of the commercial sets of Sonja Henie paper dolls from Merrill. This is #3418 in 1941. *Marge Meisinger Collection.*

Illustration 6. Sonja Henie and skaters in a scene from the 1937 Twentieth Century-Fox film *Thin Ice*, which was advertised as *Lovely to Look At* before it went into general release.

booklets, movie memorabilia and of course Sonja Henie dolls by Madame Alexander. The dolls are more collectible than ever.

Many different dolls from the Alexander Doll Company use the same mold. An example of this is the McGuffey-Ana, Flora McFlimsey, Kate Greenaway and Princess Elizabeth dolls with the heads all marked Princess Elizabeth. The head of the Sonja Henie doll, executed by Bernard Lipfert (who else?), is completely distinctive and easily recognized as Sonja with her blond hair, brown eyes, smiling mouth with teeth and flashing dimples. The dolls were marketed from 1939 until about 1943 in composition and again in 1951 in hard

be purchased separately, as well as a huge variety of original costumes on the dolls themselves. Sonja Henie was also an accomplished skier and many of her films included skiing scenes. Sonja Henie dolls also came wearing ski costumes and skis and carried ski poles. Other dolls were dressed in contemporary gowns and dresses.

Little Sonja Henie, who was so beloved by her fans, died in 1969. She was traveling on an ambulance plane from Paris to her native Oslo with her husband. Before the plane landed Sonja Henie died from leukemia at the age of 57. □

Illustration 9. Sonja Henie films were light comedies and musicals. Many of them introduced hit songs, like "There Will Never Be Another You" from *Iceland* in 1942, which has become a "standard," or a classic. This is the cover of the sheet music, which in the 1930s and the 1940s sold like records and albums do today.

Illustration 7. Advertising announcement for the 1945 film *It's A Pleasure*, Sonja Henie's only film in color (excluding her final film, *Hello London*). This picture was made by International Pictures, who later merged with Universal Pictures to become Universal-International. *It's A Pleasure* was released by RKO Radio Pictures. Movie posters, lobby cards, stills, promotional material, theater programs and product advertisements are eagerly sought by collectors of movie memorabilia as well as doll collectors.

plastic and vinyl. During the period of Sonja Henie's immense popularity other doll companies put out "skating dolls," many of which are called Sonja Henie dolls today, the most common of these being from ArranBee. But the true Sonja Henie doll is by Alexander and is a unique personality-portrait doll. The Sonja Henie dolls wore skating costumes and miniature ice skates. There was an extensive wardrobe for Sonja Henie dolls that could

Illustration 8. Sonja Henie appeared on the covers of many movie magazines and general interest magazines. In the 1930s when movies were valued only as popular amusement, libraries did not consider subscribing to "fan" magazines, let alone save them. Now that films have been accepted as an American art form these institutions regret their former attitude and wish that they had not scorned these highly collectible items that can be used for research purposes. This copy of *Hollywood* is from 1938. The announcement on the cover referred to a contest in which the winner of a suggestion for a title for a future Sonja Henie film won Sonja Henie outfits, including parkas, hoods, hats and mittens. Another magazine, *Movies,* in December of 1939 awarded similar prizes to the entrants who selected the most perfect "leading man" for a future Sonja Henie film. Twelve lucky "young readers" were awarded prizes of original Sonja Henie dolls from Madame Alexander.

Illustration 10. Cigarette card from Germany in the 1930s, before the time Sonja Henie came to Hollywood. Personality trading cards attached to packs of cigarettes were at one time as popular in Europe as baseball player cards are in packs of American bubble gum today. The actual size of this card is 2-1/2 x 2-3/4in. (6.4 x 7cm). *Marge Meisinger Collection.*

Illustration 11. 14½in (36.2cm) *Sonja Henie* designed by Bernard Lipfert for Madame Alexander, circa 1941. She is fully-jointed composition; she originally wore ice skates but her dress is original and is labeled. The head is embossed: "MADAME ALEXANDER//SONJA//HENIE." *(Photograph by John Axe.)*

A Photographic Essay

by John Axe

One of the greatest advancements in doll manufacturing during the modern era was making dolls of all hard plastic. Plastic is an organic synthetic or processed material that is usually a by-product of petroleum. The first really popular hard plastic doll was IDEAL'S *Toni* who came out in time for Christmas in 1949. *Toni* eventually came in several sizes ranging from 14 in. (35.6cm) to 20½ in. (52.1cm) and the same basic doll was used for other doll characters from IDEAL. The *Toni* doll was an "advertising doll" who had a miniature Toni home permanent kit included with her so that her hair could be curled and set in various styles. The dolls had synthetic nylon, saran or dynel wigs that could be washed and combed without causing permanent damage to them. Durable hard plastic dolls with washable hair were imitated by other doll companies during the 1950s and all sorts of dolls were produced using the concept of the *Toni* dolls.

The following illustrations show the various dolls that utilized the different *Toni* molds from IDEAL. All are dressed in original costumes; some slight variances from originality are pointed out.

The standard head and body molds used for *Toni* dolls are the following with the sizes given for standard versions:

P-90 14 in. (35.6cm)
P-91 15 in. (38.1cm)
P-92 18½ in. (47.0cm)
P-93 20½ in. (52.1cm)

(Accurate measurements may not coincide with catalog descriptions.)

RIGHT: Illustration 2. Full-page advertisement from a Sunday newspaper supplement from about 1953, showing *Toni, Miss Curity, Harriet Hubbard Ayer* and *Betsy McCall.* The original prices seem surprisingly high even when compared with today's inflationary standards:

Toni	14 in. (35.6cm)	$11.98
	16 in. (40.6cm)	$13.98
	19 in. (48.3cm)	$16.98
	21 in. (53.3cm)	$19.95
Miss Curity	14 in. (35.6cm)	$11.98
Harriet Hubbard Ayer	14 in. (35.6cm)	$11.98
	16 in. (40.6cm)	$13.98
	19 in. (48.3cm)	$16.98
	21 in. (53.3cm)	$19.95
Betsy McCall	14 in. (35.6cm)	$ 7.98

ABOVE: Illustration 1. The four sizes of marked *Toni* doll heads. These were available from a doll supply company in the 1950s to use as replacements for damaged dolls. The heads are marked, from left to right: "P-93 // IDEAL DOLL // MADE IN U.S.A.;" "P-92," same as P-93; "P-91," same as P-93; "P-90," same as P-93.

198

LEFT: Illustration 3. P-91 *Toni* head with a dark brown replacement wig from the 1950s. The original carton is in the background. (The wig is only resting on the head.) The curlers at the right came attached to the arm of various *Toni* dolls and others of the same type.

ABOVE: Illustration 4. P-90 *Toni* with bright red hair and dark eyeshadow. The back is marked: "IDEAL DOLL // P-90." The original dress is aqua and white.

LEFT: Illustration 5. Two *Toni* walkers with light blonde hair and eyeshadow. Note the walking mechanism which is attached to the head so that it turns from side-to-side when the doll "walks" when led by the arm. The larger doll is 16 in. (40.6cm) tall and has a P-91 head; the back is marked: "IDEAL DOLL // 16." The smaller is 14 in. (35.6cm) tall with a P-90 head; the back is marked: "IDEAL DOLL // 90 W."

RIGHT: Illustration 8. Two P-93 *Tonis,* the largest size. Both are wearing original dresses. The doll on the right has replaced shoes. The dress labels (as on most original Toni clothing) are: "GENUINE TONI DOLL // WITH NYLON WIG // MADE BY IDEAL TOY CORPORATION." The 20½ in. (52.1cm) size is marked on the back: "IDEAL DOLL // P-93."

ABOVE: Illustration 6. Two P-92 Tonis, both with eyeshadow. On the left is a walker with reddish-brown hair, original yellow cotton dress with attached apron; original vinyl shoes marked: "IDEAL TOY CORPORATION // MADE IN U.S.A.;" back is marked: "IDEAL DOLL // 19." On the right is Toni with dark blonde hair and a dress that may not be original. The standard P-92 doll is marked on the back: "IDEAL DOLL // P-19." On the right is Toni with dark blonde hair and a dress that may not be original. The standard P-92 doll is marked on the back: "IDEAL DOLL // P-19."

BELOW: Illustration 7. P-90 and P-91 in original dresses. (The footwear is not original.) The back of the 15 in. (38.1cm) doll is marked: "IDEAL DOLL // P-91."

RIGHT: Illustration 9. P-92 walker. This one is still in her original box that includes a cowgirl outfit and a wedding dress along with extra shoes. The original price was $17.00. This Toni has very light blonde hair and the straw hat is also original. Jean Canaday Collection.

Illustration 10. Mary Hartline was first issued in 1952, utilizing the *Toni* mold. She has light blonde hair and dark eyeshadow. The original majorette outfits, copied after those that Mary Hartline wore on the television show "Super Circus," are red cotton with white painting. The original carton and baton belong to the doll on the right. These dolls are the P-91 mold.

Illustration 11. Miss Curity came out for Christmas in 1953. She is the P-90 doll with blonde hair and eyeshadow. All of *Miss Curity's* accessories are shown with the original package. The nurse's uniform is white and the cape is navy blue lined in red.

Illustration 12. Harriet Hubbard Ayer is from 1953. On the left is the P-91 body; on the right is the P-90. The stuffed vinyl heads are marked respectively: "MK 16 // IDEAL DOLL" and "MK 14 // IDEAL DOLL." These dolls have hair color of various shades and the wigs are glued to the head. The arms are also vinyl with bright red fingernails. The dresses are gray and the aprons are white with red stripes and white with green stripes. The original ads said that "Harriet Hubbard Ayer is the *only* doll in the world with Ideal's exclusive 'Magic Flesh' —specially made for doll make-up." She had her own "non-staining, washable 8 piece cosmetic kit by Ayer, creator of famous beauty preparations."

Illustration 13A & B. Betsy McCall has the P-90 body and she came out in 1952. The vinyl head has a glued-on dark wig and it is marked: "McCALL CORP." The original costume is a white blouse and a bright red rayon jumper. The McCall's apron pattern came in the original carton that shows a picture of a *Betsy McCall* paper doll which was drawn by Kay Morrissey in McCall's Magazine beginning in May of 1951.

Illustration 14. Shown here is an IDEAL doll called *Sara Ann,* as stated on her original tag. She is identical to the P-90 *Toni* doll and has blonde hair and wears a red and white dress. The vinyl shoes are the later shoes for *Toni* and date the doll from the early to mid 1950s. This doll came in all the *Toni* sizes (thus saving royalties to the Toni Company) and without the original tag is difficult to identify.

Illustration 15. Princess Mary is a very unusual all-original doll on the P-91 *Toni* body from ca. 1954. The head is stuffed vinyl and is marked: "IDEAL DOLL // V 91." The hair is an early attempt at "rooted" hair as it is inserted like the hair on the early wax dolls. The dress is yellow rayon with an attached slip. Only the sox are replaced. The doll measures 15¼ in. (38.8cm).

"Hi! I'm Ginny"

by Jan Foulke

Photographs by Howard & Beth Foulke

All dolls from the Beth Foulke Collection.

Illustration 1. This sweet little girl, obviously *Alice in Wonderland,* dates from the early 1940s when Vogue produced a series of *Nursery Rhyme* and storybook characters. Her composition is of excellent quality, smooth and colorful. Her cobalt blue eyes look to the left; she has faintly molded hair under a blonde mohair wig; her arms are molded alike. She is marked "VOGUE" on both the back of her head and torso. Her outfit is all original, tagged with the blue and white Vogue label. Her blue cotton dress has two rows of white piping around the bottom and is topped with a white organdy apron with lace and rickrack trim. Her stockings go up over her knee, and she is wearing black snap shoes.

Illustration 2. This *Toddles* composition boy has the same body as the girl in the first illustration. Even his eyes with the widespread lashes and white highlight are painted the same. His outfit is of pink cotton knit; his shirt with blue, white and maroon stripes matches his socks; his snap shoes are pink. He is from the same early 1940s period and has a sister in a matching costume with a skirt instead of shorts. I have also seen this outfit in white and blue cotton knit. He also has the blue and white Vogue label on his clothes.

I am not really sure how my daughter, Beth, became interested in the *Ginny* dolls made by Vogue, but there are now 35 of these little imps occupying a treasured place in her doll collection. I think she is just particularly drawn to their sweet faces; there is no underplaying the appeal of these charming little dolls. With all of her accessories, *Ginny* just makes a fun collectible. There is always some goodie to look for at a doll show or flea market: in addition to her furniture (bed, chairs, table, chest, wardrobe), there are trunks, suitcases, hair bands, hangers, hats, shoes, glasses, parasols, skis, skates, purses, jewelry and even her own Steiff dog! Not to mention her extensive and fashionable wardrobe. In 1953 alone, she had more than 40 outfits!

After beginning her collecting with all *Ginny* dolls, Beth has traded off and narrowed her interests down to only those dolls made in 1953 and before. These are the composition *Toddles* and the hard-plastic dolls with painted eyes or moving eyes with painted lashes which do not have a walking mechanism. As for accessories and clothes, she has allowed herself to go beyond this date, feeling that a little girl with a *Ginny* doll would have continued to add items over a period of years.

Since the *Ginny* dolls have become so popular in the past few years (prices are up over 600% in five years), Beth has agreed to share some of the dolls from her collection in this article. Just a little background material is given on the manufacturer, Vogue Dolls, Inc. For more detailed information in an indispensable guide for the *Ginny* doll collector refer to *That Doll, Ginny,* by Jeanne Niswonger.

Up to 1937 - - Jennie Graves started her Vogue Doll Shoppe business by dressing German bisque dolls and selling them to department stores. One of the little dolls which she used extensively was the *Just Me* doll made by Armand Marseilles. The first time I saw one of these dolls with a tagged Vogue outfit, I just assumed that someone had been clever enough to put a cute ready-made outfit on the doll, but after several of these turned up, I realized that it was certainly no coincidence, and that Mrs. Graves did indeed use the *Just Me* as one of her early dolls. One of these dolls in a storybook-type outfit is pictured on page 157 of the *2nd Blue Book of Dolls and Values.*

1937 to 1947 - - With the turmoil in Europe prior to the outbreak of World War II, Mrs. Graves could no longer obtain German dolls, so she was

Illustration 3. This girl *Toddles* is made of a different type of composition from the previous two; her finishing is not as fine, and her coloring is darker, not so peachy as the first two. She has one arm bent and one arm outstretched like the *Patsy* doll. She is marked "VOGUE" on her head and "DOLL CO." down near her back waist. Her eyes are more turquoise than blue, but they still look to the left. Over slightly molded hair her blonde mohair wig is built on just a small piece of gauze running under her machine-stitched side part. Her outfit is all original, a blue organdy dress and matching hat with pink, white and blue lace trim. She is also from the **1940s.**

Illustration 4. The composition girl on the left is the same type as the doll in Illustration 3. She is clearly identified by the stamp "JILL" on the sole of her shoe, where many of the *Toddles* are stamped. She dates from 1943 and is part of the *Character* and *Nursery Rhyme* series. Beth is now looking for her companion doll *Jack. Jill* is wearing a dress with blue and white checked skirt with attached panties and a yellow bodice with blue trim. Her hat matches her skirt, and her shoes are yellow. The composition dolls came with either slip ons, snap or tie shoes of a leather-like material. As with many of the early dolls, her outfit is not tagged. Probably less than half of these early dolls had tagged clothes, but one soon learns to recognize the Vogue clothes because of their fine styling and finishing detail. (Also they nearly all have a metal hook and thread eye as a back fastener.)

The hard-plastic doll on the right is *Tina* of 1953. She has brown eyes and auburn braids. Her school dress is of brown check with green, yellow and white trim. Vogue often gave individual dolls girls' names and the doll in the center is the original *Ginny* of 1951 with the new hair which could be wet, curled and combed; in 1952 she was one of the *Ginny* series. Her dress is pink and white check with white eyelet trim. Both *Tina* and *Ginny* have the narrow white label with the blue script "Vogue."

The dolls are marked "VOGUE" on the heads and "VOGUE DOLL" on the torso. The use of "Ginny" to apply to the doll in general apparently did not come about until 1953, when she was finally named for Mrs. Graves' daughter, Virginia, who designed all the lovely little clothes.

LEFT: Illustration 5. This 8in (20.3cm) hard-plastic boy with painted eyes is the *Prince* from the *Cinderella* set of 1949 and 1950, which also included *Cinderella* and her *Fairy Godmother*. His blonde mohair wig is over faintly molded hair. His tights are of blue cotton knit with an attached white organdy top with lace trim. His plumed hat and cushion holding Cinderella's slipper are blue satin. He is missing his blue satin jacket. His costume has the white Vogue label with blue letters.

RIGHT: Illustration 6. This 8in (20.3cm) girl is another of the storybook characters from the 1948 to 1950 period, but we are not exactly sure which one, perhaps *Bo-Peep*. She matches the *Prince* in construction, and also wears her original tagged clothes. Her dress is of pink cotton with an attached pinafore of white nylon with pink flowers and white trim. Her hat matches. Her blonde wig is very full, held together with a gauze strip sewn to her side part. She has the same clothes label as the *Prince*. Both dolls are marked "VOGUE" on the head and "VOGUE DOLLS" on the back torso.

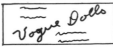

Illustration 7. The curved-limb babies with the same face as the toddler doll seem to have always been a part of the Vogue line. Beth does not have any of the composition babies in her collection (a gap which must be filled!), but she does have several of the hard plastic ones. This line was advertised as the *Crib Crowd* and featured "special ringlet wigs of real lambskin." The baby on the left is probably *Sally* from 1950; although she has a tagged Vogue dress, it is of later vintage than she is. The baby on the right is *Betsy* also from 1950; she has never been played with. Her pink dimity romper with eyelet ruffles has the same clothing tag shown with Illustration 6. She also has her original silver cardboard wrist tag.

The doll in the middle is a hard-plastic toddler with the lambswool wig, which was made in 1952 only, so is rather difficult to locate. He is *Wee Willie* from the *Frolicking Fables* series, and has his silver wrist tag, which says "Willie" on the reverse side. He is wearing a pink printed one-piece pajama and white nightcap. Blue pompoms decorate his pajama, cap and slippers. His original pink box with blue and white pasted-on label is not shown. All of these dolls are marked "VOGUE" on the head and "VOGUE DOLL" on the back torso.

forced to find a domestic supplier. During this period she apparently purchased some 8in (20.3cm) composition dolls from Arranbee, so it is not necessarily incorrect for a marked R & B doll to have tagged Vogue clothes. At this time also she commissioned an 8in (20.3cm) composition toddler doll to be designed. The company referred to these dolls as *Toddles,* but today collectors refer to them as the composition *Ginny* although at this period Vogue was not using the name "Ginny." Beth has ten of these small composition dolls in her collection, four of which are shown in Illustrations 1 through 4.

1948 to 1950 - - During this period most of the doll manufacturers turned to the use of hard plastic which turned out to be one of the most satisfactory mediums used to make dolls, and Vogue was no exception. Their dolls of this period were made entirely of hard plastic with painted turquoise-blue eyes looking to the left, still having wide-spaced upper eyelashes and white highlights. The plastic allowed for a more shapely arm and for fingers with greater detail than those on the composition dolls. Dolls from this period are shown in Illustrations 5 and 6.

1950 to 1953 - - During this period, the *Ginny* dolls were made of hard plastic with the added feature of sleep eyes. These dolls did not walk, as that mechanism was not added until 1954. Now the dolls had both blue and brown eyes with painted upper lashes. They also had both mohair and synthetic wigs in a wide variety of shades and colors from champagne blonde to bright red. This was also the period of the silver wrist tag with blue lettering: "A Vogue Doll."

Some tags had the name of the doll on the back. These dolls are shown in Illustrations 4 and 7 through 11.

Illustration 8. A prized doll in Beth's collection is this baby which was issued as a special promotion doll for the 1950 Easter holiday. She has a blonde lambskin wig with attached bunny ears of light green poodle cloth and pink felt. Her costume is also of the light green poodle cloth with pink satin bows and white net trim.

Illustration 9. Pairs of dolls were always a popular feature with Vogue. In 1952 this pair in Alpine outfits was offered along with a *Holland* pair, a *Rodeo* pair, a *Brother and Sister* series and a square dancing pair. The dolls pictured both have blonde wigs; his is mohair and hers is synthetic. They are wearing matching outfits with blue felt caps, pants and skirt, white organdy blouses and yellow felt vests. Their cheeks are soft pink.

Illustration 10. Skating dolls on both ice and roller skates were offered almost every year by Vogue. This little girl from the 1953 *Gadabout Series* is especially attractive as she has beautiful red hair, dark blue eyes, and a skating outfit of purple velvet with gold trim. Like the pair in Illustration 9, she is marked "VOGUE" on the head and "VOGUE DOLL" on the back torso. Her dress tag is slightly different, as is her silver wrist tag which says "Vogue Dolls, Inc."

ORIGINAL
Vogue
DOLLS, Inc.

Illustration 11. The doll on the left is *Ginger* of 1953. (Remember that Vogue often gave their dolls names of little girls; this is not to be confused with the Cosmopolitan *Ginger* doll.) She is a beautiful blue-eyed blonde dressed in a red velvet outfit. Her hat is trimmed with white fur and red cherries; she is carrying a red purse and some cherries; her shoes are red suede with red bows. Many Vogue dolls from this period wore tie rather than snap shoes. (The plastic "Ginny" shoes were not used extensively until 1955.) The doll on the right is from the 1952 *Kindergarten Series;* although she looks a little fancy for attending school; perhaps she is dressed for a party. She is very striking with her champagne blonde hair and dark brown eyes. Her dress is white satin with a green print, overhung with green velvet. A very large light green bow adorns her hair. Both dolls are marked "VOGUE" on the head and "VOGUE DOLL" on the back torso. They have the same label as *Tina* in Illustration 4.

Black Members of the Barbie Doll Line

by SIBYL DeWEIN

Sibyl DeWein is author of *Collectible Barbie Dolls 1977-1979* and coauthor (with Joan Ashabraner) of *The Collector's Encyclopedia of Barbie Dolls.*

Mattel's first attempt to add black dolls to its famous *Barbie* doll line was a failure. This was in 1967 when they presented a black version of the *Francie* doll; the original *Francie* had been introduced the year before as *Barbie's* younger cousin. Children found it difficult to accept a black version of *Barbie's* cousin so the doll was discontinued in 1968.

Black *Francie* was 11¼in (28.6cm) tall, had a twist and turn waist, bendable knees, medium brown skin, rooted eyelashes and was marked on the hip: " ©1966//Mattel, Inc.// U.S. Patented//U.S. Pat. Pend.//Made in//Japan." The early issue had rust colored eyes and brown hair that turned reddish as it aged; the later doll had brown eyes and brown hair that retained it's original color.

Since only a limited number of the black *Francie* dolls (called *Colored*

Illustration 1. Close-up of the *Black Barbie* doll.

Illustration 2. 11½in (29.2cm) *Black Barbie Doll,* introduced in 1980 and still on the market.

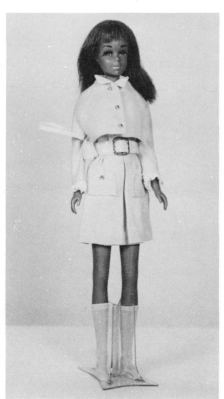

Illustration 3. 11¼in (28.6cm) *Francie,* the first black doll in Mattel's *Barbie* doll line. (This played-with, imperfect example is valued at $250.00.)

Illustration 4. 11½in (29.2cm) *Golden Dream Christie,* the 1981 version of the *Christie* doll introduced in 1968.

Francie back in those days) were produced, they are now extremely scarce; therefore they are selling for ridiculous prices. Early this year a nude, unboxed, played-with doll sold for $250.00; a NRFB (never-removed-from-box) doll lists for $500.00 and up.

Although their first black doll was rebuffed, Mattel tried again in 1968 with a *Christie* doll, this time with notable success. *Christie, Barbie's* friend, with a distinct personality of her own, is still a member of the line. Although there have been only 11 different *Christie* dolls to date, these 11 have varied so much that a good collection contains approximately 37 dolls.

In all, there have been nine black dolls, plus a black doll's doll, in the line. *Julia,* based upon the television show, "Julia," played by Diahann

Carroll, was introduced in 1969 as *Barbie's* celebrity friend. The doll came in two versions, a *Twist 'N Turn* nurse and a *Talking* doll. With variations, a good collection might have about 12 different *Julia* dolls.

Christie's boyfriend, *Brad,* the first black male doll in the line, was

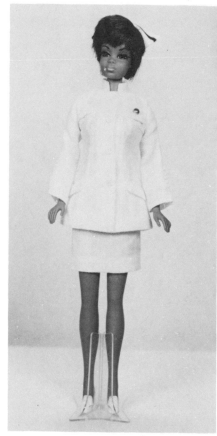

Illustration 5. 11½in (29.2cm) *Julia,* *Barbie's* celebrity friend, based upon the television show, "Julia," played by Diahann Carroll.

on the market in 1970 through 1972 in two versions with seven or eight variations.

Nan 'N Fran, a 6¼in (15.9cm) black doll holding a 3in (7.6cm) black toy doll, was on the market in 1970. Since this was another limited production item, the pair sells in the $50 to $75 range, or higher, if NRFB.

Two black dolls were introduced in 1975, 11½in (29.2cm) *Cara* and 12in (30.5cm) *Curtis.* Although *Free Moving Curtis,* the only version, was on the market only one year, collectors are finding an adequate supply at reasonable prices. *Cara,* on the market two years, came in four versions with about eight variations.

In 1976 Mattel introduced to the German market a 6¼in (15.9cm) black girl doll named *Carla.* Although not sold in the United States, the doll is still on the market in Germany and collectors can usually get one without too much difficulty. A good collection

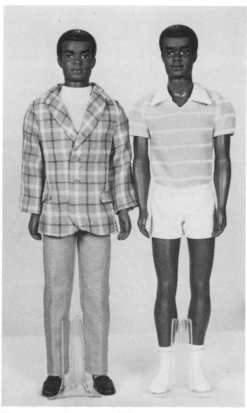

Illustration 6. 12in (30.5cm) *Brad* and 12in (30.5cm) *Curtis,* the only black male members of the line. Currently there are no black male dolls on the market.

Illustration 7. *Ballerina Cara.* There were three other versions of this 11½in (29.2cm) member of the line: *Free Moving, Quick Curl* and *Deluxe Quick Curl.*

Illustration 8. *Nan 'N Fran,* one of the "Pretty Pairs" group. Nan is 6¼in (15.9cm) tall; Fran is 3in (7.6cm).

Illustration 9. 6¼in (15.9cm) *Carla* from Germany. Not sold in the United States.

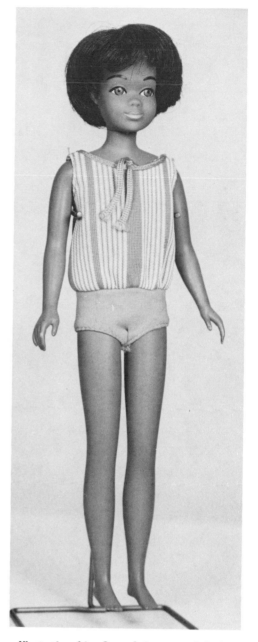

Illustration 10. Close-up of the black *Skipper* doll.

would have about five *Carlas* to have all variations.

A black version of the *Barbie* doll, herself, was put on the market in 1980 and was immensely successful. This must reflect something of the changing attitudes in the country during the past 13 years.

So from *Colored Francie* of 1967 to *Black Barbie, Sun Lovin' Christie, Golden Dream Christie* and *Carla* of 1981, the avid *Barbie* doll collector would need about 78 black dolls to have a complete, or close to complete, collection. A *complete* collection is almost impossible since "store display sets" containing black dolls are extremely hard to find; some dolls are too costly and then there is that rarest doll of all, the one-of-a-kind black *Skipper.*

This prototype black *Skipper* was bought from a former Mattel employee and is definitely a Mattel product. The doll's torso and limbs are the regular straight leg *Skipper* type, with the regular markings, that were stained brown. The head was made from a regular *Skipper* mold using a brown-colored plastic formula. The quality and styling of the hair is definitely Mattel's; the quality and styling of the swimsuit is also definitely Mattel's.

The doll's hair style is somewhat similar to that of *Bendable Leg Midge* and it's swimsuit is styled like *Bendable Leg Barbie's.* It seems a logical assumption that this prototype black *Skipper* was designed about the same time as the *Bendable Leg* dolls which were introduced in 1965. Therefore, the *Black Skipper* must have been the first black doll *designed,* although the black *Francie* was the first one *produced* for the market.

Illustration 11. One of the rarest dolls in the *Barbie* doll line. This 9¼in (23.6cm) prototype black *Skipper* was never produced for the market.

1981 TOY FAIR

by **MARY RECEVEUR RUDDELL**

Color Photographs by GARY R. RUDDELL

LEFT: Illustration 1. Three new artist dolls by Faith Wick.

BELOW: Illustration 2. Hattie Holiday attired in Easter and 4th of July costumes.

Toy Fair in New York City, February 15-17, 1981 was the annual preview showing of toy manufacturers, importers and specialty dealers. Naturally, our attention was focused toward items of interest to doll collectors. This year, collectors have much to be impatient over in awaiting your favorite dealer to receive their shipments.

At least you can do some planning (and budgeting) prior to your seeing these collectibles.

Effanbee Doll Company, who has released many doll collectibles over the years has done it again with their 52 *new* doll designs plus nearly 30

additional costume changes. Of particular interest is the second doll of the *Legend Series: John Wayne -- American, "Symbol of the West."* This 17in (43.2cm) doll is meticulously sculpted to give a likeness of this famous American Hollywood actor. He appears in red long-johns, a corduroy shirt, vest, saddleworn pants, cowboy boots and a cowboy hat. In his hand is a specially-made scaled carbine rifle. A portion of the royalty on the sale of each doll goes to the John Wayne Cancer Society Fund.

Effanbee has introduced three new artist dolls in vinyl by Faith Wick. Two of these dolls are witches: *Hearth Witch* and *Wicket Witch.* The dolls (18in [45.7cm]) sculpted with great detail even have warts on their noses. These are soft bodied dolls. The third doll is a peddler (16in [40.6cm]) carrying a tray of odds n' ends. She bears the dimpled full cheek look of Faith Wick dolls.

Hattie Holiday, a holiday ensemble doll with four changeable outfits, is an adorable 16in (40.6cm) toddler. The four holiday costumes are Christmas, Easter, 4th of July, and Hal-

210

From the April/May 1981 Doll Reader.®

Illustration 3. Effanbee's 1981 limited edition John Wayne doll from their Legend Series.

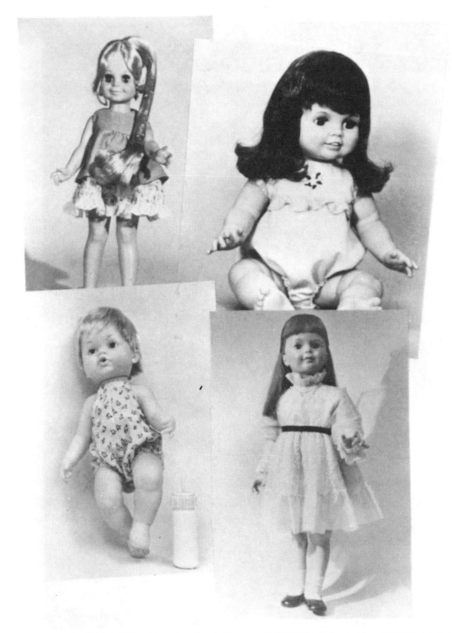

Illustration 4. TOP LEFT: Growing Hair Velvet. TOP RIGHT: Baby Crissy. BOTTOM LEFT: Tiny Tears. BOTTOM RIGHT: Patti Playpal. All dolls are being reintroduced in 1981 by Ideal.

loween. For Christmas, she is dressed in red velvet-like coat and hat. The Easter outfit is a blue organdy dress and straw hat. 4th of July is recalled by a drum majorette uniform, tall hat and a baton. For Halloween she is attired as a gypsy complete with mask. Costumes are to be available separately.

The *Four Season Doll* collection has been completely changed. The new dolls (15in [38.1cm]) are childlike with a more contemporary look replacing the high fashion look from years past.

The *Petites Filles Collection* has four sister pairs. Each pair consists of an 18in (45.7cm) soft-bodied bebe and a 16in (40.6cm) older sister dressed to match. They are porcelain

look-alikes. In this older sister group are *Denise* (16in [40.6cm]) in white satin, *Marianne* in royal blue velvet, *Genevieve* in rust taffeta and *Nanette* in light blue moire. The younger sister group (18in [45.7cm]) includes: *Bebe Denise* in white satin (with reddish hair), *Bebe Marianne* in royal blue velvet, *Bebe Genevieve* in rust taffeta, and *Bebe Nanette* in light blue moire.

The *Pride of the South Collection* consists of six new 13" dolls. The dolls are dressed to recall days of majestic southern living. In this line is *Natchez, Mobile, Savannah, New Orleans, Charleston* and appropriately a *Riverboat Gambler.*

The *Grande Dames* have all new costumes. Four new sized dolls of

11in (27.9cm) have been added. These dolls are dressed in the same grant style of the larger *Grande Dames.*

Effanbee has also introduced a line of *Pierrotts.* They are dressed in white taffeta with cherry red pompoms. Two of the clowns, 15in (38.1cm) and 17in (43.2cm) are soft-bodied. The other three are vinyl dolls which measure 11in (27.9cm), 15in (38.1cm) and 17in (43.2cm).

The *Storybook Collection* introduces *Hansel* and *Gretel, Mother Goose, Mary Had a Little Lamb,* and *Pinocchio.* Pinocchio with his pointed red nose seemed to say "so my red nose will not grow any longer - - I say Effanbee will 'touch the heart's' of collectors in 1981."

The news from the Alexander Doll Company for 1981 concerns few additions or changes to their line. A 12in (30.5cm) *Scarlett* in green taffetta, a 12in (30.5cm) *Rhett Butler* in traditional Southern gentleman's garb and a 12in (30.5cm) *Lord Fauntleroy* in black velvet are new additions. An *Elise Bride,* 16in (40.6cm) tall, is also new this year. The Portraits remain the same with color changes in costumes on Agatha and Melanie. This magazine regrets the Alexander Doll Company would not permit any photographs of the new dolls as it was the Alexander Company's opinion that showing their new dolls through photographs would be "advertising" and as such would only frustrate collectors. Once again the perennial question presents itself - - why can't the Alexander Doll supply be increased to better supply collectors?

The House of Nesbit from England shows quite a few new lavish costume dolls. They include: *Prince Charles* in the uniform of the Gordon Highlander, *Prince Andrew* in Naval Uniform, *Lord and Lady Baden Powell, Pocahontas, Sitting Bull,* and *General Custer.* A 250 set limited edition of Royal Wedding figures featuring the *Duke of York* with *Lady Elizabeth Bowes Lyon* and the *Duke of Edinburgh* with *Princess Elizabeth* will be available in 1981. There is also a signed and numbered 750 piece limited edition of *Ronald Reagan* in inaugural dress. See exciting word in the announcement following this article about Royal Doulton and House of Nesbit making fine bone china dolls!

Reeves International displayed several foreign lines of interest to collectors. Dolls made by Heidi Ott will come from Switzerland. These artist dolls are hand made on her farm. They feature vinyl heads,

ABOVE LEFT: Illustration 5. Limited edition Sasha doll.

ABOVE RIGHT: Illustration 6. Hand printed Martha Washington cloth doll by Crafted Heirlooms, Inc.

RIGHT: Illustration 7. 1981 Gerber Baby Doll attired in christening dress laying on matching pillow.

human hair wigs, soft bodies, and a mixture of soft and vinyl hands. Zanmi and Zambelli of Italy have 25in (63.5cm) vinyl Flapper dolls dressed in 1920s style. They also have two vinyl Pierrotts, as well as five high fashion dolls. The *Suzanne Gibson* line features five new drink and wet dolls. All other dolls in this line are recostumed.

Now starting to be availabe in a limited edition of 5000 is the *Sasha* doll. Each will be marked with its individual number and have a signed certificate. She is attired in dark blue velvet with lace at collar and cuffs and black patent shoes. Her eyes are painted grey blue.

Cloth dolls are becoming more popular. A hand printed *Martha Washington* doll in uncut form is available from Crafted Heirlooms, Inc. She is the first in an American made series including all First Ladies or

Illustration 8. Left to Right: Jack Wilson, Chairman of House of Nesbit, Peter Bull holding Bully Bear (note distinctive tag), and Timothy Atkins of Bear Necessities, a leading teddy bear sales organization with shops in Boston (MA), Pittsburgh (PA), Boca Raton (FL) and Providence (RI).

official hostesses. Separate costume portions with necessary trims and ribbons are included with each hand-screened doll. *Abagail Adams* and *Martha Randolph* are to be available in April. From Dean's Rag Book Co., Ltd. of England comes *Mignonne*. She is a screened doll made to mark the Church of England Children's Society Centenary. Available also are two old Teddy Bears on a rag sheet to cut and sew. Lenci dolls are still available but there is a new distributor. They have available twelve styles - - three large 27in (68.6cm) Lenci line dolls and nine smaller ones at 19in (48.3cm). These dolls are limited to a production of under 1000 and includes designs that were offered prior to this year.

There were also a number of porcelain dolls on display. Gerber Baby enthusiasts will be excited about the porcelain 14in (35.6cm) *1981 Gerber Baby Doll* introduced by Atlanta Novelty. This exquisite replica of the famous Gerber Baby, "Trademark" of the Gerber Products Company, comes in a wicker basket. It is wearing a christening dress which is an authentic reproduction and laying on a matching pillow, both of which have been embroidered in an eyelet design that dates from 1901. It's face, arms and legs are molded in bisque crafted by Shader's China Doll, Inc. and since this doll will be a limited edition of 10,000 pieces made only in 1981, the molds will be broken at the end of the production. Each doll will be individually numbered and will come with an authenticating certificate. This doll will retail in the $300

range. A smaller vinyl version in black as well as white will also be available in a basket.

Three all bisque Feltman dolls in a limited edition are available. The dolls range in size from 14in (35.6cm) to 16in (40.6cm) are attired in hand embroidered clothes. They were crafted by an anonymous designer. The production is limited to 895 numbered and notarized sets. These dolls will retail for approximately $800.00 each.

Dolls by Jeri displayed fine examples of original limited edition porcelain designs. These American made dolls are available in 1000 piece series. They are all-bisque with human hair wigs and glass eyes. The dolls which range in size from 16in (40.6cm) to 23in (58.4cm) are available in eight new designs. The new dolls are: *Mary with Lamb, Toy Soldier, Clara, Hansel and Gretel, Mistress Mary, Paul* and *Su-Tsen,* an oriental doll. Black doll collectors may find her exquisite *Miss Nanny* and *Uncle Joe* of interest.

Hazel Pearson Handicrafts showed a doll kit, *"Victoria Anne"* and Steamer Trunk, doll patterns and accessories. This kit includes a 17in (43.2cm) completed fabric doll with porcelain head, arms and feet. Also included in each kit is pattern and fabric for the lace-tipped nightgown, plus three additional period patterns and one shoe pattern. Two accessory lines are offered to embellish this doll: dresses, capes, coats and hard-to-find accessories and fabrics including small buttons, miniature trims and small-scaled print fabrics.

From Vogue doll comes a new *Ginny* attired in designer clothes

by Sasson. This doll has painted eyes and twenty designer outfits. Her clothes will be cross referenced with children's clothes by the same manufacturer.

Of great interest to collectors this year will be Ideal's 11½in (29.2cm) *Laura.* Designed by Judy Albert, this unique fashion doll features a "soft" bosom and derriere, and comes with a bra and panties. A Calvin Klein designer wardrobe is planned for *Laura* and her black counterpart *Robin.* Also of interest is *Loni Anderson,* an 11½in (29.2cm) replica of the star of the popular television show "WKRP in Cincinnati" and *Pretty Curls,* a 12½in (31.8cm) toddler with beautiful long hair which can be permanent-waved or styled in a variety of different hairdos. In addition, Ideal is reintroducing a wide range of best-sellers from the past, including 36in (91.4cm) *Patti Playpal* and 13in (33.0cm) *Tiny Tears.*

One great experience at Toy Fair was meeting Peter Bull. He was in New York to promote a new addition to the House of Nesbit line of Bears: *Bully Bear.* An enchanting conversation of the bear minimum introduced this honey-colored adult size bear. His welcoming arms, over-sized snout and humped back make him receptive to adult as well as children's problems. Mr. Bull reminded us that he has had a long interest in bears. We made the acquaintance of Theodore, his 40-year-old Teddy, which is carried in his coat pocket. Also of interest was a miniature Teddy that he proclaimed "the world's smallest Teddy Bear." It bears mentioning that this man is the author of the well known *Teddy Bear Book* (unfortunately out-of-print). A limited number of "Bully Bears," to be autographed by Peter Bull, are to be available in the U.S.

To commerorate their 101st Anniversary and to accompany the first limited edition, Stieff is offering a mother and baby Teddy for 1981 to create a family with last year's Teddy. This pair will match last year's in color, material, style, and presentation. It is planned to be an edition limited to 7500.

A bear family with a different approach is available from the North American Bear Co., Inc. These 20in (50.8cm) bears are soft and huggable. They are available in several styles: The ballet couple - - *Anna Bearlova* and *Bearishnikov;* the movie star - - *Douglas Bearbanks;* the fictional character - - *Scarlett O'Beara;* and the famous aviator - - *Amelia Bearhart.* Each is appropriately costumed and bears examination.

Discovered in Switzerland - Heidi Ott

by CLAIRE HENNIG
Photographs by MARGIE LANDOLT
of Basel

Illustration 1. Heidi Ott sewing doll bodies.

Her start as a commercial saleswoman was in 1977 with "partly-finished dolls" to be completed by customers, an idea now popular in the United States. Two models were available with two different constructions. Yet when people saw Heidi's smaller-sized ready-made dolls, they preferred these. So, for the time being, this half-ready line has been discontinued.

Today most of her dolls are part-commercialized. Heidi hands over to home workers ready-cut body material and ready-cut clothing to be partly sewn by them. Yet the final touches, like painting the eyes, mouth and hair (with the babies) are done by herself. Every doll goes through her expert hands. She sews fasteners, buttons, adds wigs and sees to it that legs are straight, a very tricky feature.

The body, made of machine-woven tricot, turns and twists which makes arms and legs turn their own way, although there is an extra strong lining inside. The dolls are filled with vinyl and similar substances and are

Illustration 2. Heidi Ott stuffing a doll's limb.

Heidi Ott, a creator of dolls, looks like a doll herself. No wonder that her dolls seem to be portraits of her. She need not be introduced to America as her dolls have been on display here for some time. Doll makers are not organized in Switzerland as are NIADA artists. Heidi works on her own, supported by her husband who does the secretarial work and by some other relatives, fully trained dressmakers. Her two children are moral supports and keep Heidi's critical capacity alive. I recommend a visit to Mettmannstetten (not far from Zürich) to see Heidi at work. She lives in a beautiful district, her home village, with a view of the Rigi mountains.

It happened thus: after leaving school, Heidi went to the French speaking part of Switzerland in order to learn the language. Her family, to tidy up the place, discarded all her "useless" dolls. When the girl returned home she was dismayed to find that her dolls had disappeared. She sat down in silence and just made dolls, seeing to it that they resembled her lost darlings. It was love for her dolls that started her on her career and it has remained love to this day, although there are now hundreds of these children sitting around in Heidi's workshop. Today she can hardly cope with orders and yet one would think each doll is a unique creation.

Illustration 3. Heidi Ott carving an individual doll head from wood.

Illustration 4. A girl and boy doll by Heidi Ott.

soft and pliable but can, nevertheless, stand on their own. Some of the heads are of rubber covered with tricot, others are of a type of vinyl, with a roughened surface in order to resemble the non-shiny human skin. Every doll is signed, marked and given an individual number and date.

A certain similarity has been detected to Käthe Kruse and also Sasha Morgenthaler dolls. This most likely springs from comparable mentality: all three artists loved natural, unsophisticated people and, in consequence, dolls. All three worked with a view to their own children. All three liked the simple life away from towns. Heidi's dolls are country-children of her own youth; they are babies or they go to school, wearing aprons and heavy black scratchy stockings held by elastic and buttons. The larger children's coiffures consist of human hair only, held by ribbons and bows. Their cotton clothes have small patterns and white lace collars.

Besides these half-commercially manufactured dolls, which are between 35cm (13¾in) and 48cm (18-15/16in) high, Heidi produces artist-dolls of about 48cm

(18-15/16in) in height. They have carved wooden heads and none are ever alike. They wear individual clothing and for these, specific wishes can be considered. They cost about eight times the price of the first dolls. They are not available through her agents but only through her directly.

There are pitfalls in home-doll manufacturing of which the buyer usually has no conception: material for clothing might have a slightly different pattern or shade from the one originally ordered and stockings or hand knitted pullovers might be slightly too big or too tight so that they take unforeseen time to readjust. To be in time for the Easter and Christmas collection often means working through the night. Worst of all was a fire which destroyed Heidi's stock, her patterns and her documentation. The Otts were not insured, unfortunately, but then they lived in a world of make-believe, play and fun and love.

Heidi sometimes regrets that her loving father, a farmer in her village, wanted to have his only daughter at home and did not fulfill her wish to let her go to an art school. She thinks she might have been an even more accomplished artist today had she

been allowed some kind of training. I am, however, convinced that it is her natural, unwarped, simple attitude and style of life that enables her to create these little people so much like herself. It is very satisfactory to see that they are appreciated in many parts of the world today.

Heidi's dolls have been included in Reeve's Toy catalog and have been exhibited in the United States.

In Switzerland they are represented by W. A. Linegger, Buchholzstrasse 120, Zürich 8053.

Heidi Ott lives at 12 Rossauerstrasse, CH-8932 Mettmenstetten, Switzerland, and can be contacted for further information at this address.

Illustration 5. Heidi Ott girl and baby dolls.

Illustration 6. Three little girls by Heidi Ott with three of her baby dolls with painted hair.

Illustration 7. A group of Heidi Ott dolls ready to be shipped to the United States.

TOY FAIR...
Guide to Collectible Manufacturer Dolls
of 1982

by EDITORIAL STAFF - DOLL READER

The job of researching the American Toy Fair to present the myriad of 1982 collector dolls by manufacturers was some experience! The manufacturers listened to the message collectors echoed in 1981 "keep those original doll designs made expressly for doll collectors!" In fact, there was such an extensive array of beautiful new doll models presented that it will take two articles in the Doll Reader to do it justice. Collectors in 1982 are in for a "feast and famine" situation. The feast is for the hundreds of new dolls to choose from whether they be porcelain, vinyl, cloth, wood or resin. The famine is sure to follow after the grocery money is spent on updating one's collection.

Effanbee Doll Corporation again silenced those who said "How can Effanbee top its' 1981 dolls?" The nostalgia and authenticity of "the Legend Series" sees two new blockbusters that will only be produced in 1982. A younger version of the Duke (No. 2981) as a frontier U.S. Cavalry soldier in blue with pistol, suspenders and hat is *John Wayne* "Guardian of the West." This 18in (45.7cm) doll is 1in (2.5cm) taller than last year's edition. This is the third "Legend" doll and the second and final version of this popular American hero. *Mae West,* the fourth "Legend" series doll, is as one remembers her - - sassy and voluptuous. The

shapely 18in (45.7cm) Miss West (1982) is costumed in a tightly fitted black taffeta gown with lace flounces. Her black hat with brim is trimmed with grey marabou and is finished with elaborate jewelry, white gloves, marabou feather boa, and a ribbon wrapped cane.

The "Craftsmen's Corner Collection" welcomes Joyce Stafford with her Effanbee debut of *Orange Blossom* (No. 7501). This 13in (33.0cm) Chinese tot is dressed in an orange peasant dress with green embroidered apron. You will not be able to forget her winsome expression. Faith Wick has two new entries. One doll is the 18in (45.7cm) old-fashioned *Nast Santa* (No. 7201). Her other new vinyl doll is a 16in (40.6cm) *Billy Bum* (No. 7007).

Among the 60 new models from Effanbee for 1982, collectors should note: "Storybook Collection" *Mary Poppins* (No. 1198), *Hans Brinker* (No. 1172), *Rapunzel* (No. 1199); 13in (33.0cm) "Absolutely Abigail Collection" of turn-of-the-century era with *Cousin Jeremy* (No. 3310), *Sunday Best* (No. 3311), *Recital Time* (No. 3312), *Strolling in the Park* (No. 3313), and *Afternoon Tea* (No. 3314); "Grande Dames Collection" with 15in (38.1cm) *Guinevere* (No. 1551), *Olivia* (No. 1552), *Claudette* (No. 1554), *Hester* (No. 1553) plus 11in (27.9cm) *Eliza-*

Illustration 1. *Mae West,* Effanbee's 4th "The Legends Series". *Photograph courtesy Effanbee Doll Company.*

beth (No. 1151), *Amanda* (No. 1152), *Katherine* (No. 1153), and *Robyn* (No. 1154); 18in (48.7cm) "Age of Elegance Collection" with *Buckingham Palace* (No. 7851), *Versailles* (No. 7852), *Victoria Station* (No. 7853) and *Westminster Cathedral* (No. 7854); and, 11in (27.9cm) *Bobbsey Twins, Flossie* (No. 1202) and *Freddie* (No. 1201) with outfits of clothes Winter Wonderland (No. 1221 boy and No. 1222 girl), At the Seashore (No. 1223 boy and No. 1224 girl), Out West (No. 1225 boy and No. 1226 girl) and Go A' Sailing (No. 1227 boy and No. 1228 girl). The new *1982 Effanbee Doll Catalog* in color is available for $2.50 from Hobby House Press, Inc.

Madame Alexander doll collectors can add some new treasures to their collections in 1982. First and foremost is the third set of six 14in

Illustration 2. Third six "First Ladies" by Madame Alexander. Left to right: *Martha Johnson Patterson, Jane Pierce, Harriet Lane, Abigail Fillmore, Mary Todd Lincoln,* and *Julia Grant. Photograph courtesy of Alexander Doll Company.*

Illustration 3. *John Wayne II,* third "the Legend Series." *Photograph courtesy of Effanbee Doll Company.*

(35.6cm) "First Ladies." *Abigail Fillmore* (No. 1514), 1850 to 1853, a brunette, wears a pink brocaded gown with pink taffeta ruffled over-skirt. Her gown is trimmed with multiple bows and braid and a knit shawl. *Jane Pierce* (No. 1515), 1853 to 1857, a blonde, wears a black jewel-tone net gown lined with black taffeta, over a pink taffeta petticoat and pantaloons, with a matching jewel-tone net shawl. The third First Lady, *Harriet Lane* (No. 1516), 1857 to 1861, with black hair, served as the hostess for her bachelor uncle, James Buchanan. She wears a white satin moire gown. A sweeping skirt has a pleated ruffle and braid trim over a white taffeta petticoat and pantaloons. In addition, *Harriet* wears a beige lace shawl. The famous *Mary Todd Lincoln* (No. 1517), 1861 to 1865 has brown hair pulled to one side in a long curl, adorned by flowers.

Mrs. Lincoln wears a purple cotton velveteen gown trimmed with cream color voille sleeves with a black shawl. The skirt is taffeta lined. Her petticoat and pantaloons are taffeta. The fifth First Lady, *Martha Johnson Patterson* (No. 1518) 1865 to 1869, has blonde hair and served as official hostess in the absence of her sick mother. She wears a pink, blue and gold brocaded gown trimmed with silver at waist and neck. Her full length crepe cape and hood is edged with gold lace and has tassels. Her petticoat and pantaloons are of white taffeta. The last First Lady of this third set is *Julia Grant* (No. 1519), 1869 to 1877, with blonde hair, wears a white and silver brocaded coat style gown with lace shawl, peach satin underskirt with white taffeta ruffled petticoat and panties.

The 21in (53.3cm) "Portrait Dolls" have two new additions. *Goya* (No. 2235) is a dark haired, brown eyed beauty wearing a black point d'esprit dress with a V-neck and puffed sleeves. The full skirt has wide black lace trim along the bottom. A black lace mantilla, black fan, and flowers and decorative comb complete her toilet. The second new "Portrait Doll" was inspired by *Manet* (No. 2225). This blonde lady doll looks as through she just stepped out of a painting with her double ruffled striped spice colored satin gown floating over her bouffant petticoat and pantaloons. The gown has long sleeves with lacy ruffles and a lace collar around the neck. Her hat and purse are of velveteen. The other new Alexander doll is a 17in (43.2cm) *Bridesmaid* (No. 1655). New fashions are sported by 14in (35.6cm) Cinderella Ball Gown (No. 1548), 20in (50.8cm) Victoria (No. 5748), 20in (50.8cm) Mommies Pet (No. 7136), and for the three sizes of *Pussy Cat* (14in [35.6cm] No. 3224, 20in [50.8cm] No. 5228, 24in [61.0cm] No. 6246.)

Mattel's newest *Barbie* is *Magic Curl Barbie* (No. 3856) and *Black Magic Curl Barbie* (No. 3989) with hair you can curl, straighten, and curl again. A *Pink & Pretty Barbie* (No. 3554) comes in a glamorous six-piece mix-and-match wardrobe with accessories. *Barbie* now has her own electronic toy baby grand piano that really works, a luxury bath, and both she and *Ken* have their own fashion signature jeans.

Athletic *All Star Ken* (No. 3553) actually flexes his muscles, has bend-able wrists, and a bending, twisting waist. Joining the *Barbie* family is the "Sunsational Malibu" series in beach attire: *Skipper* (No. 1069), *Barbie* (No. 1062), *Ken* (No. 1088),

P.J. (No. 1187), *Christie* (No. 7745), and *Ken* (black) (No. 3849).

Dazzle (No 5286) and her eight friends are introduced this year as 4½in (11.5cm) fashion dolls. With names such as *Glimmer* (No. 5292), *Rhinestone* (No. 5293), *Glissen* (No. 5295), *Glossy* (No. 5288), *Diamond* (No. 5289), *Crystal* (No. 5290), and *Spangle* (No. 5291). These little beauties have additional fashions, a horse, and their own city with change-around room.

Vogue Dolls, a division of Lesney, presents a new 8in (20.3cm) *Ginny* with a poseable body and new face painting. In addition to *Ginny* and her Sasson designer fashions, a new series is introduced: a magnificent collection of *Ginny* dolls dressed in traditional bridal costumes from 12 countries around the world. Packaged individually in window display boxes, these dolls will retail for between $10.00 and $12.00 each.

Spain, Greece and Japan have been added to the "Far-Away Lands" series.

"Glitter Girls," 5½in (14.0cm) miniature fashion dolls, have been added to the Vogue line. Named after precious jewels, these six different dolls have a Take-Along Fashion Penthouse and additional "Glitter" fashions. *Sapphire, Ruby, Crystal, Jade, Amber,* and *Pearl* each have totally poseable bodies and long silky hair that can be combed.

Sixteen-year-old Brooke Shields and her manager-mother Teri wanted the *Brooke Shields* doll to look as much like Brooke as possible. They aided designer Karyn Weiss in arriving at the final version of the doll, which looks exactly like the young star.

The *Brooke Shields* doll is all-vinyl and fully-jointed and is an 11½in (29.2cm) "fashion doll" that has 16 costumes. The sculpture for the head of the doll was done by Ken Sheller, a New York sculptor. Karyn Weiss traveled to Hong Kong twice to personally supervise the manufacture of the doll. Packaged with each *Brooke Shields* doll will be a star-shaped ring containing strawberry flavored lip gloss and a picture of Brooke signed "with love, Brooke Shields."

Brooke Shields appeared on the Johnny Carson Show on February 9 to display the doll likeness. *Time* magazine (February 8) reported that Brooke received one million dollars from L.J.N. Toys for the privilege of manufacturing the doll.

Shirley Temple, first introduced as a doll by Ideal in 1934, reappears this year in two sizes: 8in (20.3cm) and 12in (30.5cm). There are six dolls in each size dressed in costumes from the child star's most popular movies. These include: *Heidi, Stand Up and Cheer, The Little Colonel, Stowaway, Captain January,* and *The Littlest Rebel.*

Two other "classic" dolls are being revived by Ideal this year. They are: 15in (38.1cm) *Beautiful Crissy* and *Country Fashion Crissy* with growing hair; *Tiny Tears* in three 14in (35.6cm) drink and wet versions; and *Thumbelina* in four sizes.

"The Sophisticated Ladies" came to town and made a splash! Marcy, Dollspart's designer, is credited with this nostalgic and chic group of four 24in (61.0cm) dolls. Marcy has designed and selected elegant and exquisite characteristics and attire reflecting high society life throughout the years. Each doll has a soft-stuffed cloth body with a uniquely hand-painted porcelain face and poseable porcelain arms and legs. The models are *Lauren* (No. MB421), *Josephine* (No. MB242), *Clara* (No. MB243), and *Kim* (No. MB244).

Shader's China Doll Inc. has fine new musical dolls with porcelain heads and soft sculpted bodies. *Angel* (No. SS-1), dressed in all white, plays "Silent Night." The *Ballet Dancer* (No. SS-2), dressed in an elaborate white satin costume trimmed in lavender and wearing satin ballet slippers, has a fanciful white feathered headdress and plays "Music Box Dancer." The exotic *Belly Dancer* (No. SS-3) wears an appropriate costume of red and blue enhanced with glitter. She has a flowing black hairdo. The artistically costumed *Saloon Girl* (No. SS-5) plays "Deep in the Heart of Texas." Shader's *Mermaid* (No. SS-4), which plays "Ebb Tide," has an exaggerated hairdo. She is wearing a pink costume with a brilliant green tail.

Shader also has a new group of beautifully costumed dolls that are reproductions of antique classics.

The porcelain original Dolls by Jerri have several unique models for 1982. The "Mark Twain Series" includes three 18in (45.7cm) characters, *Tom Sawyer* (No. 825), *Huck* (No. 828) and *Becky* (No. 827) dressed in typical clothing from the Twain stories. These are limited editions of 1000 dolls each.

In the Walt Disney collection are two authentic doll renditions based on characters from the movie *Cinderella*. *Cinderella* (No. WD1-1) is 21in (53.3cm) tall in her blue ball gown. *Prince Charming* (No. WD1-2) is wearing red trousers and an off-white jacket with gold trim. The set also includes a satin pillow decorated

Illustration 4. *Shirley Temple* by Ideal in two sizes, 8in (20.3cm) and 12in (30.5cm). Six costumes. *Photograph courtesy of Ideal Toy Corporation.*

with gold tassels holding *Cinderella*'s blown glass slipper. Each doll is marked with the catalog number of the doll and "JERRI//Walt Disney Productions © //1982." These dolls are limited to 1500 each.

Little David (No. 829) is an 18in (45.7cm) two-faced baby in a christening dress and lying on a pillow. This edition is also limited to 1000.

A new company - Doll Classics by Al Trattner - launches its 1982 line by presenting four models in porcelain that are inspired by classical 17th century and 18th century paintings of children.

The children are *The Infanta Margarita,* the Spanish princess who married Louis XIV of France, from the painting by Diego Velazquez in 1654; *The Artist's Daughter* by Cornelis de Vos from the Low Countries, 1627; the child from *Nurse and Child* by Dutch artist Frans Hals, about 1620; and the cousin of the Infanta Margarita, *Don Manuel Osorio de Zuniga* ("the Red Boy") by Francisco Goya, 1786.

The dolls were sculpted by Howard Kalish and are made in Delaware. Only 1500 dolls of each design will be made for 1982 and they will retail for $200 each. Each doll is a faithful representation of the child in the original painting. The dolls have brown glass eyes. They are "breathers" with pierced nostrils. *Margarita* has a light blonde wig; *Don Manuel* has a brown wig; the other girls have light red wigs. All of the clothing is made from authentic materials and is faithful to the designs from the famous masterpieces of European art.

Tiderider Incorporated is introducing several new items in the Lenci line from Italy.

For the first time another classic Lenci face - the fourth one that has been used by the successor of the original Lenci dolls - will be utilized. The doll is a 16in (40.6cm) girl of felt with felt clothing. The models are *Elena* (No. 001) in red and white; *Elisabetta* (No. 002) in salmon pink; *Grazia* (No. 003) in light blue; and *Giovanna* (No. 004) in light green

220

Illustration 5. *Don Manuel Osorio de Zuniga "the Red Boy" by Francisco Goya by Doll Classics by Al Trattner. Photograph courtesy of Doll Classics by Al Trattner.*

and white. These dolls more closely resemble the traditional Lenci dolls from the 1920s and the 1930s than previous models do. The wigs on the dolls are a synthetic fiber, but they have the look and feel of human hair. The number marked on each tag matches the number marked on the neck of each doll.

A Pinocchio doll that in 1981 won an award in a contest in Italy for the best design to be used for the 100th Anniversary of Pinocchio is available in felt in 12in (30.5cm). A Pinocchio hanging ornament is also new.

Lenci also has a line of six new plush teddy bears. Four of the models are sitting and two are standing.

The Sasha Limited Edition doll for 1982 will be produced as 6000 examples. She has a fair colored natural hair wig and brown eyes. Her dress is white pintucked cotton worn over a lace trimmed petticoat. The shoes are dark green velvet. Each doll will be marked with her individual number and she will be accompanied with a signed certificate of authenticity.

Sasha introduced *Gregor Red-head* (No. 312), a new 16in (40.6cm) doll who wears a T-shirt, blue trousers and jacket, and white shoes. A 16in (40.6cm) girl, *Sasha Blonde* (No. 112) with a short hairdo, is attired in a white belted sweater, beige skirt, white knee-socks and white shoes.

Little *Baby Bear* (No. 512), 12in (30.5cm) has a dress, turned-up brimmed hat and panties all of white piqué. Her shoes are red, and she is holding a little white bear decorated with a red ribbon. Separate new clothes from Sasha include the costumes worn by these three dolls. In addition there is a blue mackintosh and red beret; and, also their holiday ensemble which consists of a T-shirt, shorts, hat striped swimsuit, socks, shoulder bag and training shoes.

Steiff "Teddy Bear Picnic." 1982 Limited Edition of 10,000 numbered with certificate. Four bears the size of "baby bear" from 1981 will be produced in four colors: brown, carmel, honey and white. Comes with "table" replete with tiny tea set with Steiff mark on tableware. More on bears next issue.

Effanbee Limited Edition Doll Club announced their 1982 selection is "A Royal Bride Diana, Princess of Wales." This 18in (45.7cm) vinyl doll wears the candlelight ecru English Royal wedding gown made of silk-like fabric. The doll is complimented by a magnificent trailing train and carries a huge bouquet of flowers. Members who bought last years "Girl with the Watering Can" are first in line for the 4220 total pieces to be made. To be put on the waiting list and for a free brochure write to Effanbee Limited Edition Doll Club at 200 Fifth Avenue, New York, NY, 10010.

We are happy to report that the wrap-up of the American Toy Fair 1982 will require two feature articles. The June/July issue will feature dolls from companies not included herein as well as photographs not received by press time because of the lateness of Toy Fair.

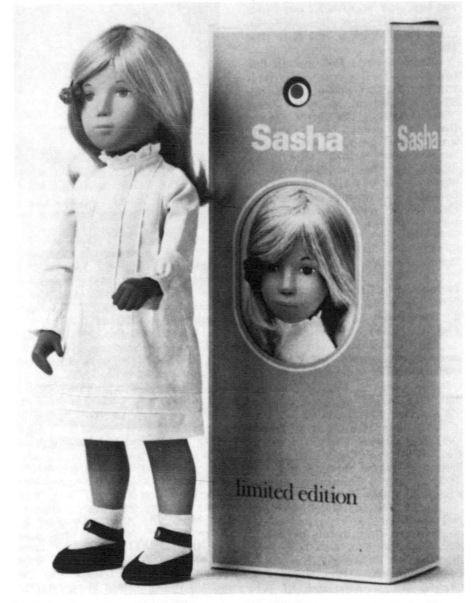

Illustration 6. Limited Edition Sasha new for 1982. *Photograph courtesy of International Playthings.*

INDEX

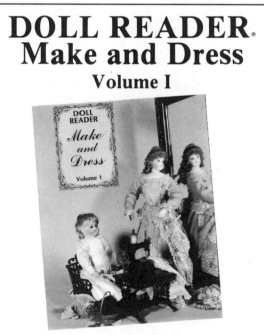